S0-BIC-134

A New Approach to Continuing Education for Business and the Professions

A New Approach to Continuing Education for Business and the Professions

The Performance Model

Philip M. Nowlen

National University Continuing Education Association
American Council on Education  Macmillan Publishing Company
NEW YORK
Collier Macmillan Publishers
LONDON

The American Council on Education/Macmillan Series on Higher Education

Macmillan Publishing Company
866 Third Avenue, New York, N.Y. 10022

Collier Macmillan Canada, Inc.

Library of Congress Catalog Card Number: 87-1616

Printed in the United States of America

printing number
1 2 3 4 5 6 7 8 9 10

Library of Congress Cataloging-in-Publication Data

Nowlen, Philip M.
A new approach to continuing education for business and the professions.

Includes indexes.
1. Professional education—United States.
2. Business education—United States. 3. Continuing education—United States. 4. Performance. I. Title.
LC1072.C56N68 1987 374'.973 87-1616
ISBN 0-02-922740-2

Contents

Preface

What is the answer? (I was silent.) In that case, what is the question?

Last Words of Gertrude Stein — *Alice B. Toklas*

THIS BOOK IS MORE ABOUT QUESTIONS than answers. It is the din of contending answers that drives the rapidly evolving field known as continuing professional education: "Mandate continuing education." "Accredit the programs." "Accredit the providers." "Relicense and recredential professionals." "Establish professional standards." "Concentrate on interprofessional programs." "Update professionals' knowledge and skill." "Teach toward the competencies required by actual job functions." "Adopt the continuing education unit." "Decentralize responsibility for providing continuing education." "Tax employers for a national continuing education scheme." "Offer postprofessional degree certificate tracks." "Build a residential conference center." "Get a satellite up-link."

In Mike Nichols's *The Graduate,* a well-intentioned friend of the family puts his arm around Dustin Hoffman drawing him aside to whisper, "Plastics!" But what is the question for which "Plastics!" is the answer? What are the questions for which continuing education has so many answers? Which of the questions are really compelling?

In what follows, the search for the right questions begins with an examination of the current state of continuing education for business and the professions and, in particular, an analysis of the contribution and limitations of its chief vehicle, the intensive short course organized with a view toward keeping professionals and executives up to date. Analysis of this update model yields a set of questions about how professionals know, about the nature of their knowledge, and about reasoned ways of choosing among educational opportunities. The search continues with an analysis of the update's growing rival, a model for educational design based on questioning both what executives and professionals really do for a living and what competencies are thereby required. The competence model offers persons a way of grounding educational choices, including update opportunities, in decisions related to descriptions of actual practice. The competence model can identify the knowledge and skills required for individual performance in the major settings of business and the professions but, how, then, do we account for day-to-day, or context-to-context, variances in the performance of the same individual? What is more, how can we account for variances in the performance of groups of comparably competent individuals? Moving beyond the critical functions of a job, what are critical cultural influences on individual as well as group performance?

Many contemporary fields of research suggest that two interactive strands of variables apply here as in all of human experience: one carries the powerful influences of culture; the other carries the traits and dispositions, knowledge and skills shaped by individual human development. The interaction of the two strands is continuous and can modify the performance code they carry. Assuming this "double helix" as a tentative model for understanding performance, what are its implications for rethinking the conceptual frameworks and operations of needs analysis, educational design, and evaluation? What research agenda does this model imply? Are current continuing education providers able to address both the cultural as well as personal dimensions of individual and collective performance? Will executives, professionals, and their organizations' leaders demand it?

The "double helix" metaphor for performance suggests a performance model for educational analysis and design that can accommodate the update and competence models but also address important variables of individual and group performance that fall outside the purview of these models. How can this possibility best be explored?

Questions about the nature of performance and a resulting model for continuing education can best be pursued by widening the conversation about continuing education in several ways. The title of the book contains the phrase, continuing education for business and the professions, as a way of insisting on widening the frame of reference from that of continuing business education or continuing professional education—phrases implicitly linked with discussion of topics that are curricular extensions of business and professional schools. The subject under discussion also must be widened to include group as well as individual performance, because most people experience professional performance as an encounter among a client, an ensemble of interacting professionals, and others.

Another way in which the conversation must be widened is by including significant voices currently uninvolved in the dialogue. Business already may be the primary employer of professionals and is a culture that strongly influences those outside its employ. Members of the helping professions counsel executives and professionals and have developed insight into the factors limiting or enhancing performance in the occupational world. Those in scholarly professions, such as human development and cognitive science, have much to offer with respect to understanding personal traits, dispositions, and proficiencies. Anthropologists and sociologists also can contribute substantially by probing culture as the interactive context of personal development, particularly in forms such as values, organizations, symbols, sacred stories, and the like. Among those who already understand that the immediate context of work influences performance, the conversation has to be widened to include other powerful cultural influences such as family, civic affairs, religion, and leisure. Among the providers, professionals, and executives who have come to identify continuing education as short-term programs of instruction by those who know for others who don't, the conversation must be widened to include the possibility of long-term teaching/learning relationships between educators, and executives and professionals in the contexts of their cultures. Guided self-reflection and the development of complex learning agendas by individuals and groups may be more important to such relationships than programs of instruction. If the examples cited throughout appear to favor certain corporations or professions such as IBM, medicine, pharmacy or accounting, it is because their role in the conversation has been long and lively.

This book enters this conversation deeply indebted to the following people. Cyril O. Houle of the W. K. Kellogg Foundation, a professor of adult education at the University of Chicago from 1939 to 1979, in *Continuing Learning in the Professions,* took an undefined but vast space and enclosed it within frameworks that provide the mind's eye with lines of sight and a sense of proportion. Alan B. Knox of the Department of Continuing and Vocational Education, the University of Wisconsin-Madison, mapped the field's major players, activities, and issues, maintained the lines of communication among higher education, major employers, and professional associations, and in *Adult Development and Learning* stimulated me to consider that the *interaction of human development with the many cultures of adulthood might be the missing link between the potential of competence and the reality of performance.* Samuel H. Kalman whose ten-year achievement as Director of Education for the American Pharmaceutical Association, demonstrates the significance of gritty determination and political savvy in translating knowledge into performance. He conceptualized a profession-wide competence framework sensitive to both the content and cultures of pharmaceutical practice, demonstrated its validity, and provided it as a model for practitioner self-assessment and self-directed learning decisions, as well as for provider educational design.

I am grateful to Carol G. Schneider, Deputy Director of Continuing Education at the University of Chicago, whose nationally recognized institutes on the ends and means of liberal learning: critical thinking, and formation of values, cognitive frameworks and higher-order reasoning I found to be suggestive of a vital relationship between liberal learning and the performance of executives and professionals. Her critical skills of mind argue strongly for acknowledging the role others have in raising the level of "personal" performance. I am indebted to Milton R. Stern and Joyce Feucht-Haviar, who urged me to undertake this book and contributed clarity and grace to several troubled passages. I am also grateful to Helen K. Bailey and Versey Cooper who greatly facilitated the preparation of the manuscript.

The book is dedicated to Jenny, Justin, and Morgan, my wife and sons, who, I trust, did not become too accustomed to life without me during this project.

Chicago, Illinois PHILIP M. NOWLEN
June 1987

ONE

Bringing the Field into Focus: The Update Model

CONTINUING EDUCATION FOR BUSINESS and the professions is an enormous enterprise. One-fourth to one-half of the practicing professionals in the United States attended one or more formal continuing education activities in 1981. According to a study by the National Center for Educational Statistics of participation in adult education during 1981, 43% of those in the allied health professions, 40% of physicians, 35.8% of teachers, and 16.8% of all employed persons participated in one or more formal continuing education experiences (NCES, 1982, pp. 19–22). Employers estimate that well over one-third of middle and upper management participate in at least one continuing education program annually. These experiences take various forms. They may be courses, seminars, tutorials, conferences, or executive development programs. They may be for credit, toward a certificate or degree, or credit free. They may meet nights, weekends, three successive days, for one to eight weeks, or for 18 months—combining nights or Saturdays with short, intensive residential periods. They may be live or mediated on film, audio, or video tape, over the radio or television (narrowcast or broadcast), through a modem or disc to a computer terminal, or on an electronic blackboard. They may meet in the home, on a commuter train or in a car, at the office or corporate training facility, on a campus, at a hotel or a conference center, in town or out of town. They may be sponsored by an employer, a college or university, a professional association, a civic or religious organization, a government agency, a community hospital, a computer manufacturer, or an office-systems purveyor or consulting firm—and this is by no means an exhaustive list.

The Department of Defense spends $18.5 billion a year on training and development, and some $700 million of this is earmarked for professional development (Scott, 1984). The annual investment of all U.S. employers in executive and professional education as well as white- and blue-collar training is estimated at more than $60 billion when fully costed, that is, when salaries and wages, travel and per diem, loss of billable time, or diversion from regular duties are added to instructional costs. This is more than twice what all 50 states appropriated for public higher education and nearly half of what all the states spent on kindergarten through twelfth grade (K–12) education in 1984. It must be said, too, that if anything, these are conservative figures and certainly imprecise. There are major difficulties in auditing dollars spent on continuing education. The public's continuing education vocabulary is blurred, with little distinction made among seminars, programs, conferences, institutes, workshops, short courses, and the like. Educational activities reported by corporations as human-resources development often represent just the blue- and white-collar training budget, which is the typical limit of the involvement of the personnel office or human-resources office in educational matters. Sometimes continuing education is expensed as affirmative action or even as job rotation (Foster and Rippey, 1985, p. 111). Continuing education costs for professionals, middle managers, and senior executives are often reflected in travel and per diem expense reimbursement figures. In addition, in costing continuing education, few businesses, law firms, or dental offices make an effort to include lost billing hours, fewer patient appointments, or business not conducted because a professional or executive is away. Approximately $30 billion is committed to opportunities conducted by employers. According to the American Council on Education's Office of Educational Credit, in 1983 some 180 employers offered 2,000 or more accredited courses, forming a kind of shadow education system. Many of the larger professional associations engage in continuing education activities on both the national and the state level and commit from $4 million to $30 million each to the effort. A for-profit seminar industry has appeared. Continuing education for business and the professions is the fastest-growing realm of higher education during a period otherwise characterized by stasis or decline. University and college efforts range from small projects undertaken with part-time staff to more typical operations budgeted at $2 million to $4 million and staffed by 25 to 35 people. Some major university-based efforts are budgeted at $13 million to $17 million and have staffs of 50 or more. A few have budgets in excess of $40 million. Registrations range from 100 to 70,000 people per institution per year.

Driving this development are the 26.9 million people in the United States with four or more years of study beyond the twelfth grade. This population is growing. The more formal education people have had, the more they participate in learning experiences of all kinds throughout their lives. The demand for continuing education will intensify for the remainder of the century (Keane, 1985, p. 93).

Other significant factors at work include the information explosion, the changing nature of knowledge, increasing organizational complexity, the drive to maintain excellence and to remain competitive, the public's demand for professional accountability, compulsory relicensure, the threat of malpractice litigation, rapid development of new technologies, and shifts in governmental regulatory patterns. These factors can be seen in the wide range of learning objectives pursued by those in business and the professions: updating in chosen fields; mastering of new technology; help with supervising other professionals; sharpening critical skills of inquiry, judgment, and choice; understanding the contextual factors likely to shape the future; rekindling the values that motivated them to pursue excellence; finding a new competitive edge; strengthening their performance; exploring changing family and societal roles; responding to midcareer challenges; puzzling out the implications of new legislation; and pursuing the ethical issues multiplied by science and technology. Education is no longer a stage in human development. In the consciousness of more and more people it has become a condition of existence inseparable from the quality of life. The integration of learning and life is evidence of higher education's astonishing success. The growing population of lifelong learners is higher education's most influential and devoted constituency.

The millennium is still on hold, however. Continuing education for business and the professions is also a disorderly marketplace, as Milton Stern maintains. Higher education's role has sometimes been abdicated or subverted; the public's selection of learning experiences is faddish and frequently haphazard; some faculty members have been seduced from institutional loyalty by entrepreneurship; and when professional associations double as continuing education providers and accreditors, there is at least the appearance of impropriety (Stern, 1983). Higher education, professional associations, and sometimes even corporate employers lack the baselines necessary to reach decisions about which learning needs to serve, which to defer, and how success is to be measured. University and college leaders face continuing education policy and planning issues involving governance, academic accountability, financial monitoring, and collaborative relationships with professional associations and major employers. Public disillusionment with the professions (*Wall Street Journal* headlines such as, "Investors Call CPAs to Account," "Inept Doctors A Growing Illness," etc.), consumer pressure for greater accountability, the growth of agencies

TABLE 1.1. Status of Mandatory Continuing Education for Selected Professions

	NUMBER OF STATES[1]		
	Required by Statute or Regulation	*Enabling Legislation Passed*	*Required Under Certain Circumstances*
Architects	1	6	
Certified Public Accountants	47		
Dentists	13		
Engineers (Professional)	2	2	
Lawyers	20		4
Nurses	11	2	7
Nursing Home Administrators	43		
Optometrists	46		
Psychologists	13	8	
Pharmacists	36	3	
Physical Therapists	4	2	1
Physicians	21	3	2
Real Estate Salesmen and/or Brokers	29		3
Social Workers	20	2	1
Licensed Practical/ Vocational Nurses	10	1	7
Veterinarians	26	1	

1. Includes District of Columbia

Source: Information obtained from national professional associations. Revised 1986. Copyrighted by Louis E. Phillips, Athens, Georgia.

regulating professional practice, and feuding and fragmentation of professional associations have continued in parallel with continuing education's growth.

These forces came together in the 1970s to energize two issues through which the field stumbled toward greater clarity and the edge of consensus. Mandatory continuing education as a prerequisite for periodic state relicensure or compelling professionals to participate in continuing education as a recertification requirement appealed to many professional associations (Shimberg, 1980, pp. 126–132). (See Tables 1.1, 1.2, and 1.3.) It was a way for associations to make a good-faith effort at holding their members accountable for maintaining their proficiency. It also served to counter the centrifugal forces that were weakening some associations. Some university-based continuing educators supported mandatory continuing professional education as a beneficial marriage of faith and reason: faith, in that continuing education sustained or improved

TABLE 1.2. Trends

	1977	1979	1980	1981	1982	1984	1986
Architects	0	1/1	1/1	1/2	1/6	1/6	1/6
CPAs	23	28	36/1	38/1	37/1	43/1	47
Dentists	8	9/1	9/1/1	11/1/1	10/0/1	10/0/1	13
Engineers (Professional)	0	1	1/2	1/2	2/2	2/2	2/2
Lawyers	7	8/8	9/8	9/0/9	10/0/8	12/0/8	20/0/4
Nurses	6/3	10	11/2/7	10/4/4	11/4/4	11/2/5	11/2/7
Nursing Home Administrators	37	42	43	44	42/1	44/1	43
Optometrists	45	45	44	46	46	46	46
Psychologists		7/6	8/6	12/9	11/9	12/9	13/8
Pharmacists	14	21	21	22	24/4	30/3	36/3
Physical Therapists		3	3	3	3	3/1	4/2/1
Physicians	17/11	20/4	20/4/1	20/4/1	20/4/1	18/4/1	21/3/2
Real Estate Sales Persons and Brokers	11	11	14/1	17/1	21	22/0/3	29/0/3
Social Workers	6	10	10	11	15	18	20/2/1
LPNs		8/3	11/1	10	12	10/1/1	10/1/7
Veterinarians	18	19	22	23/2	22/1	24/1	26/1

NOTE: The first digit represents number of states with mandatory requirements. The second digit represents number of states with enabling legislation passed. The third digit represents number of states with requirements under certain circumstances.

Source: Information obtained from national professional associations. Revised 1986. Copyrighted by Louis E. Phillips, Athens, Georgia.

TABLE 1.3. Status of Mandatory Continuing Education for Selected Professions

	Alabama	Alaska	Arizona	Arkansas	California	Colorado	Connecticut	Delaware	D. C.	Florida	Georgia	Hawaii	Idaho	Illinois	Indiana	Iowa	Kansas	Kentucky	Louisiana	Maine	Maryland
Architects			E							E						X					
CPAs	X	X	X	X	X	X	X	X	X	X	X	X	X	X	X	X	X	X	X	X	X
Dentists					X					X						X	X	X			
Engineers (Professional)																X					
Lawyers	X		S		S	X				S	X		X			X	X	X			
Nurses		E			X	X				X						X	X	X			
Nursing Home Administrators	X		X	X	X			X		X	X		X	X	X	X	X	X	X	X	X
Optometrists	X	X	X	X			X	X		X	X	X	X	X	X	X	X	X	X	X	X
Psychologists		X		E				X		X	X					X	X		E		X
Pharmacists	X	X	X	X	X			X	E	X			X	X	X	X	X	X	X	X	E
Physical Therapists		X						E								X	X				
Physicians		X	X	E	X			X	X	X		X		S		X	S	E		X	X
Real Estate			X		X		X	X	X	X	X					X	X		X	X	X
Social Workers	X			X	S	X		X	E	X		–			–		X	X		X	E
LPNs			S	S	X	X		S		X						X	X	X			
Veterinarians	X	X	X	X		X			X	X				X	E	X	X	X			X

X required by statute or regulation E enabling legislation passed S required under certain circumstances – profession not licensed

Source: Information obtained from national professional associations. Revised 1986. Copyrighted by Louis E. Phillips, Athens, Georgia.

Massachusetts	Michigan	Minnesota	Mississippi	Missouri	Montana	Nebraska	Nevada	New Hampshire	New Jersey	New Mexico	New York	North Carolina	North Dakota	Ohio	Oklahoma	Oregon	Pennsylvania	Rhode Island	South Carolina	South Dakota	Tennessee	Texas	Utah	Vermont	Virginia	Washington	West Virginia	Wisconsin	Wyoming
		E						E	E	E																			
X	X	X	X	X	X	X	X	X		X	X	X	X	X	X	X	X	X	X	X	X	X	X	X		X			X
X		X				X				X			X		X	X				X									
		E			X							E																	
		X	X		X		X			S			X		X				X			X		X	X	X		X	X
X	E	X	S			X	X	S		X			S			S		S						S					S
X	X	X	X	X	X	X	X	X	X	X	X	X	X	X	X	X	X		X	X	X	X		X		X	X	X	X
X	X	X	X	X	X	X	X	X	X	X		X	X	X	X	X	X	X	X	X	X	X	X	X	X	X	X		X
	E	E					X			X		E				X						E	X	E		X	X		E
X	X	X	X	X	X	X	X	X	X	X		X	X	X	X	X	X			X	X			E		X			X
		S			E					X																			
X	X	X				E	X	X		X				X				X					X			X		X	
	X	X	S	X		X	X	X		X	X		X	X	X	X				X	X	S	X			S		X	X
X		–	–	–	X	X	–		–	–		X	X	X	X		–			X		X	X		X	–	X	–	–
X	E		S			X	X	S		X	S												S						
			X		X	X	X	X		X		X		X	X	X	X			X	X					X			

professional performance; and reason, in that it reduced the risk in planning and marketing programs. A movement took shape in the 1970s. The continuing education unit (CEU) was devised in support of quantifying and tracking continuing education experiences. The CEU is defined as 10 contact hours of participation in an organized continuing education experience under responsible sponsorship, capable direction, and qualified instruction. The Educational Testing Service designed a data bank, called *Passport,* for recording continuing education experiences for professionals. Even so, the bandwagon slowed. It was impossible to demonstrate an explicit causal relationship between continuing education and sustained or improved performance. Attempts at defining criteria that would identify programs that would "count" toward the mandated minimum dissolved into simpler and less expensive approval of any programs from providers that met general standards. Minimum requirements differed greatly from state to state. Monitoring and recording professional participation turned out to be either prohibitively expensive processes that intruded themselves on the learning experience (Are those who are registered still present?) or uncertain undertakings, heavily dependent upon the honesty of individual professionals. Some professional groups mandated continuing education and then accredited programs they, themselves, offered and for which they charged fees, a practice worthy of the Chicago City Council.

The companion issue of the 1970s was turf. Who will mandate continuing education and on what authority? Who will accredit experiences or providers that "count?" Who should be the primary provider? Higher education, as the traditional center for the discovery and dissemination of knowledge, was widely asserted to possess a prior normative claim. Its research and teaching base, as the argument went, was already well established and could be augmented as necessary. There was the tradition of professional schools, including business schools, whose alumni were the constituencies to benefit from continuing education. There was the tradition of extension/continuing education units and their success in bringing academic resources to wider publics. Some even advanced the notion of periodic certification of postgraduate study by universities as the best recredentialling process for professionals. Educational planning, design, and evaluation could then take place along established ladders for professions and their specialties and subspecialties.

The objections to arguments of primacy and turf were persuasive. Leaders were still experimenting with how and where continuing education made the greatest difference to professionals' practice. If the aim was to sustain or improve practice, neither associations, nor universities, nor employers could claim distinctive success. The development of programs with clearer and greater impact would require the collaboration of many groups, including professional associations, universities, employers, government agencies, and foundations. Competition was seen as positive when it served to assure quality. Higher education did not (and, with rare exceptions, still does not) control the involvement of faculty in nonuniversity educational programs or in consulting. Professional associations, employers, and the for-profit seminar companies employed faculty as teaching resources without so much as a "by your leave" to their colleges and universities, whose involvement was viewed as simply increasing the cost and slowing the pace. The needs of practicing professionals were viewed by Carol Schneider in the *American Journal of Education* as

> . . . so disparate and so linked to particular organizational contexts that only observers close to the actual work can hope readily to identify genuinely helpful directions for individual professional development. . . . employers, professional associations, and professionals themselves have a far more keenly developed interest in at least the broad subject of professional competence than do universities. [Schneider, 1984, p. 536]

Within universities, professional schools and extension/continuing education units sometimes each claimed exclusive rights to design and offer programs to business and the professions. For the most part, however, universities were not even interested in arguing the case. As Lawrence Berlin suggested, the ethos of the professional schools has become increasingly disassociated from the cultures of everyday professional practice. Moreover, this detachment is rapidly being accelerated in an economic climate that forces universities to concentrate on their most significant priorities while eliminating activities on the periphery. Continuing education for business and the professions, as a relatively new—if fast growing—development, was decidedly on the periphery (Berlin, 1982).

The many in higher education who viewed its principal aim as the transmission of high culture saw any further involvement in credentialism as vulgar. The credentialling of society, many reminded us, had a kind of Keynesian quality: If the credential has value, everyone will want one, but if everyone gets one, its value will be marginal.

The issues of mandatory continuing education and turf did serve to stimulate a somewhat unexpected consensus about several points. First, patience was required. A certain amount of ambiguity and confusion, it was agreed, was bound to characterize a phenomenon as pervasive as continuing education for business and the professions. The pluralistic efforts of higher education, employers, professional associations, and voluntary organizations were encouraged and carefully examined for successful models. Second, the field needed mapping. Should it address any group that identified itself as a profession? Should it be limited to education *in* the traditional disciplines of the professions? Should it include any learning experiences organized *for* professionals? What were the contours of success and failure? How were measurable standards of practice to be identified? Until substantial work was done to develop instrumentalities for understanding and assessing professional performance, the practice of mandating continuing education as an assurance of desirable levels of performance was urged to be deferred. A National University Continuing Education Association's position paper stated, "Care must be taken to ensure that continuing professional education is not seen as a substitute for professional regulation; continuing professional education cannot be used as evidence of practitioner competence" (Nowlen and Queeney, 1984). Third, with patience and the emergence of baselines, the field's aims, methods, and theories needed to be identified with a view toward examining the merits of the field's prevailing paradigm. Many contributions to the literature and practice of the field during the last 10 years have made its structure clearer, yielding a surer grasp of its strengths and weaknesses and, arguably, pointing toward a more promising paradigm.

Continuing Learning

The much larger phenomenon of which such continuing education is a minor part is continuing learning. Continuing learning includes self-directed learning, informal learning experiences, the mentoring that is implicit in most professional and occupational settings, and human-resources-placement schemes that pass promising professionals through sequences of responsibilities with high learning potential. Professional life involves continuous reflective practice. Within this general learning environment, continuing education has its episodic uses. Its value is heightened when it is integrated with the larger realm of self-directed learning activities, as in a professional's plan to meet the challenge of new responsibilities, for example.

The Professions Broadly Understood

For baseline details and depth, Houle's *Continuing Learning in the Professions* remains a major achievement. It brings the field's dynamism and movement into manageable focus. In it, Houle takes the undefined, vast, and sometimes troubled field and encloses it within frameworks that provide the mind's eye with lines of sight and proportion. Influenced by the work of E. C. Hughes, R. Bucher, and A. Strauss, and particularly by H. M. Vollmer and D. L. Mills's edited collection, *Professionalization,* Houle rejects the static, exclusivist notion of professionalism and its cabalistic preoccupation with the question of which occupational groups are really professions. He opts, instead, for the inclusivist position that is grounded in a dynamic understanding of the professions. The one unchanging feature of the professional is unceasing movement toward new levels of performance. In the achievement of these new levels, inadequacies of performance become clear and better levels of performance possible. This is an untidy but energizing process with observable characteristics:

concern with mission/function clarification

mastery of theoretical knowledge

capacity to solve problems

use of practical knowledge

self-enhancement

formal training

credentialling

creation of a subculture

legal reinforcement

public acceptance

ethical practice

penalties

relations to other vocations

relations to users of service (Houle, 1980, pp. 34–75).

The victory of this dynamic, inclusivist definition of the professions and the consequent identification of characteristics common to all professionalizing groups make the field significantly more congenial to analysis and planning. The characteristics are facets of the professionalizing drive. As such, they impel the professional toward one or another cluster of related learning needs. The characteristics also represent a taxonomy of learning objectives related to professionalization. Continuing education's role is as self-renewing as the professionalizing drive. It enables higher levels of performance, and in the achievement of these new levels of performance, their inadequacy becomes clear and new sets of educational objectives become necessary.

Including Business

Cyril Houle acknowledges business people as a category of skilled workers having specialized segments of people within it, accountants for example, who have a highly professionalizing attitude. No traditionalist, Houle sees each group laying claim to professional status as located somewhere along a continuum represented by the characteristics typical of the professionalizing process. Even the most traditional professions are, in fact, professionalizing groups possessing only in some measure the conceptual, performance, and collective identity characteristics noted above. Recent practice in the field also views business in ways conceptually and operationally distinct from continuing education for the professions. The National University Continuing Education Association, for example, has one member-interest area for business, industry, and labor, and another for continuing professional education.

It is true that business spends relatively little effort in clarifying its mission and function (perhaps because it is so obvious), a key professionalizing characteristic. Business is occasionally given to heated controversy about its mission, as with the 1970s debate fueled by Milton Friedman over inclusion of some sense of public responsibility beyond making the highest possible profit. On the other hand, the sense of mission held by other professional groupings doesn't seem as clear as one might expect, given their effort. Dentistry's mission keeps evolving as research and technology simultaneously threaten its existence and bring it to new standards of service. Corrections is a field constantly warring over punishment versus rehabilitation as its mission. It and the nation are as divided as ever about its mission.

Business fares well when examined in light of other professionalizing characteristics, such as mastery of an organized body of theoretical knowledge. There are over 600 graduate management education programs in the United States that produce 60,000 to

70,000 professionally trained persons annually, according to the Educational Testing Service's Graduate Management Admission Test information. There are approximately 700,000 holders of the MBA degree in the United States. This is a large and growing body of formally trained, academically certified masters of a theoretical knowledge field. In addition, they are skilled in problem solving, the use of practical knowledge, and they have a commitment to lifelong learning that is the delight of continuing education leaders—other professionalizing characteristics. The point is not to insist that business fits the profile of professionalizing groups perfectly but rather that there may be something to gain and little if anything to lose by including business with the professions when searching for the aims, methods, and theories that will bring the field into more workable focus.

Individuals professionally trained in business face a number of issues, opportunities, and dilemmas common to the professions: What strategies, sequenced in what ways over a career, offer a reasonable guarantee of personal excellence? Where do formal and informal learning experiences fit in? How do I mentor, motivate, or evaluate others? What help can I expect from employers, universities, and professional associations? There are commonalities at other levels as well.

Business is increasingly the employer of choice or necessity for professionals. Business executives are drawn from law, engineering, information systems, chemistry, the military, economics, pharmacology, industrial psychology, and other sources in addition to the disciplines of the professional schools of business. Some executives from schools of business are members of professional groups such as accountants, or groups in which professionalizing characteristics are beginning to appear such as finance, marketing, and information systems.

Conversely, the more traditional context of professional practice, such as law firms, hospitals, social service agencies, schools, the military, and even symphony orchestras, have become complex, economically sensitive organizations. They demand high proficiency in critical business and management skills from the professionals who lead them and good marks in problem solving, monitoring, group process, and negotiation from professionals who staff them. Even "solo practice" has many of the characteristics and demands of the business setting. Professionals are a major segment of the market demanding continuing education programs in business and management topics.

Both the professions and business are a suitable focus because each has something to gain from the insights of the other. Both business and the professions are ultimately interested in performance as the outcome of continuing education. Business has come to certain insights earlier than the professions. Business has experienced that keeping people up-to-date in their field neither necessarily enhances nor maintains performance. Business has more sharply defined performance measures. Business finds it useful to think of performance as the result of many factors, only one of which is individual competence. The professions bring a sense of history and a tradition of examining issues in ways that transcend employment settings and next quarter's bottom line.

Business *and* professional people register in programs designed and offered by the same providers in higher education. Many educational and operational issues are common to these providers, including the fact that the employers of business and professional people typically pay their continuing education bills. The same classroom frequently holds both business and professional students at the same time, when the program addresses organizational leadership questions, economic issues, or personal impairments. Business and professional people are increasingly seeking two-profession competency as lawyers with economics degrees, physicians with management degrees or social-service professionals with degrees in public administration (Collins, 1985).

Business *and* professional people are largely self-directed learners. Professional schools have not prepared them formally for this role either with respect to designing their own learning experience or exercising critical judgment in choosing from among existing programs. Sophisticating the skills and judgment of business and professional people in self-directed learning could be a significant contribution of continuing education. There is much to learn, and many research paths will be enriched by examining situations in both business and the professions.

While Houle was working on *Continuing Learning in the Professions,* Alan Knox was gathering information about *university-based* continuing education in medicine, pharmacy, social work, education, and law (Knox, 1980). Continuing education for business and the professions includes education in the traditional disciplines and body of theoretical knowledge represented in preprofessional education, but extends much more broadly to embrace any organized learning experiences that flow from characteristics related to professionalization, especially those closely related to individual performance or impairment, the management of the settings of practice, and the general issues facing business or the professions. In each of the five professional areas, Knox provides detailed and fairly representative case descriptions, drawing together the extent and type of education provided, organizational arrangements, client characteristics, some activity of other providers, the condition and quality of faculty involvement, the ways in which program development is carried on, major influences, and issues of interest. The surveys did not include employers, associations, unions, and the like.

Activities in medicine were extensive and varied. The public universities surveyed each conducted about 40 to 50 conferences for approximately 6,000 physicians, and in 1979 100 sessions were held in cooperating hospitals for their staffs—about twice the activity of private universities. Much of this activity involved joint effort with local hospitals, often for the purposes of assisting hospitals with accreditation, providing interns and residents with gains in clinical experience, and increasing the proficiency of primary-care physicians while helping them to meet continuing education requirements. University-based offices of continuing medical education have been in existence for from 2 to 60 years; most have been operating for 5 to 10 years. They are chiefly influenced by the vision, energy, and style of their directors or leadership teams, by collaborative relationships with hospitals and professional associations, by the mandatory rubrics associated with continuing medical education and by changes in Federal funding levels. One-third of the continuing medical education directors have served for 2 to 4 years; another third has served from 15 to 20 years. Most are MDs but some are educators. They tend to have wide latitude and answer to faculty committees and/or deans of medicine. They have little to do with university-wide divisions of continuing education/extension. University-based continuing medical education offices serve highly varied publics ranging from major metropolitan areas to four-state regions to international publics in medical specialties or subspecialties for which the institutions have established preeminent reputations. Conferences and other programs are typically promoted through cooperating hospital or professional association networks and by means of direct-mail distributed brochures. There is seldom interuniversity collaboration. Most offices of continuing medical education can account for one-fourth to one-half of the continuing medical education requirements of physicians in their service areas, a decline since hospitals have been providing more and more continuing medical education to their staff physicians. One-third of the faculty are involved in teaching, and this accounts for 50 to 90% of continuing medical education teaching. The major institutional objective served is increase in the referral of patients likely to provide rich teaching material. Honoraria or extra-service payments are relatively small, and frequently sponsoring departments share in income. Program development is largely a matter of internally generated ideas. Programs are evaluated by simple reaction forms circulated at the conclusion of the sessions. The issues of some importance in continuing medical education are how to design programs that improve practice, how to evaluate such efforts, and whether more of a continuum could be constructed from preprofessional training through continuing education.

Activities in pharmacy are strongly influenced by the relatively high number of pharmacists who are in solo practice or in small hospitals and clinics and experience difficulty in staffing the pharmacy in their absence. (Large pharmaceutical firms take care of many of their pharmacists' learning needs.) Metropolitan-based activities, supplemented by media, technology, and correspondence study for those in solo practice, tend to be the common pattern. In the largest continuing pharmacy education operations, the annual budgets exceed $250,000 and a diversity of financial support seems characteristic. Where there is only one school of pharmacy in a state, it tends to provide between 60 and 90% of pharmacists' continuing education experiences and to work closely with the state pharmacy board. Associations cosponsor many of the programs. It is the associations that appear to be the major providers in states with multiple schools of pharmacy. In multiprovider states, financial considerations make many providers marginal operations with unimaginative and low-risk program development. Only in the larger offices of university continuing education in pharmacy are there frequent attempts to go beyond knowledge acquisition to applications and performance changes. Academic and practicing pharmacists equally share teaching responsibilities, with approximately one-third of the faculty members in each school contributing to at least one activity each year. Little or no honoraria for teaching are supplied by larger offices; the smaller depend upon honoraria for incentives. All offices see themselves as struggling with low institutional priorities assigned to continuing pharmacy education.

The longest history in university-based continuing education for business and the professions is the 80-year relationship between schools and departments of education and teachers, counselors, and administrators employed in settings from kindergarten through high school. During much of this history continuing education was virtually mandatory for teachers. And nowhere else is the distance any greater between individual professionals' learning and longed-for systemic improvement. As Knox observes, "In contrast with the enthusiasm and optimism regarding continuing professional education in the other professional fields studied, those who were conducting and to some extent coordinating CPE in Schools of Education seemed weary of long effort, and in a reactive and defensive position" (Knox, 1980, Part E). The future appears to hold stability or decline. Currently, larger operations serve 25,000 or more teachers each year with yearly budgets of $500,000. Many school of education faculty members consider continuing teacher education as a routine part of their responsibility, so routine in fact that in many schools there isn't an office or person responsible for coordinating efforts. Most faculty members conduct at least one continuing education activity each year and 20% are very active. A network of school district, association, and union relationships provides the context for continuing teacher education. Many collective bargaining agreements include provision of continuing education.

Interestingly, almost one-half of the institutions Knox surveyed report no continuing legal education efforts other than a few conferences a year. The largest had about 3,000 registrants in approximately 25 programs, with an annual budget of $1 million. In most states, the Bar Association, or an organization related to it, has been the primary provider. Faculty interest is modest and so are honoraria. The main barrier appears to be a lack of practitioner interest in the specialized expertise that most law professors have. Although a major trend cited was increased attorney specialization, none of the deans or directors expected major changes in the extent and type of continuing legal education in the near future. It is intriguing that the strongest demand by practitioners in many locations was evidenced during their earliest years of practice.

The picture in schools of social work or social-service administration couldn't be more different. With annual continuing education enrollments ranging from 1,000 to 6,000, the schools provided from 30 to 200 programs to metropolitan areas, the main service area defined by most schools. The schools serve a public much broader than social work, sometimes called the helping professions: clergy, nurses, teachers and counselors, personnel directors, and the like. After a decade of expansion, the schools surveyed felt that demand had stabilized. Public institutions' program activities were substantially more extensive than those of private institutions. With one exception, the institutions Knox surveyed reported that between one-half and two-thirds of the faculty members made some contribution to planning and conducting activities each year. A few faculty were heavily involved, however, and carried most of the load.

The pattern of program development was similar in each institution, with individual faculty responsible for traditional credit courses and single-instructor summer workshops. Committees drawn from faculty, potential registrants, and the continuing education office planned group activities such as conferences. The continuing education staff originated about half the ideas that eventually grew into programs. Most continuing education directors had held their positions for about a decade. Important differentiating characteristics were observed related to the role of director. In the more vital programs, the director was particularly effective in acquiring and maintaining external support, in relating to practitioners and faculty members, and in persisting with efforts to expand or improve things. Another important differentiating characteristic was the actual involvement of practitioners in planning and conducting programs. Some of the directors anticipated using practitioners and faculty members to identify emerging trends and policy issues in the field as a basis for programs to which the university could make a distinctive contribution.

For all the attention given to issues of turf and competitiveness in the 1970s, the Knox study shows that larger, university-based continuing education operations depend upon effective collaboration with state agencies, employers, and professional associations. Furthermore, even though some of these are competitive providers, the relationships often include collaborative needs analysis and program design, cosponsorship, and joint evaluation.

A collaborative survey-research effort involving the National University Continuing Education Association and the American Society of Association Executives was conducted by Lillian Hohmann at the University of Chicago in 1978 and 1979 (Nowlen and Stern, 1981). The Chicago survey found that 48% of the 110 responding professional associations and 85% of the 136 responding universities had engaged in cooperative planning and/or provision of nondegree continuing education for professionals. The range of associations and universities surveyed was broad: Ten percent of the associations and 25% of the universities each served between

9,000 and 20,000 professionals; 7% of the associations and 25% of the universities served more than 20,000 professionals each. Universities and associations initiated the relationships with roughly the same frequency; about 10% of the time, a third party brought a university and an association together. With respect to perceived benefits, 90% of the associations felt that the quality of continuing education had been improved through collaboration and 80% cited the development of rewarding professional friendships as a result. Seventy percent of the responding associations indicated that the collaborative relationship served to respond to professionals' demands for improved competence. Among the universities, 88% felt they benefited from greater public awareness of the university's continuing education capabilities and the same percentage cited the development of new and professionally rewarding friendships. Eighty-five percent felt that the quality of resulting programs had been improved as a result of collaboration. Eighty-three percent experienced additional requests for collaboration and 82% felt that the relationship had occasioned continuing education staff development in important ways.

On the downside, 47% of the associations and 43% of the universities experienced difficulty in defining the roles of the collaborating parties. Thirty percent of the associations felt that the universities' hierarchies were too complex for effective decision making. Thirty-six percent of the universities felt that their facilities were inappropriate for adults, particularly for professionals (interestingly, this was not reflected by professional associations). Twenty-six percent of the universities had underestimated the indirect cost of the collaborative relationship. As to the financial nature of the relationships, associations and universities were asked which party took the greater financial risk in the venture. Sixty-seven percent of the universities and 64% of the associations felt that they had carried the greater risk. This response represents different perceptions of risk with respect to some of the *same* ventures by the cooperating parties themselves. Twenty-five percent of the universities surveyed found that the problems of role definition and indirect cost would inhibit them from considering a future collaborative effort. Only 17% of the associations replied that role definition would inhibit them in the future and 14% felt that the universities' ponderous hierarchies were seriously inhibiting.

Despite such extensive collaboration, communication within the field is poor. Those in continuing education for nurses or accountants rarely read journals devoted to continuing education for engineers or physicians. The National University Continuing Education Association (NUCEA), the American Society of Allied Health Professions (ASAHP), and the American Society for Training and Development (ASTD) are among the few places where sustained conversation across professional boundaries can be found among those who analyze needs, design programs, and evaluate outcomes in continuing education. However, in NUCEA the conversation is almost entirely among higher education providers; in ASAHP the conversation rarely strays from issues particular to health-related technicians and therapists; and in ASTD conversations occur within the conceptual framework of employing organizations. The American Association for Adult and Continuing Education (AAACE) has created a Commission for Continuing Education for the Professions that shows promise of addressing the preparation, performance, and continuing education needs common to all who conduct continuing education for business and the professions. Occasionally a foundation, government agency, or national educational association will convene a group of continuing educators that transcends professional and provider categories, but to date such efforts have been intermittent and unrelated. A fragile network has emerged, but only at the most senior levels of leadership. This network is neither strong enough nor catholic enough to act as a field-wide catalyst for adapting successful educational innovations; for identifying the special strengths universities, professional associations, and employers bring to continuing education; and for addressing the major issues that confront business, the professions, and the public interest.

In what we have seen of the field so far, continuing education comes into focus as the more formal, episodic, and visible expression of the sustained drive for learning that pervades professional life. In continuing education experiences, professionals are directed by others toward explicit sets of closely related learning goals. In continuing learning, the context for continuing education, professionals direct themselves, usually informally, and often pursue several unrelated learning strategies simultaneously. Continuing education is only occasionally a tactical choice flowing intentionally from continuing-learning strategies. Whether measured by the rate of participation by professionals, the dollars committed, the number and kind of providers, or by the variety of programs available, continuing education is a major fixture of American professional life. Continuing education is, at present, heavily didactic and is directed toward keeping professionals up-to-date. This overarching and ambiguous aim provides continuing professional education with conceptual unity without wedding it to performance outcomes. Employers are the largest provider. Among programs provided by others, employers are the largest consumer. A characteristic of major providers is the number and extent of collaborative efforts with associations, universities, and employers. Providers evaluate programs by assessing participants' opinions about the value of the just concluded update (most instruments are exit polls) and by registration counts. There is relatively little assessment of participating professionals. Two dominant issues confronted the field in the 1970s: whether continuing education should be mandatory; and whether higher education or professional associations had some form of primacy. These have led the field to a set of current issues dealing with teaching, learning, and performance and, increasingly, to serious doubts about the prevailing "update" paradigm.

Several other dimensions must be added to this picture for the field to come completely into view. Continuing education for business and the professions represents theory and research as well as practice. Some of the intellectual streams that define and nourish it are to be found in the field of study and application called adult education. Professional-school planners, association executives, and corporate-education directors, pondering the right policy, structuring an organization, choosing staff, analyzing needs, designing or evaluating programs, will want to engage the accumulated literature on the historical, philosophical, and operational issues of adult education.[1]

The research literature on actual program operations is abundant. It addresses questions of needs analysis, adult student mo-

[1]A comprehensive discussion of adult education as a movement and field is available in the work of M. Knowles and C. H. Grattan. Adult education's intellectual fonts include R. Kotinsky and E. C. Lindeman's applications of J. Dewey's pragmatism; the many theoretical formulations of program planning processes heavily influenced by R. Tyler; C. O. Houle's detailed analysis of program origin settings and his fundamental design system; the descriptive research by D. Walker and others suggesting a very low ratio exists between explicit educational planning decisions and those reached implicitly; applications, especially L. P. Bradford's, of K. Lewin's work on group process and change theory; the community development movement so influenced by H. McClusky; systems analysis, as in applications by G. Odiorne and M. Toye; H. M. Kallen's observations of the influence of values in the education process; and adult development theory from R. Havighurst's application of role concept and E. Erikson's studies of the life cycle to A. B. Knox's comprehensive consolidation of human development research and its implications for adult educators.

tivation, patterns of adult student anxiety, the range of organizational models for the continuing education function, guidance and counseling, marketing, measurement and the appraisal of results, financial patterns, and budgetary models.

Many who are engaged in continuing education for business and the professions are aware of the literature and traditions of the field of adult education, actively participate in one or more of the field-wide professional associations, and contribute to the literature of the field's research and practice. Others, some of whom have come to business and professional continuing education from disciplines found in relevant professional schools, from successful management of professional association meetings, or from corporate human-resources management, are unfamiliar with the field. The latter sometimes fate their professional schools, associations, or corporations to muddle through questions and issues that the field of adult education had already successfully addressed—a distinctly wasteful form of ontogeny recapitulating phylogeny. A superb bibliographic essay on the literature of adult education is available in Houle's *Design of Education* (1972, pp. 237–302).

The field's intellectual history and the literature of its practice yield major frames of practical reference. These frames of reference act like sensitive scanning devices, which, in the manner of infrared photography, can be used to probe each of the many levels of a situation (Nowlen, 1980, pp. 14–17). Scanning the various settings of practice is a diagnostic process designed to identify the widest possible range of continuing education interventions.

The scanning devices might include a needs-assessment instrument drafted and applied under the influence of learner-centered interests. Research on adult life roles might suggest a scan for educational needs that relate generally high motivation for improvement to the powerful engine of successful past performance. Using a systems-theory framework, the practitioner might scan a situation for possible use of continuing education experiences as temporary systems to influence organizational restructure or to improve generic tasks such as project management. From the conceptual viewpoint of human-resources development, the practitioner might scan for strategies to democratize knowledge and information throughout the organization.

From such a list, those educational strategies likely to make the most critical contribution in the most cost-beneficial way can be identified, interrelated whenever possible, and sequenced for maximum effect. Multiple scans of this sort cannot fail to identify the difference that continuing education is expected to make to the nurse supervisors, teachers, and securities analysts or to the pharmaceutical company, public library, or architectural firm involved in the scanning procedures. The number and kind of scans need be limited only by ignorance of the field's frames of reference and the lack of resources to act upon the results. Looking at business and professional life through the many conceptual lenses available suggests extraordinarily varied continuing learning and, hence, continuing education needs. Unfortunately, the continuing education response doesn't generally reflect this variety.

The Update Model

What is the structure of the field?

> At minimum, continuing professional education appears to be a complex of instructional systems, many of them heavily didactic, in which people who know something teach it to those who do not know it. The central aim of such teaching, which is offered by many providers, is to keep professionals up to date in their practice. But the achievement of this goal is usually evaluated indirectly, chiefly by counting the number of people involved in an activity or assessing their attitude toward it. [Houle, 1982, p. 254]

This picture still accurately captures the field. (See Figure 1.1.) As a complex of instructional systems, the field can be quite varied. The tools of the field: teleconferences, decision trees, interactive computer terminals, video-taped case studies, executive-behavior simulations, city-planning games, and the like—are widely adaptable, often stimulating as well as instructive, and their relative contribution to learning objectives can be evaluated. These tools are sometimes orchestrated in programs and systems that vary individual and group activity, study and discussion, challenge and reassurance.

Although the landscape of the field is dotted with such innovative practices, it is dominated by the informational "update." In what is typically an intensive two- or three-day short course, a single instructor lectures and lectures and lectures fairly large groups of business and professional people who sit for long hours in an audiovisual twilight, making never-to-be-read notes at rows of narrow tables covered with green baize and appointed with fat binders and sweating pitchers of ice water. Billed variously as a "knowledge update" or "technology transfer," the updates are more

Figure 1.1. UPDATE MODEL

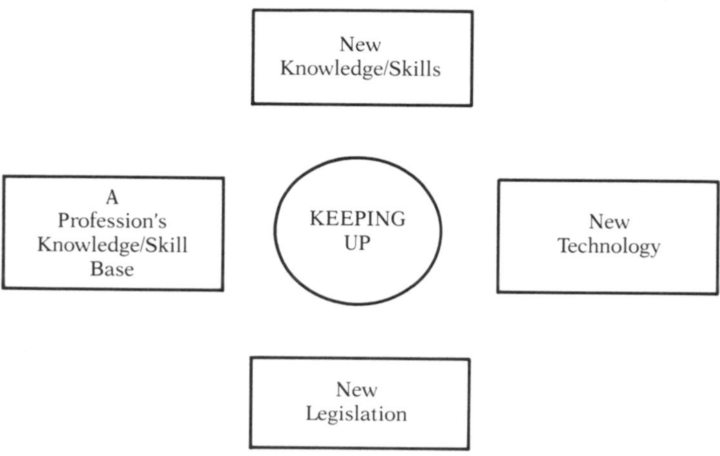

specifically promoted as "Finance for the Non-Financial Executive," "Principles of Microbial Control of the Hospital Environment," "Environmental Engineering Update," "Theory and Practice of Jaw Orthopedics," and "New SEC Regulations." These heavily didactic short courses pursue the central aim of keeping professionals up to date in their practices. This aim unifies the field but only in the same ambiguous way in which astrological signs can be said to unify the heavens. Allowing for the traditional American love of new gadgetry and dread of being caught up in a fad past its prime, what is the content of the phrase "being up to date" as applied to professional practice? How is it related to competence, proficiency, and performance? In what ways are clients, patients or customers better off? Nonetheless, ambiguous though it is, keeping up to date is as close to a unifying aim as the field currently has. The information-intensive, short-course update is overwhelmingly the characteristic continuing education response.

How can we account for the dominance of the update model, given the varied conceptual frameworks and tools of adult education and the equally varied continuing-learning agendas of business and professional persons? Unfamiliarity with the concepts and practices available in adult education may be part of the explanation. The prevailing view of the structure of knowledge and of the ways professionals "know" has also strongly (if imperceptibly) limited the continuing education response.

When there is a strong consensus about knowledge and the ways of knowing, there is broad agreement about the methods and purposes of investigation, teaching, and learning. Until recently, the view prevailed that knowledge is certain, hierarchical and determinate, and that the relative value of knowledge is determined by the extent to which it can be mathematically validated. As Donald A. Schon demonstrates in *The Reflective Practitioner,* this positivist construct places basic science, expressed in general principles, at the apex. Applied science, including related skills and attitudes, is one step down. Problem solving, basic science mediated by applied science, is one more step down. Researchers create knowledge, providing basic and applied science from which methods of solving problems are drawn. Practitioners consume knowledge and provide researchers with opportunities for study and tests of utility. Higher education's research and teaching and the resulting "knowledge base" particular to each profession had until recently reflected broad agreement with this paradigm. The positivist model is also the dominant epistemology of professional practice. Professionals often say that they feel "most professional" when they are applying a research-based technique or protocol, that is, when their problem solving is firmly grounded in the world of certainty, stability, and rigor (Schon, 1983, pp. 21–69).

There should be little surprise, then, that continuing education's updates express this framework. Updates view professionals as if they were at the passive end of a series of mediatory steps, each at increasing distance from the world of "real" knowledge. New knowledge of this sort is created by scientists and scholars doing basic research in the strongest institutions. Their specific research interests and opportunities are often influenced by the dynamics of their own scholarly profession and institution but are almost never troubled by issues of immediacy or application for practicing professionals. Other minds in other institutions work at applied science and produce decision trees, protocols, and technologies that, in turn, may enhance the problem-solving proficiencies of practitioners. The advance of knowledge, at several removes from practitioners, creates a gap between what practitioners know and do and what they could know and might do. Informational updates have the unending task of closing such gaps and "keeping up" is the imperative driving professionals to continuing education.

The update is thus tied to positivism that was well established early in the century, and that still influences the way professionals view themselves. Yet the positivist paradigm is now, everywhere, under attack. First rocked by Einstein's theory of relativity, the positivist paradigm has rested on increasingly shaky ground ever since. Einstein demonstrated that measurement is relative and thus weakened the application of mathematics to science. The tremors turned into a full scale quake with Heisenberg's uncertainty principle and Goedel's demythologizing of mathematics as self-validating. As Kenneth Bruffee puts it,

> Whereas Einstein cast doubt on our ability to measure things and Heisenberg cast doubt on our ability to observe them, Goedel insisted that the results of measured observation (even if we could measure, even if we could observe) cannot be validated within the frame of reference which governs the measuring, or with the symbolic system which expresses it. [1981, p. 180]

By the 1970s the positivist model had been jolted from its dominance by Thomas Kuhn, who demonstrated in *The Structure of Scientific Revolutions* the extent to which the so-called laws of nature remain in force through consensual (not mathematical) validation (1970). Kuhn maintained that the privileged position accorded to the "hard" sciences is unwarranted. With others such as Stephen Toulmin, Kuhn argued that the positivist paradigm of knowledge is naively empiricist and ahistorical because frames of reference are in fact continually negotiated and renegotiated, that is, knowledge is social. Frames of reference are determined by *communities* of interpretation and it is in these communities that knowledge grows.

Business and the professions, broadly defined, are just such active interpretive communities in which collaborative learning, the formation and reformation of frames of reference, and the growth of knowledge take place. These processes can most easily be seen at work within professions that represent several differing interpretive communities. Psychiatry, social work, and urban planning, for example, each contain groups that sharply disagree about ends, and, therefore, these professions, as such, have no consensual context, no established decision trees guiding the application of techniques and no profession-wide agreement about the problem to be solved. In other professions, such as dentistry, a major paradigm shift occurred in the last decade when the frame of reference changed from treatment to prevention.

The positivist epistemology of professional practice is also under attack because as Schon writes,

> . . . [it] invariably ignores problem setting, the process by which we define the decision to be made, the ends to be achieved and the means

> which may be chosen. In the real world, problems never appear as such without the intervention of the problem setting or defining mind. It is a process in which interactively we name the things to which we will attend and frame the context in which we will attend to them. [Schon, 1983, pp. 21–69]

An example from medicine: In a Chicago hospital recently, a surgical resident was reviewing for the benefit of some colleagues the workups on a case with a large pancreatic mass. The resident had recommended a biopsy. A colleague inquired about the personal characteristics of the case, "Who is the case? What are the family circumstances? What's the prognosis?" The "case" was, in fact, an 86-year-old widower with no immediate family. From the size of the pancreatic mass, there was no doubt that the old man had a reasonably short time in which to live. The biopsy was unnecessary for arriving at a reasonable diagnosis and would certainly not positively affect the prognosis. The resident was not at all sensitive to the role of her defining mind that viewed the problem in the narrowest of settings, "a case with a large pancreatic mass," thereby locking it into a particular decision grid. The typical continuing medical education update would only enhance the sophistication of the radiological workups, the rapidity of the diagnostic conclusions, or the skill with which the surgical procedure itself would have been performed.

The emphasis on problem solving, as opposed to problem definition, is a natural consequence of the positivist model of knowledge. The process of problem definition is, after all, filled with uncertainty, uniqueness, instability, and values conflict—dimensions of reality better addressed by "soft" knowledge such as artistry, craft, and wisdom.

Positivism often leaves the professional torn between rigor and relevance. The resident dealing with "the case with a large pancreatic mass" protested that she could only view the "case" as an 86-year-old who didn't have long to live by stepping outside her professional role. As Schon points out, very little of the topography of professional practice is high, hard ground where a problem can be smoothly mapped on a decision tree. "The professional who tries to confine his practice to the rigorous applications of research-based techniques would find not only that he could not work on the most important problems, but that he could not practice in the real world at all" (Schon, 1984, pp. 12–13).

Yet, most people in business and the professions do deal successfully with situations in which there are collisions of value systems. They cope every day with uncertain, indeterminate, complex, unique, and unstable circumstances. They do demonstrate art, craft, and wisdom. They are often at a loss to explain how they do it and they are uneasy because the application of specialized knowledge to self-defining tasks doesn't seem to be involved. They have difficulty showing others how to do it. Descriptively, professional knowing and professional doing appear to be far richer and more creative than the prescriptions of positivism would suggest.

To question the positivist view of the structure of knowledge is to do more than question the prevailing model of continuing professional education. Positivism still reigns prescriptively in many professional schools and there will be implications for preprofessional curricula as continuing education moves beyond the informational update model. Moreover, to reject the positivist view of knowledge and of the way professionals "know" is to shift continuing education's fundamental orientation from the professional as passive consumer to the professional as an active source of knowledge about the critical elements of professional performance.

While the pace of contemporary life and, particularly, the speed with which knowledge is expanding will continue to motivate business and professional people to participate in continuing education, the impossibility of any single person ever being fully up to date has caused some to make more discriminating continuing education choices and others to question whether being up to date has value in and of itself. The better newspapers are always up to date, but their value often fails to outlive the day. The drive to be current is inevitably in some tension with the need to be well-informed. No president was more current, more on top of details, than Jimmy Carter. No president was better informed than Thomas Jefferson. Especially now, when the very pace of technology has made it possible to store the latest information at arm's length in a desk-top personal computer, minds are potentially freer for more significant activity than information storage.

Keeping professionals and business people up to date is a means, not an end in itself. When the educator chooses among possible updates to offer, and when the learner selects one update opportunity rather than another, there are criteria at play that carry each well beyond considerations of simply keeping up to date. Universities and professional associations are concerned with the relative impact on the professions and their clients of new information, legislation, conceptual frameworks, skills, procedures, and technology. Business and professional people are concerned with the relative difference the conference, seminar, or course is likely to make in their professional practice, agency, or organization.

References

BERLIN, LAWRENCE. "A Contrary View." In *Power and Conflict in Continuing Professional Education,* edited by M. R. Stern. Belmont, CA: Wadsworth, 1982.

BRUFFEE, KENNETH A. "The Structure of Knowledge and the Future of Liberal Education," *Liberal Education,* Fall, 1981.

COLLINS, GLEN. "Young Professionals Flock to Night School," *New York Times,* February 22, 1985.

FOSTER, BADI G., AND RIPPEY, DAVID R. "By Any Other Name . . . Continuing Higher Education and the Corporation," *Continuum* 49(2), 1985.

HOULE, CYRIL O. *The Design of Education.* San Francisco: Jossey-Bass, 1972.

———. *Continuing Learning in the Professions.* San Francisco: Jossey-Bass, 1980.

———. "Possible Futures." In *Power and Conflict in Continuing Professional Education,* edited by M. R. Stern. Belmont, CA: Wadsworth, 1982.

KEANE, JOHN G. "Higher Education: Some Trends Stressing the Need for Strategic Planning," *Continuum* 49(2), 1985.

KNOX, ALAN B. *Adult Development and Learning.* San Francisco: Jossey-Bass, 1977.

———. "University Continuing Professional Education." Occasional Paper No. 10. Office for the Study of Continuing Professional Education, College of Education, University of Illinois at Urbana-Champaign, 1980.

KUHN, THOMAS. *The Structure of Scientific Revolutions.* Second edition. International Encyclopedia of Unified Science, 2(2). Chicago: University of Chicago Press, 1970.

NATIONAL CENTER FOR EDUCATIONAL STATISTICS. *Participation in Adult Education 1981.* Washington, D.C.: National Center for Educational Statistics, 1982.

NOWLEN, PHILIP M. "Program Origins." In *Developing, Administering and Evaluating Adult Education,* edited by A. B. Knox. San Francisco: Jossey-Bass, 1980.

NOWLEN, PHILIP M., AND QUEENEY, DONNA S. *The Role of Colleges and Universities in Continuing Professional Education.* National University Continuing Education Association Occasional Paper. Washington, D.C.: NUCEA, 1984.

NOWLEN, PHILIP M., AND STERN, MILTON R. "Partnerships in Continuing Education for the Professions." In *Partnerships with Business and the Professions,* 1981 Current Issues in Higher Education. Washington, D.C.: American Association for Higher Education, 1981.

PHILLIPS, LOUIS E. *Mandatory Continuing Education for Selected Professions: Status and Trends.* Athens, Georgia: Louis Phillips and Associates, 1986.

SCHNEIDER, CAROL G. "Power and Conflict in Continuing Professional Education Reviewed," *American Journal of Education* 92(4), 1984.

SCHON, DONALD A. *The Reflective Practitioner.* New York: Basic Books, 1983.

———. "The Crisis of Professional Knowledge and the Pursuit of An Epistemology of Practice," Paper presented on the occasion of the Harvard Business School's 75th Anniversary Colloquium on Teaching by the Case Method. The President and Fellows of Harvard College, 1984.

SCOTT, WILLIAM. "Remarks on Department of Defense Commitments to Training and Development." National Consultation on Continuing Higher Education. Washington, D.C.: NUCEA, 1984.

SHIMBERG, BENJAMIN. *Occupational Licensing: A Public Perspective.* Princeton, NJ: Educational Testing Service, 1980.

STERN, MILTON R. (ED.). *Power and Conflict in Continuing Professional Education.* Belmont, CA: Wadsworth, 1983.

TWO
The Competence Model

What competencies make the greatest difference in a professional practice, agency, or organization? On what competencies are professionals drawing when they deal successfully with the uncertain, the unique, the unstable? What competencies are actually at work in successful professional performance? How can such competencies be taught? Can continuing education for business and the professions be advanced as a competence model?

Assessing, creating, maintaining, renewing, enhancing, or assuring competence is frequently not only the goal that providers and consumers have in mind, but also a goal that immediately reveals the limitations of the update paradigm. Competence is most generally defined as marked or sufficient aptitude, skill, strength, judgment, or knowledge without noticeable weakness or demerit. Implicit in definitions of competence are two ideas: context, that is, a job, role, function, or task; and, requirements, that is, context-related demands or standards expressed in terms of level of expectation or sufficiency. (See Figure 2.1.)

Being up to date is only one aspect of the relationship of knowledge and skill to competence. Updates rarely address competence-related aptitudes and strengths such as interpersonal skills and motivation, or the events and personal weaknesses that impair competence. Updates maintain or enhance the competence of only some persons, some of the time.

Continuing educators who have moved beyond the update paradigm have entered a lively discussion about the nature of the new goal. Generally accepted definitions of competence refer to both the presence of characteristics or the absence of disabilities that render a person fit, or qualified, to perform a specific task or to assume a defined role. To be competent is to possess sufficient

Figure 2.1. COMPETENCE MODEL

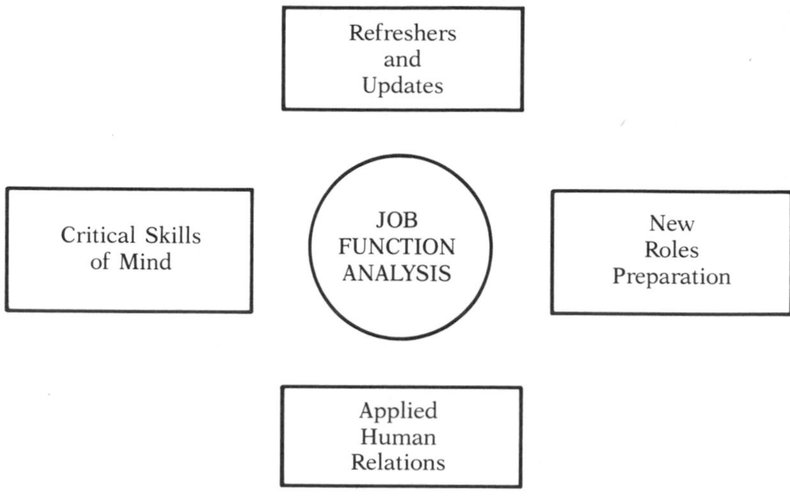

knowledge and ability to meet specified requirements in the sense of being able, adequate, suitable, and capable. A competence-based approach in pharmacy (Cyrs, 1978, p. 1) adopts G. E. Hall and H. L. Jones' definition:

> Competence is acquired intellectual, attitudinal, and/or motor capabilities derived from a specified role and setting and stated in terms of performance as a broad composite or domain of behavior and which is, in effect, an integration or synthesis of behavioral objectives as well as some elements of covert behavior. [Hall and Jones, 1976, pp. 29–30]

Arguably, the most serviceable competence definition emerges from the McBer firm's studies of professional and executive performance:

> Competence is generic knowledge, skill, trait, self-schema or motive causally related to effective and/or outstanding performance in a job.
>
> - knowledge, a category of usable information organized around a specific content area, for example, knowledge of math;
> - skill, an ability to demonstrate a set of behaviors or processes related to a performance goal, for example, logical thinking.
> - trait, a consistent way of responding to an equivalent set of stimuli, for example, initiative;
> - self-schema, a person's image of self and his/her evaluation of that image, for example, self-image as a professional;

- motive, recurrent concern for a goal, state or condition which drives, selects and directs behavior of the individual, for example, the need for efficacy. [McBer, 1978]

Many agendas, such as the development of standards, evaluation of performance, certification and recertification, licensure and relicensure, planning and implementing continuing education programs, and reevaluation of professional school curricula energize associations, higher education, and other agencies to identify the competence actually required by professional or business practice. Some of the work has taken a decade to complete. Other projects have been underway for 10 years and are still not complete. The consistent starting point is identification of the basic functions performed. Variously called job or function analysis, a practice profile, or (sometimes) role delineation, the first step establishes what businesspeople or professionals really do for a living. This is also the case for professionals who function as organization executives.

Anyone imagining this to be an exercise in demonstrating the obvious might be surprised by doing an easy experiment. Choose someone who reports to you. Jot down a description of what you expect from that person, that is, the chief functions of the position, their relative priority, and their demands on time. Note briefly the knowledge, skills, and attitudes that you consider of particular importance to the position. Ask your subordinate to perform the exercise with respect to the same position. Compare what you think the subordinate does for a living with the subordinate's judgment. Where judgments are congruent, compare notes about relevant knowledge, skills, and attitudes. Where there are significant differences in judgment, who is right and how do you know? Try the same exercise with a subordinate who holds essentially the same kind of position as the one first chosen, but in your judgment performs at a different level of competence. Does a comparison of the subordinates' judgments suggest explanations for variance in performance? With your experiences freshly in mind, consider the following major efforts.

Seven Competence-Model Cases

In 1975, the University of Minnesota's College of Pharmacy decided to develop a competency-based curriculum in order to improve teaching effectiveness. The college was chiefly interested in the issue of predictive validity. Can students' future competence be predicted from knowledge of test results, grades, or degrees? Can competence be certified for the purpose of licensure? Although the focus of the project was a professional school's curriculum, the issue of predictive validity is very close to continuing educators' concern with developing programs that will maintain or enhance competent practice.

Thomas E. Cyrs directed the Minnesota project by building back toward curriculum evaluation and change from the assessment of professionals in practice. Cyrs did not have traditional student evaluation methods in mind, but insisted that assessment must be conducted in an environment that simulates the real-world setting and role in which the performance is expected to take place, and from which an understanding of the requisite competence could be inferred. Cyrs' approach applied criterion sampling and was predicated on assessing those behaviors that actually sample skills utilized in a variety of pharmacy settings and are arrived at through analysis of job requirements (Cyrs, 1978, p. 2).

Initially, panels of faculty, students, practitioners, and consumers addressed the nature of competence in the practice of pharmacy and arrived at a set of tentative statements. Interestingly this preliminary effort generated two categories of competence statements, one labeled "must have" (core competencies, frequently found) and the other, "should have" (desired but not necessarily found at all). These and other panels subsequently provided words and short phrases that would describe core competencies and actions evidencing individual mastery. The College of Pharmacy staff then reviewed these statements. Six hundred Minnesota practitioners, students, and faculty evaluated them, 93% "highly valuing" all except two of the competence statements. On-site job analyses in 14 different pharmacy settings provided comparative data for final confirmation and validation of the statements.

Through similar processes, a number of groups examined the validated statements in order to identify their major content and to describe the terminal performance that would demonstrate the underlying competence. The typical statement was supported by five or six such descriptors. Resulting lists of performance or behavioral objectives in hierarchical relationships were then evaluated for comprehensiveness and appropriateness by professional review panels.

Cyrs maintains that such a schema is promising for either continuing education needs assessment or for licensure and relicensure, particularly if used in an assessment-center mode. (The literature devoted to assessment centers is abundant. An assessment center refers to a cluster of methodologies rather than a physical place.) Cyrs' methodology cluster favors work simulations; multiple measurement techniques such as independent, systematic, objective observations by multiple raters; role-playing, gaming, situational problem solving and criterion-referenced paper/pencil tests. Behaviorally anchored rating scales are used in what amounts to a holistic rather than an atomistic approach. Used in continuing education circumstances, the businessperson or professional can formulate a significant learning agenda and the continuing educator can gain evidence of need as well as case-rich data for developing programs serving specific competence objectives.

In 1976, the American Association of Colleges of Pharmacy (AACP), the American Pharmaceutical Association (APhA), and the Educational Testing Service (ETS) began working together. Their objectives were to develop professional standards of competence; to identify a mechanism for applying the standards to practice; and to establish a voluntary system in which the standards and mechanisms could be tested. The project leader, Samuel H. Kalman, has been a model of openness and generosity to other continuing educators, freely sharing the AACP-APhA experience. As a first step toward developing a comprehensive checklist of the pharmacist's job description and tasks, AACP and APhA provided ETS with descriptions of pharmacist responsibilities and functions. Project staff reviewed the occupational literature and made site visits to practitioners in varied settings such as research, solo practice, and large corporate multipractitioner settings such as drugstore chains. The site visitors observed and interviewed pharmacists who reviewed a preliminary schema of job-description tasks.

AACP and APhA then reviewed the checklist of pharmacist tasks. A committee of practitioners was formed, representing a variety of practice settings. This committee was concerned to see that the checklist included all the major dimensions and tasks of pharmacist practice. The committee also advised on the checklist-survey's wording and format. Project staff revised the checklist a third time. After it was then pilot tested by pharmacists, reviewers realized there were problems with its length as well as with the number of rating scales. The final draft was approved by the project's steering committee and distributed to a broad geographical random sample of 5,000 pharmacists. Preliminary survey data was available three months later, 18 months after the two associations and ETS had begun working together.

In comparing the first draft with the final checklist, one is struck with the shift of focus from the pharmacist to the pharmacist-patient relationship. For example, the first item in the first draft under the general responsibility of processing the order is "Receives order from an authorized prescriber." Item one under the same general rubric in the final checklist is "Determines necessity of immediately handling the preparation and delivery of the medication to the patient (emergency or stat)." Another general responsibility in draft one was "Dispensing and compounding." In final form, it had become "Patient-care functions." Another, more subtle, shift was made from the detached, rational order of draft one to the final form's listing of responsibilities as they generally occur in practice.

Considerations of organization behavior as well as survey research were well served. For the responsibility-task checklist to become the basis of a set of practice standards in a voluntary system required that many constituencies in each association and among pharmacists in various settings of practice invest themselves in the checklist process and thereby come to the view that they owned and believed in what they had had a hand in developing.

With a validated checklist of responsibilities as a baseline, the AACP and APhA began to address issues of practice standards: What must pharmacists do to fulfill these responsibilities? What are the subfunctions involved? How often should each be performed, and with what degree of accuracy or completeness? Another committee of practitioners was formed and the now-familiar process began again.

In 1979, Pennsylvania State University began a five-year effort that built upon the practice-audit experience of the AACP-APhA project. Penn State's objectives were:

- to bring the university and the professions into collaboration;
- to focus continuing education activities as closely as possible on the needs of the profession at the point of practice;
- to develop the basis for a long-term relationship by institutionalizing the continuing professional education development process in both the university and the respective professional associations.

Collaboration, practice orientation, and institutionalization are the concepts that appear again and again in the detailed and extensive publications the project has occasioned. (For example, Toombs and Lindsay, 1985; Crowe et al., 1984; Queeney and Melander, 1984; and "Continuing Professional Education Development Project News," published by project staff.) Five professions are engaged in designing, executing, and evaluating the project: architecture, accounting, clinical psychology, clinical dietetics, and nursing.

The "Practice Audit Model" (see Figure 2.2) provides a sense of the project's flow. The project is centered in Pennsylvania State University's Office of Planning Studies and funded by the W. K. Kellogg Foundation. The five collaborating professions were selected on the basis of their being established bodies, represented by organizations whose rolls included most of the practitioners. Project staff felt the professions selected had to be characterized by a generic body of practice, a set of knowledge, skills, and applications that everyone was expected to know, serious interest in setting up practice standards, and a commitment to continuing education. The size of the profession within the state, relevant academic resources within the university, and willingness to commit to a five-year process were also among the criteria for selecting collaborating professions (Queeney and Melander, 1984). Project staff selected associations as collaborating organizations rather than professional schools, government licensing bodies, or consumer-advocate groups. Associations certainly have richer and more varied contact with professionals than do government agencies and consumer groups, and associations are generally perceived as being more representative of practice-related needs than are professional schools. With each profession, the baselines of practice, that is, the knowledge, skills, and judgment called forth by practice in key segments of the field, had to be established (Toombs and Lindsay, 1985).

The first step taken toward this objective with members of the clinical division of the state psychological association, one of the five key collaborating groups, involved panels of experts from professional schools, the American Psychological Association, the Pennsylvania Psychological Association, and the American Association of State Psychology Boards. Project staff, together with these panels, reviewed the occupational literature. The focus was general, examining the practice of clinical psychologists rather than ex-

Figure 2.2. PRACTICE AUDIT MODEL

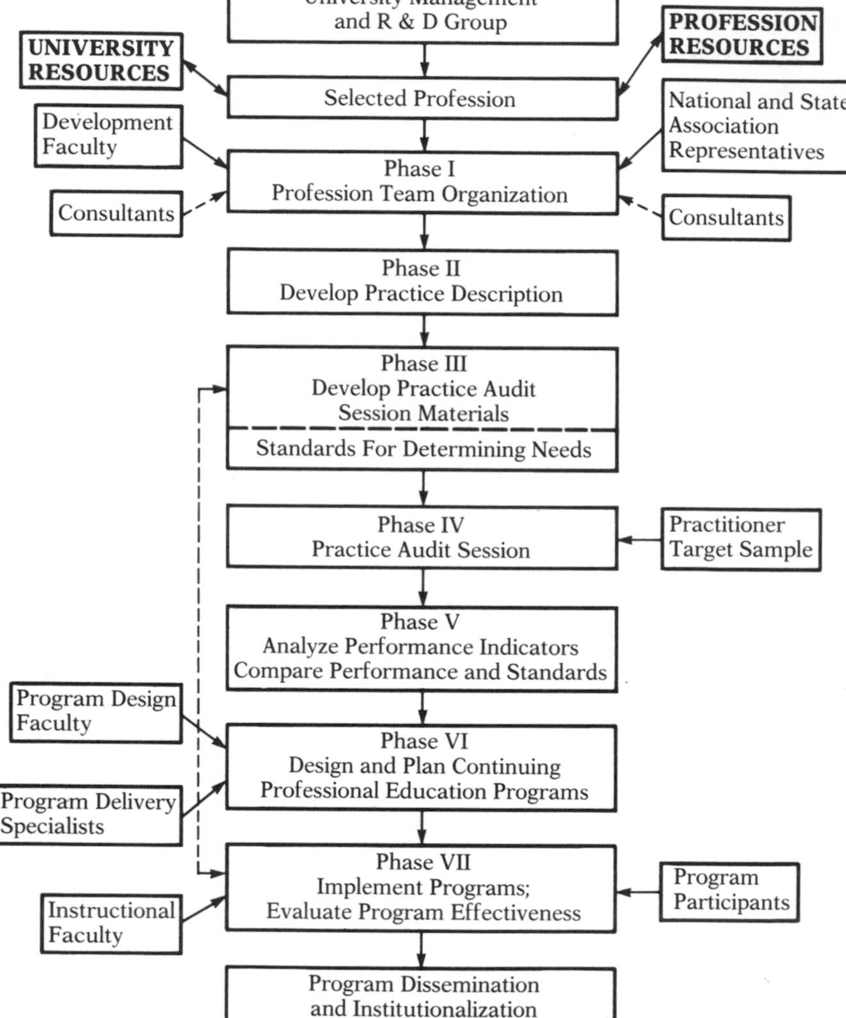

Source: Continuing Professional Education Development Project, Office of Continuing Professional Education, Planning Studies, The Pennsylvania State University, 1985.

amining an individual practitioner, an individual application to a particular set of problems, or one or another specific practice setting. Staff and expert panels of faculty and practitioners (the "Profession Team Organization") concentrated on developing and refining a description of dimensions of practice, for example:

Direct client services

Collects information for clinical inference

Integrates sources of information

Recognizes own limitations

Develops intervention plan

Implements intervention plan

Evaluates intervention plan periodically

Establishes and maintains a professional relationship with client

Maintains confidentiality

Organization and administration of services

Organizes service setting

Trains and supervises interns and staff

Establishes an information-management system

Establishes new client services

Promotes the welfare of the client

Professional activities

Maintains personal and professional standards

Participates in training of clinical psychologists

Promotes the profession of psychology

Promotes mental health through prevention

Conducts research and evaluation studies

Staff and panel members then generated task statements for each responsibility, for example:

Direct client services

Develops intervention plan

Sets goals in conjunction with client and/or significant others for intervention considering costs, time, and resources

Plans intervention in accordance with assessment findings, agreed-upon goals, and theoretical perspective

Assures client's understanding of, and obtains client's agreement to, intervention plan; explains risks, costs, duration, shortcomings, alternatives

Establishes a realistic expectancy in the client regarding accomplishment of goals (Crowe et al., 1984).

The practice description or role delineation was then submitted to the 858 members of the Pennsylvania Psychological Association's clinical division. There were 302 responses (35%). Each task was rated for importance and time required. The ratings were then used to form profiles of practice for the overall sample and groups based on primary professional role, level of experience, and type of professional training. Discriminant function analyses indicated that (a) therapists spend more time on and ascribe more importance to direct client services, and nontherapists spend more time on and assign more importance to administrative tasks; (b) experience is negatively related to the time therapists spend on direct client services but positively related to the time nontherapists spend on administrative tasks; (c) as experience increases, therapists become more concerned with standards and client welfare and yet spend less time on direct client services; and (d) nondoctoral nontherapists spend more time on client information-related responsibilities. Project staff neither intended nor concluded that the practice description was exhaustive. Overall results did confirm that those tasks listed were seen as important as well as frequently performed (Crowe et al., 1984).

With detailed profiles, validated in this way, the Clinical Psychology Profession Team reconvened in order to develop and pilot test practice "audit" approaches. The team planned a practice audit lasting two days scheduled at the conclusion of the annual state-association meeting. The team specified that the participants should be those who spent at least 10 hours weekly delivering direct client services and viewed their primary role to be that of therapist. Through an assessment-center approach, 40 clinical psychologists participated in two streams of activity: a simulated client interaction, videotaped, followed by written questions about participants' assessments and treatment plans; and exercises addressing cross sections of clinical cases, such as viewing a videotaped simulation and evaluating both client and therapist behaviors. Following the practice audit, the Clinical Psychology Profession Team recommended that a continuing education program should be designed for improving clinical skills, especially sensitivity in making clinical observations, and broadening their range. The program was designed and offered in 1984. All participants reported that their clinical practice had been influenced by the program, many contributing anecdotal evidence. The program was presented again in 1985.

The same pattern of progress can be followed with respect to accountants. Having developed a preliminary practice profile, CPAs who were members of local or regional firms and had been in public practice for five years were invited to participate in the practice audit. Using an assessment-center approach again, accountant-client interactions were simulated, tax-return preparation reviewed, and data-gathering techniques evaluated. The practice-audit session yielded 752 separately scored items. The Accounting Profession Team carefully sifted through this assessment of skills in tax practice, financial statement reporting, and effective client relations. Four areas of need were identified for program development: the client goal-assessment process; development, documentation, and audit plans for small businesses; direct adaptation of the accounting practice audit-session exercises; and development of alternatives to the standard short-form opinion provided at the conclusion of an audit. A program was designed for firm partners and those at managerial levels who have direct client contact. It used fields of activity such as tax and estate planning, management-advisory services and financial statement reporting as vehicles for improving accountants' information-gathering skills, client-communication skills, capacity to generate alternative plans of action and to judge their relative value.

In evaluating the project, professional association and project staff, and faculty and practitioners, concluded that the process was at least as valuable as the resultant educational programs. The process suggests some general, if still preliminary, conclusions to project staff.

- Almost no one practices a profession in isolation.
- The simple definition of "client" for many professions has become complex, including families, corporations, communities, and agencies as well as individuals. Most have tiers of client groups, at relatively proximate or remote interactive distances.
- Practitioners find high value in informal exchanges within structured activities.

- The practice-audit model that stressed small groups, collegial atmosphere, peer interaction, opportunity for informal feedback and, particularly, a performance orientation has been identified as a paradigm for future programs. This approach is also relatively more costly than the knowledge-oriented program model (Toombs and Lindsay, 1985).

The benefits of the process cannot be overestimated. Pennsylvania State University has come to be perceived as far more than another competing provider in the crowded field of continuing professional education. It is now regarded by many state professional associations as a reliable ally in the long process of establishing the data base necessary for professional assessment, the weighing of continuing education alternatives, and the development of responsive educational experiences. Any continuing professional education programs developed by the university are likely to be regarded as grounded in practice-related needs. The project's process has, in other words, given Pennsylvania State University a distinctive market position and, thereby, provided project staff with significant external leverage for the internal tasks related to institutionalizing continuing professional education research and teaching. The way in which the process has already involved significant internal academic constituencies also served to build the consensus necessary for continuing professional education to become a normal part of the institution's life.

The leadership of many professional associations have discovered the utility of conversations about educational issues outside the association's specialized orbit of related organizations. As a result, association-based continuing educators have come to experience their identity as members of a professional field and have deepened themselves in the field's research literature and traditions of practice.

In 1981, the board of directors of the American Society for Training and Development (ASTD) charged its professional development committee with producing a detailed and updatable definition of excellence in the training and development field. To the usual competence-model development process, definition of roles, identification of role-related competencies, and specification of behavioral anchors, ASTD added a projection of technological, organizational, educational, sociological, and political factors likely to modify the training and development role in the next decade. The project concluded that training and development's central focus is "identifying, assessing—and through planned learning—helping develop the key competencies which enable individuals to perform current or future jobs" (McLagan and Bedrick, 1983, p. 14). Interventions of training and development personnel focus on individuals, not groups and organizations.

The ASTD project also produced a set of role profiles defining critical outputs and competencies for each of the 15 roles established. A resulting matrix shows critical competencies for all roles and roles for which each is critical. For example, see Table 2.1.

Since project completion, ASTD has used the study to audit its development activities for its member professionals: How well do the activities track with the role/competence matrix? Are the experiences that fit the matrix well adequate? What are the gaps and how shall they be filled? ASTD has used its own experience in helping others to do similar studies of the entire human-resources area, forging useful alliances with other organizations by so doing. ASTD will also reexamine certification and accreditation questions in light of the competence study (McCullough and McLagan, 1983, p. 28).

Alverno College, an 1,800-student women's liberal arts college

TABLE 2.1. ASTD Competence/Roles Matrix

	Manager	Marketer	Instructional Writer	Media Specialist
Presentational Skill	•	•	•	•
Relationship Versatility	•	•	•	•
T & D Techniques Understanding			•	
Industry Understanding	•	•	•	
Organization Understanding	•	•		
Cost/Benefit Analysis	•	•		•
Futuring Skill	•	•		
Model Building Skill			•	
Performance Observation Skill				
Negotiation Skill	•	•		
Research Skills				
A/V Skill				•

Source: McLagan and Bedrick, 1983, p. 20.

located in Milwaukee, engaged in a thorough reexamination of its mission in the early 1970s. It emerged with a commitment to teach "abilities that last a lifetime." Alverno's faculty reexamined its curriculum and orchestrated courses around eight broad competence domains: communications, analysis, problem solving, valuing, social interactions, civic responsibility, involvement in the contemporary world, and aesthetic response. Faculty as well as outside assessors drawn from business and the professions have established that liberal education at Alverno has indeed nurtured specific critical skills of mind, and these are reflected in performance. (Alverno College faculty, 1979, revised 1985; Loacker, Cromwell, Fey and Rutherford, 1984). There is also substantial evidence that Alverno's graduates have continued to develop these core abilities.

As Alverno moved to consider other critical abilities, particularly skills related to career development, almost 1,000 students, alumnae, and professionals served as models for determining what abilities were desirable in particular fields. Establishing the validity of teaching toward core and special abilities for later careering and professional performance is described in Alverno's final report to the National Institute of Education, "Careering After College" (Mentkowski and Doherty, 1980). Alverno has been attentive to the generic abilities required by the responsibilities and tasks of a profession but has been even more interested in identifying the particular competences that distinguish effective performance. This interest governed development of a professional competence model to validate Alverno's faculty-designed management education curriculum. This curriculum has the following outcomes:

- The ability to effectively and consistently integrate and apply managerial concepts and decision making principles in a variety of problem solving contexts
- The ability to organize, direct and control those activities that lead to task accomplishment and the achievement of objectives
- The ability to identify and choose the leadership styles which facilitate task accomplishment and the achievement of objectives.

The American Management Association (AMA), with the help of McBer, had developed a competence model of managerial abilities, compared for effective and ineffective performance. The AMA model clusters abilities in four general areas:

- Socio-emotional maturity
    - Self-control
    - Spontaneity
    - Perceptual objectivity
    - Accurate self-assessment
    - Stamina and adaptability
- Entrepreneurial abilities
    - Efficiency orientation
    - Proactivity
- Intellectual abilities
    - Logical thought
    - Conceptualization
    - Diagnostic use of concepts
    - Specialized knowledge
- Interpersonal abilities
    - Development of others
    - Expressed concern with impact
    - Use of unilateral power
    - Use of socialized power
    - Concern with affiliation
    - Positive regard
    - Management of groups
    - Self-presentation
    - Oral communication (Evarts, 1982; Boyatzis, 1982)

Each competence is defined, in turn, by a set of behavioral descriptors. Alverno chose this model for a validation study because Alverno and McBer define competence similarly. Briefed by Alverno staff, Milwaukee business leaders nominated 146 women managers and executives from the private sector as effective. Of these, 103 from 53 organizations were interviewed using the behavioral-event-interview protocol (McClelland, 1978). This interview process is of use in reconstructing situations in which effective and ineffective performance may have been demonstrated and differs significantly from interviews that survey opinion about the relationship of abilities to performance. Those interviewed are asked: What happened? What did you do? What were you trying to do? What were the consequences? and so on.

Example of One Situation Illustrating the Behavioral Event Interview

WHAT HAPPENED? WHAT LED UP TO IT?

I had worked for a consumer-product company. When I first came to work here, the nature of this company's products was new to me. I was very uncomfortable with the terminology people used. These people I was dealing with had been with the company many years. I set up meetings with various divisions to review their marketing plans with them.

WHO WAS INVOLVED?

Fifteen marketing directors and myself.

WHAT DID YOU DO?

I went individually to get acquainted with some of the directors before our meetings. I reviewed their marketing plans prior to meeting with them.

From that I developed a year-long public relations plan: "Here's a schedule of various releases and literature you should send out relative to the product. This product is significant enough to have a news release."

Through talking with them I also set up parameters based on the products and customers. By giving them parameters I could ask them of their new product, "Does it fit this bill? OK. The trade show you'll be introducing it at would be an ideal time for a news conference." We also discussed any articles that could be written.

I followed through, kept them informed of what we had done, the timing of it, and mailed them news clippings.

WHAT WERE YOUR THOUGHTS AND FEELINGS?

I was not sure of the products and to whom they were sold. I was very confident in setting up these meetings, reviewing marketing plans, and developing P.R. plans, sure of my ground in that area.

I was very aware I was asking extremely basic questions. I was aware of being new and different. I was very careful and didn't want to embarrass this department by appearing too "green."

WHAT HAPPENED AS A RESULT?

It's helped this division to get acquainted with the markets.

The meetings not only helped directors but also helped me become acquainted with the various products we market. Our department might have put out the same type of work, but I don't think I would have understood it as well.

It took time, but I was also helping my assistant to learn. I was putting my organizational skills and his knowledge of the company together.

I don't have that feeling of having to account for my background (Mentkowski et al., 1983, p. 329).

Such interviews produced descriptions of over 500 situations. These were then coded using the American Management Association's competence model. The competences, ordered from most to least frequently performed, were as follows:

Proactivity

Diagnostic use of concepts

Development of others

Accurate self-assessment

Efficiency orientation

Expressed concern with impact

Conceptualization

Self-presentation

Perceptual objectivity

Oral communication skills

Use of unilateral power

Self-control

Management of groups

Positive regard

Use of socialized power

Logical thought

Stamina and adaptability

Spontaneity

Specialized knowledge

Concern with affiliation (Mentkowski et al., 1983).

All those interviewed also completed an inventory of their perceptions about effective performance-related abilities, using an independent, Alverno-designed set of 162 statements of manager abilities (Bishop, Mentkowski, O'Brien, Birney, Davies, and McEachern, 1980). Findings were then directly related to the American Management Association's schema. Perceptions of abilities and their relative importance generally did *not* differ markedly from performance of competencies implicit in the situations reconstructed during interviews, except for a few. For example, managers said that use of socialized power and stamina/adaptability were important but did not commonly manifest these in the interviews. Use of socialized power was especially noted by managers who had completed formal educational programs in management and it was this cluster of persons interviewed who did demonstrate the ability.

Two abilities that the inventory did not identify as very important for effective performance were frequently observed at work in the behavioral situations emerging in the interviews. These abilities were self-control and positive regard.

The same management performance characteristics inventory also served to distinguish the manager's opinions of abilities possessed by outstanding managers from those abilities believed to be characteristic of average managers. The managers viewed outstanding performance to be related to abilities such as

- Maintaining objectivity under stressful conditions
- Creativity

- Making decisions under conditions of risk
- Addressing conflict directly and tactfully
- Presenting a clear position and pressing for a decision when required
- Motivating others.

Abilities viewed by managers as related to average performance included

- Trustworthiness
- Relevant technical skills
- Intelligence
- Carrying out directives appropriately
- Maturity
- Accountability (Mentkowski et al., 1983).

Alverno researchers then asked the same question continuing educators would raise: How might these abilities be mastered? The approach Alverno took to answering the question was to examine how the abilities that were coded in the interviews appeared to be linked with each other in a developmental sequence. A number of factor, cluster, and path analyses were undertaken and the competence model emerged (see Figure 2.3). Assuming the model is realistic, accurate self-assessment, diagnostic use of concepts and the development of others are of primary importance, given the way other abilities appear to be linked with them. Some abilities seem to be prerequisites of other abilities, although they generally are seen as representative of distinct clusters of skills.

The Alverno management competence model does not imply that specialized knowledge—financial analysis and accounting, for example—traditionally associated with managers is not important. Such fields of knowledge may be thought of as the indispensable media in which relative effectiveness is judged by a person's exercise of such skills as the Alverno study highlights. Development of the distinctive clusters of interrelated skills hypothesized by the Alverno management competence model could be, in fact, the intentional outcome of an otherwise traditional management curriculum. Students could develop similar clusters of skills through

Figure 2.3. HYPOTHETICAL MODEL OF COMPETENCE IN WOMEN MANAGERS AND EXECUTIVES

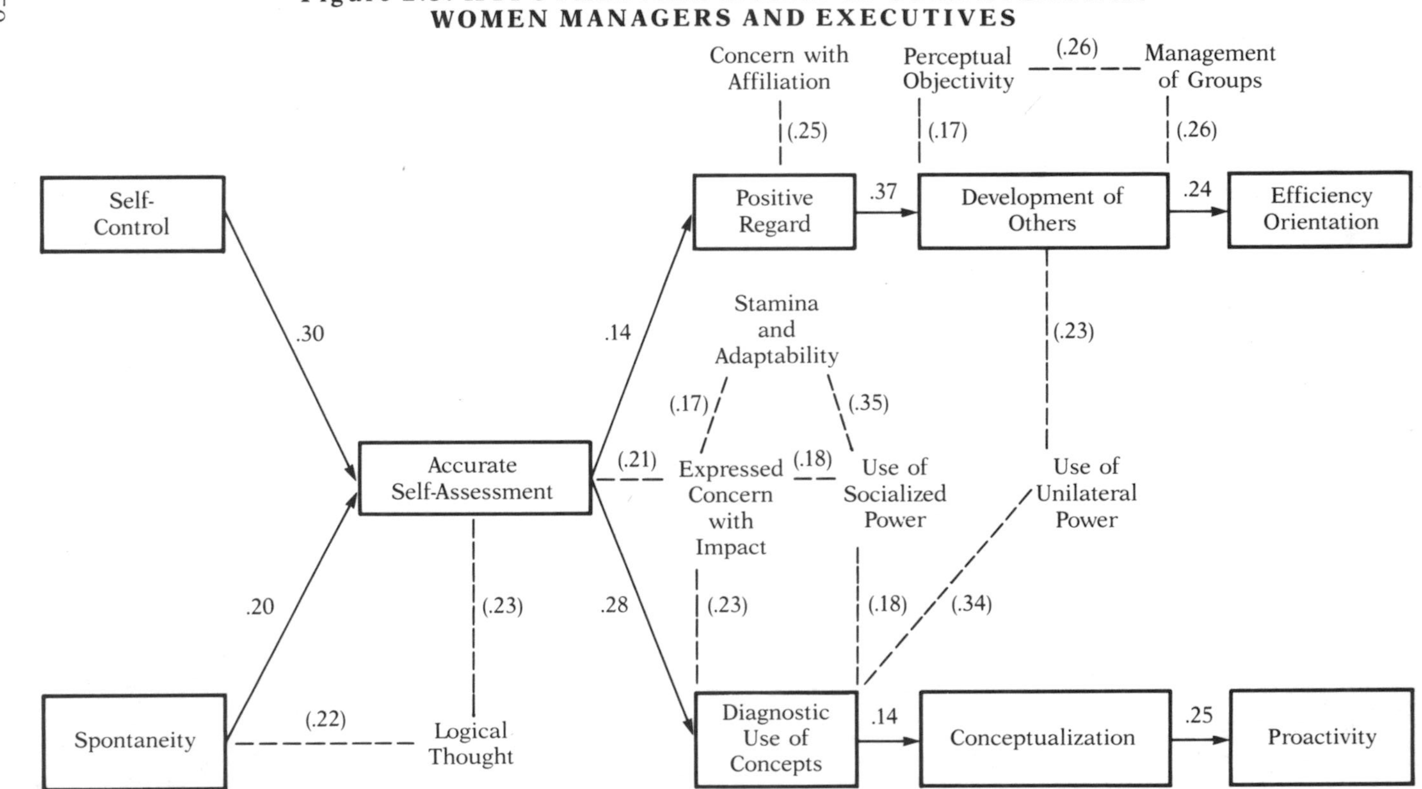

NOTE: Bivariate correlation coefficients are placed in parentheses. Numbers not in parentheses are path coefficients.
Source: Mentkowski et al., 1983, p. 114.

the traditional liberal arts curriculum, but the result would not yet be *management* competence, due to the specialized knowledge involved.

Melany Baehr, an industrial psychologist with The University of Chicago's continuing education unit, has developed a managerial and professional job-functions inventory consisting of 140 items distributed in 16 separate dimensions that describe work activities occurring in higher-level executive positions. The inventory has been administered to representative samples of personnel in nine key positions in three, three-rung management hierarchies: line hierarchy, first-line supervisors and their middle- and executive-level managers; professional hierarchy, university-qualified professionals such as engineers, pharmacists, architects, or social-service professionals and their middle- and executive-level managers; and sales hierarchy, sales representatives, sometimes with bachelor's degrees in relevant fields such as chemistry or pharmacology, and their middle- and executive-line managers. Details concerning the construction and reliability of measurement, together with instructions for administration and scoring, may be found in the inventory's interpretation and research manual (D.C. Allen, 1984). Respondents determine the relative importance of functions described as well as their relative ability to perform them.

The results indicated that there were clear differentiations among the functions performed at the three levels in each management hierarchy. In some instances there were qualitative differences. For example, the supervisory-practices function is important at the middle-management level in all three hierarchies but does not occur as an important function at the senior-executive level in line or professional hierarchies. Objective setting is important at middle and senior levels in the line hierarchy but relatively more important at the senior level. Other results indicate that senior executive-level managers perform largely similar functions regardless of the functional department or hierarchy through which they have risen. Some differences in emphasis seem to exist among senior executives, possibly owing to career path and formal education. For example, those with line-management backgrounds tend to emphasize financial planning and review; whereas managers of professional personnel emphasized interdepartmental coordination; and those with sales-management experience tended to consider handling of outside contacts and supervisor practices to be important functions.

The same groups of personnel in the same key positions were

sampled for perceptions of their ability to perform functions in each of the 16 dimensions. Comparing the group mean scores for importance and self-perceived ability, the greater the discrepancy between pairs of scores, the greater the probable developmental need. Differences of at least five standard score points (one-half standard deviation) for the national sample were identified. (Key: I–Senior Executives; II–Middle Managers; III–Entry Level Management; I–Importance, and A–Perception of Ability.) See Table 2.2. Communications (that is, monitoring and improving both external communications channels and internal upward and downward lines; developing, testing, and seeking feedback on one's own communication skills; conducting effective meetings; and the like) is the job function in which executives most frequently perceive themselves to be deficient. Deficiencies in setting objectives are perceived in two of the three hierarchies at the senior-executive level. The executives with the greatest range of perceived deficiencies are the middle managers of professional personnel, persons who have moved from staff professional or specialist positions to positions in which they are required to supervise their former peers. Their greatest perceived need is for supervisory practices (that is, clarifying subordinates' job functions and responsibilities, motivating employees while maintaining discipline and control, seeing that subordinates maintain established standards of performance and accepting personal responsibility for those who do not.)

The inventory items are generic and describe underlying behavior such as the ability to anticipate future events on the basis of history and experience. Businesspeople who make forecasts as well as professionals who design experiments, lay courtroom strategy and so on, display this behavior routinely. These generic items need to be translated into specific behavioral strategies for successful performance. Melany Baehr suggests that one way of accomplishing this is through brainstorming sessions in which executives generate examples of the kinds of problems that arise within a general performance area such as supervisory practices or setting organization objectives. These examples can then provide experientially-grounded problems for role-playing exercises or for small-group experimental learning (Baehr, 1984, pp. 157–167).

Another approach is the use of representative "critical incidents" of good and poor performance in the work setting (Flannigan, 1954). As they did in the Alverno management competence study, executives reconstruct incidents in which their own behavior may have

Table 2.2.

	Line Personnel	I	A	Professional Personnel	I	A	Sales Personnel	I	A
I	Setting objectives	67	61				Setting objectives	64	58
	Communications	56	48	Communications	53	46	Communications	58	46
II	Communications	56	48	Communications	51	44			
	Self-development	49	44	Supervisory	56	48			
				Developing employee potential	55	50			
				Developing group cooperation	55	49			
III	Supervisory practices	53	49	Setting objectives	55	49	Coping with emergencies	55	50
				Self-development	53	45	Communications	53	48

resulted in significant improvement in performance or led to unexpected difficulties. Those who design educational programs can study critical incidents to identify promising behavioral strategies, develop rich case material, and the like. More elaborate versions of the critical-incident approach, such as the Chicago study of teachers and mentors in degree programs for adults, involve the identification of behavior that successful performers have in common and that distinguishes them from the merely average. Critical-incident self-reports from both groups provide highly informative insights into the subtle differences that distinguish outstanding outcomes from the mediocre. Comparative examination of key incidents from stronger and weaker performers enables the adult learner to consider, in a neutral and unthreatening way, alternative strategies for managing various job functions (Schneider, 1981).

The behavioral-event interview (McClelland, 1978) resembles the critical-incident interview and, like it, is highly useful in developing competence models, performance standards, and continuing education programs. It differs from the critical-incident approach in that those interviewed are asked to identify experiences in their current positions in which they felt most effective and experiences in which they felt particularly frustrated. A nondirective yet structured interview format is followed. Detailed descriptions are elicited, including thoughts, desires, and intentions that accompanied behavior, not just the behavior itself. Resulting data can be examined for thematic content.

The behavioral-event interview was at the center of a study of the competence required for teachers and mentors to perform effectively in degree programs for adults. The study was jointly undertaken by continuing education staff of the University of Chicago and McBer and Company, a behavioral-science research firm that has worked on the identification of competence that differentiates superior from average performance in more than 100 studies of educational, government, and private-sector organizations. The study, supported by the Fund for the Improvement of Postsecondary Education, was made in order to identify skills, abilities, and other characteristics that were directly linked to effectiveness in teaching or mentoring adult students. Frameworks were established for (1) selection; (2) faculty members' self-assessment in relation to their own developmental agendas; and (3) the choice of developmental activities that will be helpful to faculty members undertaking new modes of teaching and learning. Mentoring was defined as assisting students, in one-on-one interactions, to plan and implement their particular degree programs. Underlying tasks vary from assistance with the evaluation of prior learning to direct tutorial instruction. Mentors function as essential links between individual student's expectations and those of the program in which the student is matriculating. Most programs for adults continue to rely heavily on the more traditional role of faculty member as classroom teacher. The resulting competence model is not a complete picture of all the possible skills and abilities that faculty members may call upon in the course of teaching and mentoring. Rather it illustrates the competence that differentiates average from superior mentors and classroom teachers.

The institutions involved represent a cross section of adult degree programs. Two are free-standing institutions, privately funded, whose sole focus is the adult student. Two are traditional institutions with special adult baccalaureate programs. All require new learning, whatever the extent of prior learning might be. All designate curricular goals that they expect their students to achieve. Two employ part-time adjunct faculty, some of whom teach full time elsewhere, some of whom are employed primarily in professional roles. One has a full-time faculty of its own. One relies almost totally on the full-time faculty of its parent institution. Each campus nominated individual faculty who were perceived as effective teachers and mentors in their respective educational settings. On each campus polled, three or four faculty members were selected who had not been nominated as outstanding in either category. These were deemed average in their effectiveness and became the comparison group.

An average of six behavioral events were sought from each person interviewed. Interviews were transcribed from tapes, and the transcripts analyzed for values, attitudes, skills, and other aspects of competence demonstrated by each interviewee in mentoring or teaching. The first step in this analysis was the study of half the interviews with a view to isolating themes that were recurrent among the study-group members and absent among members of the comparison group. Hence, a list of behaviorally grounded themes that differentiated the study group from the comparison group was created. The second step involved coding occurrences of the various behavioral themes as they appeared in the initial half of the transcripts as a way to verify their presence in the study group as well as their capacity to differentiate between the two groups. Refinement of the list of behaviors based on this coding produced a competency "codebook," against which transcripts were read and scored, forcing a careful refinement of the competence and competence-indicator statements. Finally, all interview transcripts were analyzed and coded against the final competence model:

1. Student-centered orientation
   Positive expectations of students
   Attends to students' concerns
2. Humanistic learning orientation
   Values the learning process
   Views specialized knowledge as a resource
3. Provides context conducive to adult learning
   Works to understand students' frames of reference
   Works to establish mutuality and rapport
   Holds students accountable to their best learning interest
4. Grounds learning objectives in an analysis of students' needs
   Actively seeks information about students
   Diagnoses
   Prescribes action
5. Facilitates the learning process
   Links pedagogy to students' concerns
   Structures processes to facilitate students' active learning
   Adapts to situational demands
   Responds to nonverbal cues

A set of positive and negative indicators correspond with each competence statement, for example:

1. Student-centered orientation
   Has positive expectations of students
   (+) Positive regard: expresses view that average students are capable; identifies and affirms others' capabilities
   (+) Expresses view that students are capable of change

(+) Permits student-initiated modifications of the learning contract when they are consistent with the student's learning objectives

(−) Negative regard: expresses view that students are stupid and incapable of change; treats students with disdain; identifies students' weaknesses without suggesting ways to help

(−) Expresses negative stereotypes of others, their personality or potential

As Carol Schneider notes in the project's final report,

> We have called this report 'The Balancing Act' because we found the faculty interviewed for the study attempting to hold in balance two different roles, each of which appeared central to actual effectiveness in working with adult students. On the one hand, the faculty members' own reports on their interactions with students revealed a pervasive student-centeredness, i.e., a determination to respond to adult students as persons, individuals, and adults, with their own legitimate needs, perspectives and concerns. On the other hand, the faculty members were clearly balancing their student-centeredness with highly directive and prescriptive roles as well. It was their ability to hold these two elements together which made a difference in effectiveness over time. [Schneider, Klemp, and Kastendiek, 1981, p. 66]

Confirming the experience of other competence-model processes, this project was rich in implications for professional development and the selection and organization of professionals for the tasks studied. Conducting the project also centered the project staff in ongoing networks of faculty and academic administrators for whom the competence of teachers and mentors in degree programs for adults is of growing concern. A resultant series of national institutes on teaching and learning issues has been attended by some 2,000 college faculty members.

A Major Step Forward

There can be no sure answers to the field's many questions without finding out what business and professional people really do for a living. This is the great strength of the competence model. It does not assume that the prescriptions of professional-school education are descriptions of practice any more than it assumes that the continuing education needs of practitioners are merely extensions of the lines of inquiry pursued in professional school. The predictive validity, sought by the Minnesota College of Pharmacy, demanded a reality orientation. The joint project of AACP and APhA developed a checklist of pharmacist tasks, then checked and rechecked it through site visits, literature searches, and surveys across significantly different practice settings. Concern for reality shifted the AACP-APhA focus from the pharmacist to the pharmacist-patient relationship. The Pennsylvania State University competence project added the varied simulations of the assessment center and the cross checks of time spent versus relative importance, getting readings on how experience and advancement can alter tasks and the competence required by practice. Alverno College tested the American Management Association's competence model in over 100 interviews in which managers' and executives' perceptions and demonstrations of competence were generally comparable. The Baehr research compares the line, sales, and professional executive hierarchies at entry, middle, and senior levels, discovering that while there are differentiations at each level, senior executives perform largely similar functions, despite differing perceptions and emphases. The behavioral-event interview process was used at the University of Chicago in order to construct a competence model of the superior teacher/mentor, differentiating abilities related to successful performance. Baseline data of the kinds illustrated here have been achieved and validated for many roles played by business and the professions.

University professional schools and continuing education units, professional associations and the private sector have frequently come together in order to establish competence models. Formal collaboration has deepened each party's sense of what the other parties bring to the educational needs of business and the professions. Associations have discovered adult education as a relevant field of research. Professional schools have benefitted from university-based, continuing educators' creative approaches to teaching and mentoring. Adult learners have seen both associations and universities as supportive and challenging. Stereotypes, such as the view of professional societies as trade associations and the suspicion of the quality of any research performed outside the academic setting, have been dispelled. In many cases, state and regional cooperation on competence-model research has resulted in collaborative continuing education programs. Individuals involved in the surveys, simulations, and site visits integral to competence-model development, have increased their own sophistication about professional competence and continuing education as a result.

If the discoveries produced so far by the competence model fall short, they nonetheless contribute to the definition of a practicable and focused research agenda, a higher range of challenges that has only come into view because of the field's experience with the competence model.

A Long Way to Journey's End

Competence understood as knowledge and skill is more easily investigated and defined by research. It is also more easily provided, maintained, or enhanced by continuing education. Competence understood as knowledge and skill is also more frequently addressed by research and by competence-oriented continuing education.

Competence is also properly understood as a trait, such as initiative and consistency. It may be understood as self-schema, an affirming consciousness of the self as centered around certain values, or the self-expectations arising from identification as a professional. Competence includes motivation, that is, the process of values and goals recurrently driving behavior. Competence, at least at times, includes specific attitudes, such as positive regard or a judgmental orientation, and excludes others. Competence is not always understood in these ways and when it is, competence is neither easily nor widely researched, nor is it commonly addressed by continuing education. Furthermore, if competence is understood as a complex of knowledge, skill, trait, self-schema, motive, and attitude, it becomes important to examine their interplay and relative impact on performance.

This richer concept of competence has to receive more careful attention if the relationship between competence and performance is to be better understood. Do apparent differences in the settings of practice require significantly different kinds of competence? Do the successive plateaus of career paths pose challenges that might be generalizable across the professions? Why do some executives flourish in one organizational culture and flounder in another while other executives thrive in culturally-varied organizational settings?

Reference to the absence of noticeable weakness, demerit, and impairment is usually included in the definition of competence but has been rarely addressed in practice by competence-model research. While this may be a failure of imagination or an example of a research objective deferred but in view, it may be a serious conceptual flaw in the model itself. Just as dictionary editors see quite limited utility in saying what something is not, competence-model builders concentrate on defining the knowledge and skill generally present and operative in acceptable performance. The problem is that those performing acceptably today may perform unacceptably tomorrow, or for the next six weeks, and without any sudden deficiency in knowledge or skill.

Business firms, social service agencies, hospitals, and architects' offices can anticipate, if not predict, impaired performance from otherwise highly competent professionals. Some cannot handle their private lives. The failure to make lasting friendships, the onset of mid-life crises, the stress of caring for aged parents or troubled children, anger over occasional marital battles, or the distraction of messy divorces with custody fights can and do seriously diminish the job performance of otherwise competent people for weeks or even years. Perhaps more surprisingly, so can charitable and civic overcommitments, an unexpectedly sizable inheritance or the shift of a hobby into an obsession. Others lack the insight and skill to weather fatigue and depression, to overcome the numbing effect of repetitive activities, and to find help in dealing with compulsions and dependencies such as gambling, alcoholism, or drug abuse. Few seem capable of sealing a troubled dimension of their lives from the balance of their activities. Competence models fail to identify competence in personal affairs as job related, and yet the absence of knowledge, skill, and maturity in managing private lives unfailingly affects the performance of business and professional people. Like good health, maturity in personal matters is more greatly valued in its absence.

The most serious flaw in the competence approach is its implicit assumption that performance is entirely an individual affair that leads the model logically, if erroneously, to an exclusive focus on the individual. Even in the models that are sensitive to the organizational context of business and professional activity, it is the individual and his or her individual competence that is at the center of inquiry. To be sure, some of the key influences on performance are found in the professionals' interior life, the critical higher order skills of mind, specialized knowledge and skill, motivation for excellence, the maturity to manage personal affairs well, and the grit to overcome setbacks. There are other influences, however, and they stem from the quality of the relationship individuals have to one another in the organizational setting: the ensemble of peers, subordinates, superiors, and systems. It is this ensemble that can cripple or enhance individual effectiveness. Performance is as much a function of the ensemble as it is of the individual. Symphony orchestra conductors' memoirs are replete with tales of superbly competent solo performers who, in fact, diminished an orchestra's performance when they occupied a chair in one of the orchestra's sections. Similarly, excellent chamber players who together make sounds of grace and beauty are sometimes drab and uninteresting soloists. Is ensemble performance simply the sum of individual competence? Ensemble performance sometimes appears to be less than the sum of its parts ("The doctors there are each wonderful but I don't go to that clinic anymore because one doctor will tell me this and another will tell me that and I'm never sure whose advice to follow"). Sometimes it seems greater than the sum of its parts ("They're playing way over their heads tonight; it's as if they had six people on their basketball team"). Individual performance is heightened by the stimulation of some peers and the challenges and supportiveness of some bosses, senior partners, or chief engineers. On the other hand, dull and rancorous peers, unnecessary and endless meetings, weak and visionless leaders make it more difficult for an individual to remain effective.

Business and other employers of professionals may believe in the long-range development of individual competence but they finance participation in continuing education that is likely to have a favorable impact on individual and organizational performance. The Panel on Continuing Education, part of the National Research Council's study of engineering education and practice in the United States, acknowledges the focus on group performance rather than individual competence and recommends development of tools for linking continuing education to engineering performance and the "competitiveness of organizations" (National Research Council, 1985, pp. 44–48).

Still other influences on performance stem from the quality of the relationship between the profession and society, the prevailing climate that can provide business and the professions with great latitude or severely restrain them. Banking and airlines have been deregulated. Hospitals and physicians face growing controls that more closely than ever circumscribe the physician-patient relationship, no matter what the individual physician's or hospital administrator's competence may be. A loss of faith in the efficacy of peer review has triggered wider support for reexamination and relicensure and a search for publicly accessible data by which to measure physician and hospital quality. The effort to achieve a cap on malpractice awards is a grim reminder of the restrictive change of climate that has occurred between society and health care professionals. A spate of unrelated scandals in the accounting profession brought the headline in the Wall Street Journal: "CPAs Called to Account." Accountants and their firms will be considering the steps needed to restore public confidence before the climate of public opinion triggers restrictive policies and regulatory practices.

The challenge is complex. It is necessary to link the competence model's productive focus on individuals' knowledge and skill with an inquiry into all performance linked traits, including attitudes and motivations. The influence of different settings of practice on performance merits examination. Effective professionals and business people should be compared with performance impaired people so as to establish much more clearly the critical differential factors at play. The interaction of competent solo performers in group-performance settings needs study as does the interplay between national policies and attitudes and the performance of professions and companies. These paths of inquiry begin at the same point, actual performance, and reveal the relative impact on performance of knowledge, skills, attitudes, motivations, personal impairment, and group and organizational settings. When performance critical-learning objectives drive the design and selection of continuing education experiences, the field will have progressed from updates, through the competence model, to a performance model.

The competence model requires serious reconstructive surgery before a performance-related, continuing education model can emerge. A strikingly different frame of reference may yield surer results.

References

ALLEN, D. C. *Management and Professional Job Function Inventory Integration and Research Manual.* Park Ridge, IL: London House Press, 1984.

ALVERNO COLLEGE FACULTY. *Assessment at Alverno College.* Milwaukee, WI: Alverno Productions, 1979 rev. 1985.

BAEHR, MELANY. "The Empirical Link Between Program Development and Performance Needs of Professionals and Executives," *Continuum* 48 (3), 1984.

BISHOP, JAMES; MENTKOWSKI, MARCIA; O'BRIEN, KATHLEEN; BIRNEY, ROBERT; DAVIES, ELIZABETH; AND MCEACHERN, WILLIAM. *Management Characteristics Inventory.* Milwaukee, WI: Alverno College Productions, 1980.

BOYATZIS, RICHARD. *The Competent Manager.* New York: Wiley, 1982.

CROWE, MARY BETH; GROGAN, JANET; JACOBS, RICK; LINDSAY, CARL A.; AND MARK, MELVIN. "Delineation of the Roles of Clinical Psychology: A Survey of Practice in Pennsylvania," *Professional Psychology, Research and Practice* 16 (1), 1984.

CYRS, THOMAS E., JR. "Design of a Competency-Determined Curriculum Model for Pharmacy Education." Chicago: Office of Continuing Education, The University of Chicago, 1978.

EVARTS, HARRY F. *The Competency Program of the American Management Association.* New York: Institute for Management Competency, American Management Association, 1982.

FLANNIGAN, J. C. "The Critical Incident Technique," *Psychology Bulletin* 51 (4), 1954.

HALL, GENE E., AND JONES, HOWARD L. *Competency-Based Education—A Process for the Improvement of Education.* Englewood Cliffs, NJ: Prentice-Hall, 1976.

KALMAN, SAMUEL H. "Report on the American Pharmaceutical Association/ American Association of Colleges of Pharmacy Continuing Competency Project." Chicago: Office of Continuing Education, The University of Chicago, 1978.

LINDSAY, CARL A.; TOOMBS, WILLIAM; QUEENEY, DONNA S. *Continuing Professional Education News.* University Park, PA: Office of Continuing Professional Education, Pennsylvania State University, 1983–1985.

LOACKER, GEORGINE; CROMWELL, LUCY; FEY, JOYCE; & RUTHERFORD, DIANE. *Analysis and Communication at Alverno: An Approach to Critical Thinking.* Milwaukee, WI: Alverno Productions, 1984.

MCBER AND COMPANY. *Understanding of Competence.* Boston: McBer and Company, 1978.

MCCLELLAND, DAVID C. *Guide to Competency Assessment.* Boston: McBer and Company, 1976.

———. *Guide to Behavioral Event Interviewing.* Boston: McBer and Company, 1978.

MCCULLOUGH, MAC, AND MCLAGAN, PATRICIA. "Keeping the Competency Study Alive," *Training and Development Journal,* June, 1983.

MCLAGAN, PATRICIA A., AND BEDRICK, DAVID. "Models for Excellence: The Results of the ASTD Training and Development Competency Study," *Training and Development Journal,* June, 1983.

MENTKOWSKI, MARCIA, AND DOHERTY, AUSTIN. *Careering After College: Establishing the Validity of Abilities Learned in College for Later Careering and Professional Performance.* Final Report to the National Institute of Education. Milwaukee, WI: Alverno Productions, 1983. (ERIC Document Reproduction Service Nos. 239 557–239 566.)

MENTKOWSKI, MARCIA; O'BRIEN, KATHLEEN; MCEACHERN, WILLIAM; & FOWLER, DEBORAH. *Developing a Professional Competence Model for Management Education.* Milwaukee, WI: Alverno Productions, 1982.

NATIONAL RESEARCH COUNCIL. "Continuing Education of Engineers." Report of the Panel on Continuing Education, Morris Steinberg, Chairman. Washington, D.C.: National Academy Press, 1985.

Queeney, Donna S., and Melander, Jacqueline. "Establishing Foundations for University/Professional Association Collaboration: The Professional Selection Process." University Park, PA: Office of Continuing Professional Education, Pennsylvania State University, 1984.

Schneider, Carol. "A Selection and Development Strategy Predicting Effective Leadership, *Continuum* 45 (4), 1981.

Schneider, Carol; Klemp, George O., Jr.; and Kastendiek, Susan. "The Balancing Act: Competencies of Effective Teachers and Mentors in Degree Programs for Adults." Chicago: Office of Continuing Education, The University of Chicago, 1981.

Toombs, William, and Lindsay, Carl A. "Continuing Education for Professionals: A Practice Oriented Approach," *Journal of Continuing Higher Education* 33 (1), 1985.

THREE
The Performance Model

A LARGER FRAME OF REFERENCE than the update or competence model is required in order to take into account the widest possible range of factors that determine performance. Such a window has begun to take shape from conversations within quite diverse streams of research, such as: the critique of positivism; anthropology's insight into the interplay of myth, ritual, sacred stories, art and craft with organizational life, business and the professions; cognitive science, problem framing, and problem solving; the sociology and politics of knowledge; critical theory as a new form of knowledge; constructive-developmental psychology; and organizational behavior. Work on the window is by no means complete, but the view it provides is liberating for persons searching for secure links between continuing education and performance.

The Individual Is Never Just an Individual

"Constructive-developmental psychology reconceives the whole question of the relationship between the individual and the social by reminding us that the distinction is not absolute, that development is intrinsically about the continual settling and resettling of this very distinction." So Robert Kegan writes in "The Evolving Self" (1982, p. 115), a major contribution to understanding the interaction of the individual and culture with respect to personal growth. Culture is taken here to mean the context or network within which individual meaning-making and personal growth take place. Culture includes human behavior as expressed in thought, speech, action, systems of thought and values, organizations, artifacts and the like. For Kegan and others, culture is also the psychosocial "holding environment" in which an individual at any particular moment is embedded (Kegan, 1982, p. 116).

Genetically the individual is both unique and a composite. The individual is the creature of both rational and random causes and experiences him- or herself as sometimes random, sometimes rational. The development of the fetus occurs, under normal conditions, while it is embedded in the mother. Human individuality is from the first simultaneous with embeddedness in another. For development to continue, there must be a successful transition to another form of embeddedness, that of the infant in the mothering culture. The success of the mothering culture is marked first by its protective embrace and yet, subsequently, by the growing child's increasing recognition of the mothering culture as "the other." As the developing child loosens ties with the mothering culture it becomes progressively and intensely attached to the parenting culture that considers the child more responsible for behavior as time passes. Repeated exercise of responsibility over time promotes self-sufficiency and a growing away from the parenting culture, but detachment from the parenting culture occurs at the same time that new attachments to new cultures are formed, and the progressively self-sufficient child begins to become imbedded in social and peer-group cultures. The young adult develops through embeddedness in what Kegan calls the culture of self-authorship (1982, p. 259). Ambition and decision making are celebrated by assuming responsibility in a student society or political movement, pursuing professional school studies, joining a profession, or making a commitment to a life partner. The successful development of the young adult is impossible apart from host cultures such as business and the professions that both beckon it and give it expression. Another level of self-development is reached when the self-affirming quality of the adult's embeddedness in business or the professions, civic life, and interpersonal relationships is tempered by the growth of intimacy and the capacity for interdependence. Kegan's useful perspective is that human development occurs appropriately through cycle after cycle of disengagement from one set of moorings at the same time that new strong linkages are forged, a process that provides progressive definition to the self.

The Individual and Culture Are Active Agents in Personal Growth

The corollary is that both the individual and culture are active agents in this process, functioning as two interactive strands of influences, supporting or thwarting development. One person burrows more deeply into a culture looking for safety but finding the prison of dependence. Another has a pattern of weak attachments, finding risk easy but commitment difficult. Others seem to strike just the right balance. Some cultures prevent a person from bonding with them at all while others develop a death grip locking the person into one developmental stage. Still other cultures seem to let go appropriately and even promote links with successor cultures. Family-life examples come easily to mind. Older infants attempt to walk. Parents carry them less and less frequently and create circumstances that encourage toddlers to walk unassisted. If a parent is maldeveloped, the parent may not reinforce the infant's early tendencies toward solo steps but rather reward the would-be toddler for inappropriately clinging behavior. Parents' stereotypes can sometimes result in their being overprotective toward daughters and insufficiently nurturing toward sons. Some preadolescents regard even loose ties with family culture to be constraining and pull away dangerously early; others will need a gentle push from the nest. Whether the individual in question is a developing child or a developing parent, the active interaction of individual and culture encourages or retards growth.

Developmental Stages Are Fragile Partnerships of Environment and Self, Past and Future

Each stage of development is a fragile truce as an individual both differentiates the self from the environment while integrating the environment with the self (Kegan, 1982, p. 114). Mastering a new skill differentiates an individual but frequently people must "lose themselves" in the task in order to attain a level of mastery. Parents are separate from their children but often feel their children's pain as intensely as the children do. The individual must strike a truce between the sense in which he or she is attending to the present environment and yet is also travelling through to a successor culture frequently already in view. For example, the senior high school student already has a specific college and college life in mind, often quite vividly, and yet must attend to the responsibilities of senior high school classes. Past history and future vision are lively influences upon the individual's present.

These uneasy truces between the self and culture have terms that evolve. For example, the married person on the wedding day evolves to the married person/parent on the sixteenth wedding anniversary, and the youthful son or daughter of parents in their prime of life evolves to the prime-of-life son or daughter of parents in their declining years.

Performance Is Never Merely Individual

The value attached to achievement, whether expressed in the drive to perform well or in flight from challenges, develops early as the child, and the major figures in the child's life, address the child's relationship with the environment. If the child's embedding in a protective culture as well as differentiating from it is appropriate, the child will feel secure enough to risk toddling the first few steps in discovering the self and the otherness of mother or father. If, as well, the principal figures in the child's environment are appropriately embedded in providing security as well as encouraging and rewarding the risks of differentiation, such as the child's early walking, those first few toddling steps will take the child beyond self-discovery to a gratifying experience of self-achievement and successful performance. In this way, the possibility of better performance as well as the motivation to strive for it brings the child to a cycle of stronger efforts and higher levels of achievement. This is the rhythm that both Houle and Schon recognize in the mature, reflective professional: unceasing movement toward new levels of performance. When these new levels of performance are achieved, they seem inadequate because better levels of possible performance come into view.

Whether experiences with psychosocial environments result in an individual attributing a positive or negative value to striving for achievement, the value is never permanently fixed. Even an individual who begins school life with a strong drive for high performance will experience recurring tides of growth, crisis, and renewal as the relationship between personal growth and culture is faced again and again.

In early life individuals move slowly through successive cultures. By adulthood, individuals hold multiple cultural citizenships as they move daily among occupational, civic, interpersonal, and familial environments. Individuals play a variety of cultural roles in each environment and each role experience can strengthen the individual's drive (some would say "will" or "resolve") for excellent performance when the role aids developmental balance by fostering security as well as risk taking, the sense of belonging as well as of individual recognition. Reinforcement of the performance drive also occurs when the individual brings to a new cultural role the residual of prior successful role performances, particularly the capacity for commitment balanced by critical thinking and for independent action balanced by collaboration.

Performance in Business and the Professions Is Structured by the Double Helix of Human Development

If an individual is never merely an individual, so too a job is never merely a job. A job, particularly if held over a number of years, is part of the unbroken succession of holding environments and contains on-going subcultures of loyal friends, working peers, subordinates, bosses, allies, hostile tribes, rituals, values, and webs of favors performed and favors due. A job is both across town and deep within the consciousness, connected with self-esteem, fantasies about the future, and feelings of security and insecurity. These, in turn, exist within a larger organization and/or profession with a unique culture of its own, its own sacred stories and myths, interpersonal climate, and economic and societal niche. People routinely "take the job home" just as family problems are routinely taken to work, related galaxies within the same universe. The job description is to the job culture as a prevailing wind is to the sea: It suggests the right tack, but only if the course has already been charted.

Performance can never be fully understood by studies of the decontextualized individual. The relationship between continuing education and performance is unsatisfying when it is based simply on the relationship between a job description and an individual's knowledge and skills. Any human-development framework will be concerned with jobs and job-related competence as they are elements of the more complex problems and dynamic cultural processes at work.

Through the contribution of constructive-developmental psychology it is possible to see that even the performance of the solo-practice professional or small shop owner is shaped by a lifetime of social interaction that has either steeled the will for achievement or diminished the capacity for sustained commitment. Some are excited by challenges and thrive on overcoming obstacles. Others look for the safety of undemanding practices, for protection against the unexpected. There are overachievers, leaders, and energizers as well as underachievers, followers, and enervators among solo-practitioners and mom-and-pop grocers. Not just the psychosocial past is at play. The solo-practice professional's interactions with clients, patients and customers, neighbors, community and professional leaders matter greatly. What distinguishes the performance of one from another is sometimes individually achieved competence but frequently it is that culturally achieved balance that others describe as "drive," "concern," or "maturity." Even when successful performance appears to result directly from individually achieved competence, constructive-developmental psychology reminds us of the influence of successive environments that appropriately took in, held, and let go, thus motivating the person to achieve a level of competence, to practice it consistently and, thus, to move on to new challenges.

Solo-practice, the family farm, and the corner mom-and-pop store are no longer characteristic of American life. More and more business and professional people are salaried members of large, complex organizations. Even when they are not, as with members of small law firms who must nonetheless practice in complicated civil and criminal justice systems or doctors in small physician groups who must practice in large medical centers, much of the work is done within sizable, intricate organizations and institutions.

These are environments in which others mediate the culture to the individual, just as the individual mediates the culture to others. Cadets enter the police academy with notions about police culture nourished by some personal experience, novels, movies, news articles, and perhaps the stories of a relative who is on the police force. The academy faculty mediate the official ideals of police culture to the cadets and cadets are placed in circumstances that favor mediation to one another of elements of police culture such as comradeship. Following the academy experience, the culture is mediated to the rookie by the squad-car partner, by life at the precinct or district stationhouse, by the command structure, and by the public. If the rookie's first partner is on the take, or if 4 of the first 10 traffic ordinance violators stopped hand the rookie officer their drivers' licenses wrapped in $20 bills, the rookie will form a new vision of police culture and his performance as an officer will be affected.

Table 3.1 shows the many dimensions involved in making a distinction between the individual as differentiated and the individual

TABLE 3.1. Schema of Roles, Modes, and Orientations

Roles	Modes	Orientations
Reporting Roles	Leadership Styles	Controlling
peer	team builders	demanding
superior	official	domineering
subordinate	expert	directing
	counsellor	guiding
Project Roles		
solo expert	Preferred Approaches	Accommodating
team member	action	protecting
	awareness	supporting
Development Roles	analysis	trusting
student	planning	cooperating
mentor		
	Learning Styles	Yielding
Political Roles	accommodator	respecting
lobbyist	diverger	accepting
ally	assimilator	submitting
opponent	converger	conforming
enemy		
	Action Styles	Opposing
Assessment Roles	innovator	avoiding
evaluator	adapter	resisting
validator	structure keeper	compelling
disciplinarian	avoider	attacking
counsellor		
rewarder		Expressive
		cheerful
		confident
		dramatic
		earnest
		Self-Contained
		dour
		hesitant
		reserved
		relaxed

as embedded. In virtually any work experience, the businessperson or professional will have many roles, and will be exercising each of those roles in one or more modes and orientations.

In Table 3.1, roles noted in the first column to the left can be combined with any styles found in the middle column and expressed in any orientations found in the third column on the right. Each person in a classroom, on a hospital ward, or around a corporate board room will represent several roles, styles, and orientations. Multiple, simultaneous, role combinations are tellingly descriptive of the culture of organizations in the most ordinary circumstances of organizational life such as negotiation.

Many times each week an architect, school principal, or state-agency manager faces the task of negotiation. A person negotiating with peers in a demanding or suspicious tone may be mentoring an assistant at the same time who understands that the boss is expressing confidence in him or her. The chances of negotiation success depend partly on the quality of argumentation and partly on the way in which others present identify one another with the prevailing climate of decision making and advancement within the organization. The sensitive subordinate will learn that being right isn't the same thing as being convincing. Being right as well as convincing calls for internal qualities such as logic as well as the capacity to read correctly the relative needs and political strength of others. Being right as well as convincing also requires that qualities such as presence have been validated by the culture and that other qualities such as credibility have been conferred by the culture.

The capacity to negotiate is one of the keys to personal social intelligence and is highly prized by large organizations as critical to performance. It requires a finely developed sense of balance between identification and individuation, embedding and differentiation. Negotiation involves stepping out of an interaction's intensity without fully leaving it in order to look simultaneously at all points of view. It involves individuals sensing others' feelings without either losing contact with their own feelings or having their own get in the way.

Qualities such as this have been studied since the 1930s with general agreement that they have their beginnings in early childhood when some children learn to read what is wanted or what is being felt from parents' nonverbal cues. In observations reported by Kegan, many such cues must be sent and received as infant grows into child and the mothering culture into the parenting culture. The simple act of a child learning to ride a bicycle involves a parent's comforting arms around both bike and child for a while. It is sometimes difficult for an outsider to know which person is really guiding the bike. Between parent and child, however, the sense of touch alone can express the balance of control: first security, then the invitation to risk a little, and finally the giving and taking of complete control. This is nothing less than an episode in the forming of developmental balance. The cues express shifting but appropriate mixtures of hanging on and letting go, identification and individuation, giving and taking. The child senses the parent's feelings through nonverbal cues without losing touch with his or her own feelings or letting them get in the way. In a family culture with frequent interaction of this sort, the child is well on the way toward an adulthood characterized by social intelligence such as negotiation skills.

Performance is structured by a double helix in which there are two complex interactive strands, each bearing only part of the performance code. One carries cultural influences, the other the individual's characteristics. The strand representing culture-based performance code carries the history, values, mission, character, style, symbols, resources, and structures of each culture in which an individual moves. It carries each culture's performance expectations, motivation, recognition, reward, and punishment. It carries coded indicators of each culture's own future performance: competitive edge or obsolescence, expansion or decline, the esteem or disfavor of the public. The strand representing individual-based performance code carries information from the individual's lifetime of prior cultural interactions, from every context within which meaning was developed and growth took place. It carries the individual's attributes, limitations, and predispositions. All previous individual–social interactions are made present as coded residuals: drives, needs, tendencies, and fears; knowledge, skills, intuition and competencies; character traits, self-knowledge, and self-deception; physical health, strength, and energy. The pairing of these strands, matched or mismatched, results in performance. Combinations of individuals in various cultural structures affect one another's individual performance as well as the performance of the group or organization.

Performance Is Rarely Changed by Any Single Variable

Understanding the complex reality of performance realistically limits expectations of change from any single intervention. The impact of consistently positive or negative early childhood experiences of cultural interaction is not easily altered. Engineers, accountants, and librarians numbed by years of routine are not often restored to health by a three-day seminar. Correctional personnel can be told that they are part of a helping profession, and instructed in the mysterious rites of behavior modification by continuing educators, but if correctional personnel are fired only when a prisoner escapes, they will perform as guards, not as social workers. Business executives, public administrators, and attorneys with failing marriages or deeply troubled children have depressed performance levels no matter how sophisticated their knowledge and skills. Professionals and businesspeople who enjoy collegiality find authoritarian, hierarchical structures stifle their performance. People who prefer highly structured situations are often at sea under leadership that enables rather than directs. The drug impaired are not going to perform with consistency until they are no longer drug impaired. Architects, physicians, and accountants who intentionally operate on the edge of ethical practice are more interested in sophisticating their shadowy performance than in walking in the light. The most intimate theater of professional performance, the client or patient relationship, has been imperiled by adversarial fears of clients' legal action and of professionals' incompetence, thus adding self-defense to the performance goals of professionals and clients.

The issue of identifying the client adds labyrinthian twists to the performance path. Is corporate management the client for rocket-propulsion engineers, or is the client the federal agency, or the astronauts, or the taxpaying public, or all of the above in different ways? If each is the client in some sense, what performance is owed by the engineers to each? Is the parole or probation officer's client the judge, the parole board, the offender, the criminal justice system, or the community? What are the standards of performance and who has the right to say?

Maintaining the developmental balance requires some care and energy. Superior performance is often described in terms such as "critical but loyal support," and "firm but not mindless commitment." Such terms imply that a truce or balance between being present and being at a critical distance is healthy for superior performance. This truce, with its many tensions, may be at the root of the distinction between the lawyer as representing a client and the lawyer as an officer of the court. Beckett and More were kings' servants and more. Many Nazi military officers were professional soldiers sworn to obey orders and nothing more.

This truce between the individual as embedded and the individual as differentiated is difficult to maintain because both the individual and the environment are evolving. The person who entered medicine or accounting 20 years ago is not the same person today. The practices of medicine and accounting today are significantly different from what they were 20 years ago, and the public climate in which medicine and accounting take place has changed perhaps even more significantly. Circumstances alter what it is to be a clinical psychologist, nurse, or social worker. The reasons why a person became a clinical psychologist, nurse, or social worker are not the same as the reasons a person is still practicing. The terms of an individual's commitment to the holding culture (the profession or business) shift; more is wanted, something different is needed, a new motivating value is sought. If satisfying new terms cannot be discovered or negotiated, the executive or professional may accept a lower level of fulfillment (and its companion, a lower level of performance) and "go through the motions" for a while, hoping that improvement will occur. Others may begin looking for a radical shift in careers, a change of professions, that is, a new psychosocial holding environment. Seriously pursuing a major career change requires considerable focus and energy and this cannot help but threaten individuals' already precarious performance balance. Still other executives and professionals only notice the problem as a dull but constant pain. They almost imperceptibly (and sometimes quite unconsciously) slide toward some new source of needed fulfillment: a new marriage partner, some all-consuming hobby, or other escape.

Consider the path of individual career decision making. Early childhood is filled with career fantasies of lives fighting fires, nabbing criminals, or healing the sick. Between the ages of 11 and 16, typically, a more tentative choice period occurs, with career fantasies based on a person's interests, capabilities, and values. These are significant periods in the evolution of the self, and as we have seen, involve interaction between the changing individual and a succession of environments. Toward the end of secondary school, the young person enters a more realistic choice period that begins to implement and test choices: how broadly or narrowly focused an education, at what college, taking what major? This realistic choice period may continue for many years, long into adulthood, as the person goes through several cycles of exploring-crystallizing-specifying in this or that organizational culture in an attempt to find a career that fits with needs, interests, abilities, and values (Ginzberg et al., 1951).

A "final" realistic choice is often made in professional school, based to some extent on successful experiences with preferred course content. With the increasing distance of professional schools' culture from the culture of professional practice, the subsequent shock of practice reality can disturb performance patterns as the young careerist looks for the professional school's intellectual challenge, frequent personal assessment, and socialization in the practice. The initial performance problem of professional practice is not typically the zesty challenge to knowledge and skills anticipated in professional school. It is the difficulty of becoming accepted, credible, established; of overcoming the boredom of insignificant initial challenges, the feeling of unused potential and low self-actualization; and of grieving over the loss of the warm comradery of professional school. For example, the newly ordained priest's theological formation is not challenged; and hearing confessions doesn't turn out to be the frightening test of pastoral counseling expected. The challenge is, rather, as James Carroll puts it "the ferocious rectory chill inside which most American priests must make their lives" (1984, p. 144).

Floundering can last into the thirties for people with advanced education. The realistic choice process is also reactivated in many cases for people in their forties, in what has come to be known as the "mid-life crisis." "The process of career choice takes place at several times throughout a person's career. It is not a one-shot selection of an occupation in the early twenties" (Hall, 1976, p. 24). The rhythm is one of maintenance and reexamination, reinforced by the first intimations of mortality, reduced goals, repetition, a growing sense of obsolescence, diminished career mobility, heightened interest in security, changes in family and work relationships, and unconscious self-parody. Performance in late career is challenged by aging, a sense of marginality, sometimes consignment to a safe shelf, and possibly the death of a spouse.

In early, middle, and late career, persons face distinctive sets of task-related needs. The young professional or business person must develop action skills and the mid-careerist should develop mentoring skills, for example. Each stage has a companion set of socioemotional needs. Socialization is important to the new professional, and the mid-careerist must deal with the transition from a competitive orientation to a collaborative outlook.

The cultures to which the professional belongs, small groups as well as complex organizations such as the law firm, court system, and local bar association, have similar cyclical patterns. Kim S.

Cameron and David A. Whetten have compared 18 models of group stage development (Cameron and Whetten, 1984, pp. 40–42). Cameron and Whetten found widespread agreement that groups progress predictably through a series of six sequential stages. These are:

1. Isolation, orientation, and testing stage—in which group members try to identify acceptable roles for themselves, dependence on a leader is present, individuals feel isolated, information-gathering activity is focused on, and members become familiar with rules and expectations.
2. Formation of "groupness" and unity stage—in which members begin feeling integrated and a part of the group, group issues take precedence over individual issues, and feelings of cohesion and unity develop.
3. Conflict and counter-dependence stage—in which group members react against the "sweetness" that has developed, the leader of the group is resisted, and rivalry and dissatisfaction increase.
4. Conflict resolution and coordination stage—in which rivalry and competitiveness is resolved, individual roles are coordinated into a smooth functioning group, and pairing and intimacy occur among group members.
5. Separation, elaboration, and independence stage—in which group member roles are differentiated, unique identities of individuals are reestablished and entrepreneurial activity increases.
6. Effective group functioning (or termination) stage—in which problem solving occurs effectively, personal issues among group members and role conflicts are resolved, and efficient task accomplishment occurs (Cameron and Whetten, 1984, p. 39).

At any given moment, a business or professional person may belong to several such cultures at various stages of development, some working well and providing satisfaction, others toiling with the task of coming together collaboratively. Groups are a primary theater in which most professionals are expected to perform as they move along their own career path. When the small group *is* the organization, as with small law firms and group medical practices, for example, failure to reach effective group functioning or a serious and lasting breakdown in effective group functioning will diminish the quality of individual performance and, eventually, bring about the dissolution of the organization. However, most groups of business and professional people exist within a larger organization with a life cycle of its own. Cameron and Whetten have developed a four-stage summary model based on 10 major organization life-cycle models. The stages are:

1. Entrepreneurial stage—in which there is marshalling of resources, multiple and diverse ideas, entrepreneurial activities, little planning and coordination, formation of a "niche," and the "prime mover" has power.
2. Collectivity stage—in which there is informational communication and structure, a sense of collectivity, long hours spent, the development of a sense of mission, continued innovation, and high commitment.
3. Formalization and control stage—in which there is a formalization process, stable structure, an emphasis on efficiency and maintenance, conservatism, and institutionalized procedures.
4. Elaboration of structure stage—in which the elaboration of structure is accompanied by decentralization, domain expansion, adaptation, and renewal (Cameron and Whetten, 1984, pp. 46–51).

At any point, the organization may develop a sometimes terminal loss of resiliency. The symptoms are overexpansion during times of abundance; inadequate management controls; lack of collaboration and self-protection; rigidity in problem-solving approaches; and the curtailing of long-range planning (Cameron and Whetten, 1984, p. 32).

One of the engines driving performance might therefore be seen as a three-chamber combustion model: individual, group, and organization, each chamber with its own firing cycle. Performance will be high when the cycles are tuned and will be at least uneven when the firing cycle of any one chamber needs work.

The Many Performance Variables, Creatively Orchestrated, Can Enhance Individual and Collective Performance

Understanding the complex reality of performance discourages the expectation of lasting change coming from any single variable such as a single educational intervention. On the other hand, understanding the relationship of performance to the double helix of human development multiplies the strategies available to individuals, educational institutions, employers, professional associations, and counselors for influencing performance. Performance, like music, depends upon interactions among: player concentration, technique, mood, knowledge, and satisfaction; the composition being played, for example, the strategic plan, architectural concept, or the public agency's mission; the quality of instruments, for example, systems, protocols, laboratories, funding, and the like; the conductor, other individual artists, and orchestral sections, for example, other engineers, departments, and executives or other teachers, schools, and the system superintendent; the acoustical environment, for example, the reverberation in parent companies and the investment community, among senior law partners in the prevailing climate of public policy, or between hospital administrators and major insurers; and the chemistry between the orchestra and its public, for example, the devotedness of both professionals and patients in a community-based Health Maintenance Organization (HMO), or the product loyalty of the public to a pharmaceutical firm, or the excitement felt by certain architects and cities toward one another.

A culture that is orchestrated for performance can galvanize individuals who have been ambivalent toward performance achievements and give them a taste for consistently superior performance. Among those already predisposed to excellence, the performance-orchestrated culture can sustain effectiveness, assimilate innovations, and provide for personal and organizational development. It does so through formal processes such as performance assessment, assessment-based learning agendas and the matching of individuals' agendas with organizational needs in experiences advantageous to both. Equally important, the performance-orchestrated culture acts informally through exemplars and models, through sacred success stories (particularly come-back tales) often told in mentoring and coaching, and the like. It is through such devices that the performance-orchestrated culture speaks to its members, encouraging them to appropriate levels of risk taking, and providing them with a climate in which inevitable periods of impaired or diminished performance are anticipated, planned for, and approached maturely.

Identifying the developmental balance appropriate to the culture is key. Sometimes the organizational culture of a specific professional or business setting is Weberian, that is, rules and regulations predominate in specifying desired behavior, and rewards are based on explicit performance measures. Sometimes the organizational culture is professional collegiality or industrial democracy (sometimes referred to as Type Z, self-authorizing, or high-process style), in which implicit, organization-wide customs, traditions, and values predominate in defining desired behavior. Whether the bureaucratic or the participative characteristics seem controlling, the balance of security and venturesomeness, holding on and letting go, must be appropriate to the organization's function. Reasonable risk taking in a new product research-and-development unit ought to have a high allowable (and even desirable) failure rate. The climate of risk taking among bankers and investment counselors is usually less vigorous. The allowable margin for risk among oral surgeons and nuclear engineers will be smaller. Each culture can encourage the appropriate developmental balance and do so consistently through policy, procedures, and promotions as well as through informal signals. The culture may provide individuals who are anxious for a new challenge with a greater degree of autonomy, or an expanded and more demanding assignment, or both. The culture must also be sensitive to signs that individuals have stopped growing, for example, that they are shrinking from the risk of accepting new responsibilities, or distancing themselves from issues that energize their environment, or burrowing more deeply into essentially routine matters. The performance-orchestrated culture intervenes supportively when acceptance of a new challenge triggers a series of mistakes or eventually proves to be too much. It also intervenes when growth appears to be on hold.

The performance-orchestrated culture consciously addresses its future well-being in whatever it does in the present. For example, when a special problem-solving committee needs to be appointed, task, speed, and proven skill will not be the only factors considered. A promising but unseasoned professional and a senior colleague no longer making quite as vital a contribution as in the past would be deliberately added to a group otherwise reflecting task urgency, experience, and current performance. One experienced and energetic member of such a temporary group would be specifically charged with mentoring the junior professional and another would be asked to make a special effort to draw the senior colleague into the immediacy and excitement of the task. The effort to bring a young person along and to reanimate a senior colleague costs, at least, time; that is, the special committee will take relatively longer to complete its primary objective, and there is no guarantee that the secondary objective, mentoring and motivating, will be achieved. However, the performance-orchestrated culture understands that there is also a cost in failing to move a promising young person ahead quickly enough or in allowing a senior colleague to slip into the middle distance before his or her retirement is official.

Above all, the performance-orchestrated culture will watch the life cycle of individual careers and will respond supportively, for example, to the young careerists' needs for socialization into the organization, for feeling that they make a difference, and for forming a kind of psychological contract for personal growth with organizational leaders. In this way the initial reality shock and floundering described by Ginzberg and the recurrent career reexamination described by Hall will be anticipated and dealt with in ways encouraging growth and perhaps even having a positive effect on performance. Such a culture will also closely watch the vitality of its subgroups and temporary systems, and be sensitive to their life cycles and performance and the interaction of these groups with the life cycle of the larger organization. The older and more complex such an organization becomes, the more likely it is that creativity will need to be expressed in enclaves such as research and development units or special task forces. Special-purpose groups within older organizations often must be protected against the very degree of bureaucratic formality appropriate to the larger organization but stifling to small-group needs. Small-group success often depends upon thinking the unthinkable, taking high risks, or maintaining the distance from daily emergencies or quarterly profit pressures sufficient to permit long-range planning.

Even with prudent concern in such matters, the self-renewing performance-orchestrated culture is subject to today's major organization culture shocks: mergers, acquisitions, and hostile takeovers. These are seen today not only among oil companies, air carriers and manufacturers, but also in electronic and print journalism, the health care industry, and social science research firms. Machiavelli was an enemy of cultural imperialism and mindful of the interplay between culture and performance. His advice to Lorenzo de' Medici was to control the results, not to meddle with a culture that appears to work:

> . . . allow them to live with their own laws, forcing them to pay a tribute and creating therein a government made up of a few people who will keep the state friendly to you. . . . There is nothing more difficult to execute, nor more dubious of success, nor more dangerous to administer than to introduce a new system of things. . . . [The Prince, Chaps. V and VI]

Individuals in touch with their own developmental histories, sensitive to the strong role culture plays in performance, and skilled in interpersonal relations are frequently called upon to look after the developmental needs of groups such as temporary task forces and committees. Often an entire generation of leaders can look back on their common experience of such mentors and guides as the most formative experience of their careers. A succession of national leaders, including Franklin D. Roosevelt, shared two or three uniquely inspirational mentors at the same prep school. This is a recurrent theme in McBer studies of the U.S. State Department and Navy officers and corporate executives. The performance-orchestrated culture recognizes that not every successful law partner, head nurse, or vice-president for operations will be a natural mentor or even generally sensitive to the interplay between culture and individual performance. Some can be educated or enculturated into such roles. Some national accounting firms require that their key staff identify two or three persons who might be capable of succeeding to their positions and, further, insist that key staff develop a plan for the growth of their possible successors. Of equal importance, the culture will find creative ways to use those persons who are effective mentors, that is, those who are sensitive to the power of culture, who share more than is absolutely essential with subordinates, who explain why a problem has to be handled in a particular way or who take a colleague to a meeting to see how a plan plays itself out. Some law firms make sure that every new member of the firm will spend a certain amount of time working with a senior partner gifted in this way. There are corporations that organize career paths to insure that as wide a corporate constituency as possible gets exposure to executives who are outstanding mentors. The quality of a culture's performance and that of its members, individually taken, can be enhanced by those who have been successful with their own personal developmental balancing act and who modify the culture accordingly: same ship, same crew, different captain . . . different performance level.

Individuals Can Make Developmentally Discriminating Choices among and in the Cultures Available to Them

Persons who understand something of the pattern of their relationships with the succession of cultures in their lives, who have at least an intuitive sense of personal growth as determined by the interaction of cultural influences with their individual characteristics, know that they perform well in some settings and not nearly as well in others. There is every reason for this awareness to be brought to bear as they interview for their first job, experience successive positions, and consider major changes in career path. More things have to be right than salary, title, and location. Performance-oriented individuals will look for the developmental configuration that they associate with their past best-performance situation, the mix of cultural values that provides the necessary balance for sustained excellence. They will guide their careers toward business or professional cultures relatively better suited to stimulate their performance. Persons with high needs for achievement may choose aggressive, achievement-oriented organizations. Power-oriented persons may choose influential, prestigious, power-oriented organizations. Affiliative persons may choose warm, friendly, and supportive organizations (Hall, 1976, pp. 36–37).

Individuals who are familiar with the cyclical patterns of groups and larger organizations can anticipate difficulties and plan for them, recognizing them either as healthy signs of growth and opportunity or as evidence of decline and possible collapse. The capacity to understand which problems should be ridden out at some distance and which should be taken on immediately with the utmost seriousness is crucial to the performance of those who lead business or professional organizations.

A change in cultures is often necessary, for example, a transfer within the corporation, association with a new medical group, or a portfolio shift, as from divorce litigation to chancery matters. The change may simply be made for convenience, usually the convenience of the employer. On the other hand, a change of this kind may represent an intentionally provided developmental opportunity or the self-correcting of a career misstep. Sometimes a group of persons in the daily contact resulting from shared work and office space perceives the growth of a member of the group as somehow alien to the group's comradery, a form of distancing. Subtle as well as direct pressure will be exerted in order to hold the colleague in question within the informal norms set by the group. This is easiest to see in the case of someone given temporary coordinative or supervisorial responsibilities for the first time. Someone newly appointed to a leadership position will often be transferred, therefore, so that leadership will not be exercised over a group of former peers. Less bureaucratic organizations approach the issue by giving peers at least partial ownership of the process through which new leadership is selected and the peers thus develop a stake in the success of their new leader. Culture is rarely neutral to individual growth. The risk of failing to orchestrate culture in support of development and performance is that, left to itself, its more sinister tribal spirits will be controlling.

A change in cultures is appropriate as a developmental experiment. People are reluctant to try out new behavioral patterns within a group that has grown accustomed to the way they usually behave. An eighth grader who is relatively more mature than the class often defers to freshman year in high school the relatively more mature behavior that is thought inappropriate to the controlling culture of the eighth grade. A professional or business person who had been hesitant in communication or uncertain in negotiation rarely finds it possible to practice or to experiment with newly mastered skills in the setting that is used to the person's former ineffectiveness. The person who has mastered a significantly higher level of related skills, often thanks to the opportunity of practicing them in the nonthreatening culture of fellow learners, seriously doubts that colleagues will find the new behavior credible. Some groups will not only express disbelief but may be threatened by a colleague's new strength, having depended upon or benefited from the colleague's past ineffectiveness. The bureaucratic culture, orchestrated for performance, will make sure that the person is transferred or otherwise provided with a new performance environment. The high-process style culture, orchestrated for performance, will insure that colleagues have an investment in the person negotiating or communicating more effectively, that colleagues will expect a different behavior pattern, and will support it by allowing a period of experimentation.

The Performance-Orchestrated Culture Has Key Partners Whose Contributions Must Be Coordinated for Maximum Effect

- The individual brings each of the several psychosocial cultures in which he or she is presently embedded (familial, religious, civic, recreational, educational, and occupational) as well as their enabling and/or disabling consequences; the residual developmental balance or imbalance of all prior psychosocial cultural interactions (both their collective effect on the individual as well as the individual's explicit recollections and judgments about them); the advantages and disadvantages of age and health; knowledge and skill related to occupational responsibilities, narrowly defined; and explicit knowledge and skill related to the behavior and effect of groups and organizations like those in which occupational responsibilities are expressed.

- The small group, formal and informal, brings not only its several individual universes but also: the residual of their shared developmental history as well as explicit individual recollections of successful and unsuccessful interactions; normative values and expectations with respect to personal growth and group performance; a mix of competitive and collaborative tendencies; factors of age, roles, styles, and orientations; the interpersonal qualities of their current stage in group development; perceptions of the group's mission and relative location, power, and influence within the larger organization; knowledge or ignorance of the life cycle of such groups.
- The larger organization brings the cultural qualities of its current stage of development; the formal structures (the official groups) and informal networks (the unofficial groups) that both reflect and set culture-wide values and express them in rewards and punishments, symbols and rituals, webs of favors owed and favors due; a climate of consistency or inconsistency; widespread participation or elitism in analysis, planning, and decision making; leadership with a style, if not a set of policies, related to investment in human capital and to management of the organization's culture in support of personal and group performance.
- The professional association brings its experience in defining qualifications for entering the profession, for setting and monitoring standards of practice, and for disciplining its members; representation of the general needs of its members and practice specialties (as distinct from their contextual needs); and the capacity to affect the public climate in which the profession is practiced.

- The counseling professions bring tools and experience to guide people toward developmental self-insight; to assist them in discovering the full range of their skills; to reinforce their efforts in forming developmental agendas; and, to provide help to those dealing with specific career-performance options.
- The continuing education community brings a tradition of experimentation and practice; pluralistic research and teaching perspectives; an international network that facilitates rapid interprofessional and organizational adaptation; and (in the case of higher education and professional associations) a distance from the organizational context that can represent neutrality or ignorance or both.
- The clients or customers bring the collective experience of the quality of the business or profession's performance; expectations of performance quality; operational resources desired by business and the professions; and the capacity to enlarge or restrict the freedom in which the business or profession operates.
- State legislatures, licensing and registration bureaus, and state and local prosecutors bring responsibilities for occupational regulation, consumer protection, product liability and criminal prosecution; and greatly varying policies and laws related to mandatory continuing education and professional relicensure.

The Performance Model in Continuing Education

Performance is a function of both individuals and ensembles. Even as an individual matter, performance is the result of interacting social and personal influences. To the extent that a double helix models the structure of performance, continuing education's interaction with personal or organizational performance can also be modeled. (See Figure 3.1.) In this model, persons as well as organizations engage in guided self-assessment, a kind of performance triage. The focus for the triage brings more than job functions into view. The focus also includes any other variables that are demonstrated to have a strong influence on performance: baseline knowledge and skills; the challenge of new roles; requisite skills in human relations; critical skills of mind; proficiency in self-managed learning; individual developmental progress, organiza-

Figure 3.1. PERFORMANCE MODEL

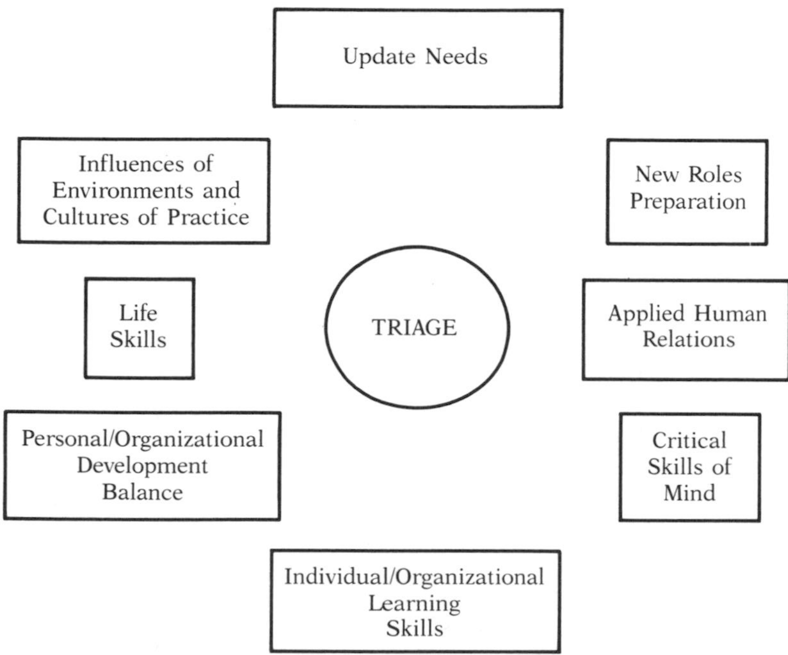

tional developmental balance, and the fit of individual and organization to one another; skills in coping with life's surprises as well as its anticipatable transitions; and understanding of the influences of environments and cultures and the skills to orchestrate them. The products of the triage for individuals and ensembles are learning and development agendas. The products for continuing education providers are referrals to their programs of potential service and performance related assessment data, in generalized form, useful in designing responsive new programs. Subsequent reapplication of triage processes serves as a measure of the performance utility of the agendas and resulting programs.

Beginnings are simple for providers who work with a profession or business field that has already developed a competence framework, self-assessment instruments, and national profiles against which individuals can compare themselves. Professionals and executives begin to set the base lines for learning and development agendas by undergoing competence assessment. Confidential conversations with counselors lead to the identification of competence areas that fall below the norms and appear to coincide with performance concerns. The agenda setting continues through behavioral event and critical incident interview processes, simulations of peer relationships or client/patient/customer encounters, and reviews of prior performance evaluations. Through these and other approaches, clients and counselors work back from instances of failed or weak performance to identify the oftentimes multiple sources of difficulty.

These and other approaches confirm the results of competence assessment yielding a well-defined continuing learning agenda of the traditional sort, pointing to other causal patterns, or both. The triage may identify the distraction of unresolved problems in other areas of life such as the disintegration of a marriage or the accumulation of debt as a seriously dysfunctional influence on performance. The triage may trace performance problems to simplistic analytical tools, even among persons in sophisticated specialities, or to a dysfunctional fit between a person's values and style and those of his or her peers or organization. The triage may point toward inappropriate risk taking or risk aversion, or a marginal capacity for commitment as a factor in troubled performance. The triage can assess whether, over time, the absence of skills in self-directed learning has diminished performance. During this process the relatively more favorable learning style of a professional or executive can be identified.

Sometimes a judgment of inadequate or spotty performance is accurate enough, but the analysis is faulty, leading some to see the causes as resting entirely in incompetent organizational leaders, ineffective organizational structures, or insufficient resources while others wrongly blame only themselves. The triage process itself can help professionals and executives make more sophisticated analyses of their performance.

Once the person's or organization's performance profile has been compared with appropriate profiles of successful performance and key contributing factors have been identified and analyzed, development and learning agendas begin to emerge. Many approaches are used: self-directed learning paths, mentoring, counseling, formal educational programs, and sequences and special assignments. Counselors, triage clients, and continuing education program development personnel begin to design responsive learning and development paths. Knowing the learning styles of participating executives and professionals helps form criteria for choosing among learning options. Counseling may be required. Mastering influence strategies for organizational improvement may be needed. Locating a context of practice or employment more supportive of personal performance may be appropriate. With an agenda in hand, support and reinforcement are organized among groups of executives and professionals pursuing similar objectives, negotiated with leaders of their organizations and—this is important—sought from participants' families.

Providers will already have some programs well suited to emerging learning agendas. When the triage processes of the self-assessment center reveal consistent patterns for persons who share a particular profession, level of executive responsibility, context of practice, or personal development issue, providers can develop responsive new programs with little risk, confident of inferring a general need. New categories of programs for professionals and executives are likely to emerge in areas such as self-directed or self-managed learning, the interaction of human development patterns and occupational life, the enhancement of developmental or life skills, and higher-order reasoning skills.

The performance model is also used to look at a single situation in a particular context, such as the one-on-one interaction of occupational therapists with children in school settings. Using observation techniques, building videotape data bases of successful, marginal, and unsuccessful therapist–client transactions, identifying consensually validated practitioners of excellence and having them (and those in the control group) behave their way through the same set of simulations for purposes of comparison and analysis, a rich description of successful performance in a single critical transaction over a wide range of client physical, mental, and attitudinal stimuli is established. Such a vivid picture of excellence is then analyzed so as to identify the elements at play in sustained, successful interactions as opposed to those characterizing spotty or unsuccessful interactions. Competence traditionally taken as proficiency in the preprofessional knowledge/skill base is among the variables hypothesized. The performance model tests a number of other hypotheses ranging from the influences of personal traits such as positive regard for children to the skilled use of voice, posture, vocabulary, clothing, pace, and touch to reassure, motivate, and reinforce. The roles of pluralistic cognitive strategies and life-coping skills are also examined. Ultimately a second round of simulated videotaped therapist–client interactions is compared with those used in the original assessment for measures of therapist performance improvement.

Examination of sufficient cases of individual performance by professionals in similar settings yields useful information about the social strand of performance's double helix. Such cases begin to suggest questions about the structures, policies, attitudes, operations, and physical resources of school-based occupational therapy. The emerging picture of strengths and weaknesses leads to learning and development agendas for the school system, school, teachers, and parents. Before-and-after measures of organizational and client satisfaction, case reviews, and parent and teacher interviews would assess improvements in the organizational variables.

On the other hand, the model's initial focus can be on the ensemble: the group practice, partnership, or organizational unit. In such cases, it engages in the triage as an ensemble with a view toward developing an organizational learning and development agenda. Residuals of this approach include identification of supportive individual learning agendas.

Bringing performance and continuing education into widespread interaction involves serious research work and design, but some implications for continuing education program development can already be seen. These perspectives will be treated in the chapters that follow.

References

CAMERON, KIM S. "Assessing Institutional Ineffectiveness: A Strategy for Improvement," *Determining the Effectiveness of Campus Service.* New Directions for Institutional Research, no. 41. San Francisco: Jossey-Bass, March 1984.

CAMERON, KIM S., AND WHETTEN, DAVID A. "Models of the Organizational Life Cycle." In *College and University Organization,* edited by James L. Bess. New York: New York University Press, 1984.

CARROLL, JAMES. *Prince of Peace.* Boston: Little Brown, 1984.

GINZBERG, ELI; GINSBURG, SAUL W.; AXELROD, SIDNEY; AND HERMA, JOHN L. *Occupational Choice.* New York: Columbia University Press, 1951.

HALL, DOUGLAS T. *Careers in Organizations.* Santa Monica, CA: Goodyear, 1976.

HEALTH DATA INSTITUTE, INC. "Final Report of Quality of Care Pilot Demonstration Project." Department of Defense Contract MDA 903–83–C–0291. Newton, Mass.: Health Data Institute, 1985.

ISENBERG, DANIEL J. "How Senior Managers Think," *Harvard Business Review*, November-December, 1984.

KEGAN, ROBERT. *The Evolving Self*. Cambridge, Mass.: Harvard University Press, 1982.

KEIDEL, ROBERT W. "A New Game for Managers to Play," *New York Times*, December 8, 1985.

KLEMP, GEORGE O., JR., AND MCCLELLAND, DAVID C. "What Characterizes Intelligent Functioning Among Senior Managers?" In *Practical Intelligence: Origins of Competence in the Everyday World*, edited by Robert Sternberg and Richard Wager. New York: Cambridge University Press, 1986.

MACHIAVELLI, NICCOLÒ. *The Prince*. Translated by George Bull. Baltimore: Penguin Books, 1975.

MENTKOWSKI, MARCIA; O'BRIEN, KATHLEEN; MCEACHERN, WILLIAM; AND FOWLER, DEBORAH. "Developing a Professional Competence Model for Management Education." Milwaukee: Alverno College Productions, 1982.

MORGAN, MARILYN A. *Managing Career Development*. New York: D. Van Nostrand Company, 1980.

SCHEIN, EDGAR H. *Organizational Psychology*. Englewood Cliffs, NJ: Prentice-Hall, 1980.

SCHNEIDER, CAROL; KLEMP, GEORGE O., JR.; AND KASTENDIEK, SUSAN. "The Balancing Act: Competencies of Effective Teachers and Mentors in Degree Programs for Adults." Chicago: Office of Continuing Education, The University of Chicago, 1981.

SCHON, DAVID A. *The Reflective Practitioner*. New York: Basic Books, 1983.

VOSS, JAMES F.; GREENE, TERRY R.; POST, TIMOTHY A.; AND PENNER, BARBARA C. "Problem Solving Skill in the Social Sciences," *The Psychology of Learning and Motivation*, vol. 17, Academy Press, 1983.

FOUR

The Search and Research Agenda

THE SEARCH FOR RESEARCH APPROPRIATE to performance-related continuing education is specified by the performance variables judged to be significant by those who assess needs and develop continuing education programs. As has been noted, most continuing education programs for business and the professions assume that acceptable performance is sustained by professionals periodically updating the knowledge and skills generally provided by professional schools, with occasional detours to take note of the impact of new technology or legislation. When professional-school–based research is at all vocational, it spans the gap between particular, occupationally specified knowledge and skills with ideal and generalized representations of the function of the profession and its specialties in society (Lynton, 1983, p. 21). Bar exams, medical-specialty boards, and placements that ornament a professional school's reputation are among the telling representations of a profession's idealized function. The research base that emerges includes lines of inquiry such as mechanical engineering, product liability litigation, multivariate analysis in marketing, the detection and treatment of cervical neoplasia, statistics, measures and evaluation, and the like. These paths are not trivial but certainly they are narrow. It may be argued that there is a prescriptive rather than descriptive quality about applications of such research. Schools of pharmacy, for example, engage in research related to pharmacy as an academic science or as a career spent at the laboratory benches of major pharmaceutical firms. This is an idealized representation of the profession's function somewhat distant from the reality of the corner drugstore's prescription counter, even in Florida where pharmacists may now prescribe drugs in a limited way.

Although updates are in wide demand among professionals and business people, exclusive use of the update model and its narrow research base is not easily defended. It cannot explain why fully updated and highly skilled professionals' performance flags during periods of serious family strife, financial crisis, or ethical dilemma. It cannot address the failure of talented professionals to be fully present to their work or clients for months following upon their being passed over for advancement within the firm. It fails to explain why many professionals are discharged because they "don't fit" or "simply can't get along." It is of no help in interpreting why a professional's discharge from a long-held position will often be followed by binge eating, heavy drinking, and abuse of family. It cannot account for the $100 billion annual cost of substance abuse expressed in the overuse of paid sick leave, depressed performance, more frequent on-the-job accidents, increased counselling costs, and the distraction and expense of more frequent executive and professional searches.

The competence or proficiency model is a significant step forward. Its research base is concerned with identifying what professionals actually do for a living, those professionals who do it well, and the key variables in their successful performance (Boyatzis, 1982; Schneider et al., 1981; McClelland, 1978). The research agenda among those using the model includes many promising questions. If competence is understood as a complex of knowledge, skill, trait, self-schema, motive, and attitude, what is their interplay and relative impact on performance? Do apparent differences in the settings of practice require significantly different kinds of competence, or, put differently, what is the nature of the elusive quality of portability across organizations and cultures? There has been relatively less research regarding the affective elements of competence than on its knowledge and skill elements. Although competence definitions include the intriguing concept of the absence of impairments, little has been done to investigate the developmental strengths of those whose performance has rarely or never suffered from impairments. The major limitation of this model and its research base, however, is its exclusive focus on the individual as if individual performance was not the result of a lifetime of cultural interaction and as if ensemble performance (the typical mode of professional performance in today's complex organizations) were the simple arithmetical sum of all individual performances.

What has been styled here as the double helix of performance is the interaction of culture (including the psychosocial environment as well as the organizational) with the individual. One strand structures performance through the intelligence, craft, and determination of cultural leadership; the maturity of its intragroup and intergroup behavior; the sum of individual performances; the appropriateness of structure, personnel, processes, policies, physical and financial resources to mission; the care and continuity with which these and other elements are orchestrated to form a climate favoring personal growth, the weathering of inevitable crises, periodic renewal of the terms of commitment; and, finally, the latitude and support provided by clients and the public. The other strand structures performance through an individual's knowledge and skill as related to job functions and explicit employer expectations; knowledge and skill more broadly taken, for example, in human development and organizational behavior; special cognitive skills such as critical thinking, pluralistic frames of reference, judgment and choice; self-regard and self-insight; traits, particularly those associated with developmental balance, for example, the capacity for commitment and critical distance, for stability and risk, for multiple role-culture involvement as well as focus; values, such as those attached to achievement, excellence, and discipline; and physical and mental health.

Each strand contains something of the other. It is immediately clear that culture includes individuals and is directly related to the quality of their interactions. It is less understood that the individual includes traits that are formed over a lifetime of interactions with culture and will continue to be influenced by those interactions. It is little recognized and even less dealt with that even the individual's thinking and knowledge have a social character. For Piaget, adults, even in their most personal and private thoughts, even when engaged in an internal inquiry incomprehensible to most others, think socially and engage contemporaries as well as sources from the past in a silent version of the continuing conversation of mankind (Piaget, 1955). Within the mind of a lawyer, Jefferson and Hamilton still engage one another as well as speak with lawmakers, judges, and society about contemporary issues. Architects pondering alternative designs may be in dialogue with Palladio, Louis Sullivan, or Walter Gropius. Thought patterns followed by city planners, engineers, and teachers in representing and defining an issue or solving a problem are fresh conversations with Aristotle or Aquinas. When professionals catch themselves "thinking out loud," they hear a conversation in progress. "Human thought is consumately social: social in its origins, social in its functions, social in its forms, social in its applications" (Geertz, 1971, p. 77). Frames of reference, even for the physical sciences, are negotiated and renegotiated and so-called laws remain in effect through consensual validation. Learning, the formation, growth, and reformation of knowledge take place within interpretive communities such as the scholarly disciplines, business, and the professions (Campbell, 1983, pp. 6–10).

There is already a substantial research base for performance's double helix. Supporting the cultural variables are organizational development/psychology/behavior/culture, sociology, social organization studies, social psychology, group-process theory, history, systems analysis, cultural anthropology, public-policy analysis and management, the economics of human capital, and the politics and sociology of knowledge, to cite but a few. Supporting the individual variables are human development, career studies, change theory, cognitive science, epistemology, decision-making studies, psychology (particularly constructive-developmental psychology), psychohistory, adult education, leadership and participation studies, values clarification, opinion research, ethics, medicine, and studies of middle age and aging, marriage, and family life. Some of these research fields, such as organizational behavior, cognitive science, epistemology and constructive-developmental psychology, take a special interest in junctions of the cultural and individual strands of performance variables, junctions in which the social or cultural is both "other than" the individual as well as "present within" the individual. The social sciences reign in most of these fields of inquiry but, as will be seen, the humanities also play a significant, subtle, and unnecessarily quiet role.

It is within the scholarly associations and journals devoted to human development, the professions and profession-related knowledge and skills, and organization behavior and public policy that performance issues are sometimes joined, interests shared, the quality of research instrumentalities discussed, and research published. The conversations and debates that really energize the research are not found in these clusters, however. They are found within smaller networks of scholars concerned with the nature and development of higher-order reasoning (Vygotsky, 1978; Piaget, 1978, 1985; McPeck, 1981); the role higher education plays in cognitive and ethical growth (Perry); whether the predictable crises of adult life define development or provide the contexts and opportunities for development (Basseches, 1984; Levinson et al., 1974; Neugarten et al., 1964); whether there is a theory of occupational choice and career development with identifiable patterns of performance or productivity (Ginzberg, 1972; Hall, 1976; Schein, 1980; Stoner et al., 1974); occupational enjoyment and play versus boredom or anxiety (Csikszentmihalyi, 1982; Berlyne and Madsen, 1973); how work and love are related in adulthood when skills and challenges are mismatched (Smelser and Erikson, 1980); the effect of individual, group, and intergroup relations on attitudes toward development (Alderfer, 1971); the interaction of individual and organization (Argyris, 1957); the congruence of individual needs, organizational climate, job satisfaction, and performance (Downey et al., 1975); the psychology of success and failure (Lewin, 1936); age and achievement (Lehman, 1953).

These lines of inquiry represent networks of scholars who are not in touch with one another with specific respect to performance in business and the professions. The research devoted to analyses of interwoven family, occupational, and developmental tasks and processes is neither abundant nor widely known (Havighurst and Orr, 1956; Lowenthal et al., 1975; Pascal, 1975; Bartunek et al., 1983). Researchers in psychology, sociology, cognitive science, or organization behavior are largely unfamiliar with adult education research: for example, that devoted to the influences on adult participation in systematic learning activities or to teaching-learning transactions (Knox, 1977b). The few splendid exceptions to this carrel blindness include the journals, *Organizational Behavior and Human Performance, Journal of Vocational Behavior, Journal of Applied Psychology, Journal of Counselling Psychology, Academy of Management Journal, American Sociological Review, Harvard Business Review* and *Administrative Science Quarterly*. Although these journals often join the issue of performance across disciplinary boundaries, business is overwhelmingly the culture and businesspeople the professionals of interest to most of the journals. Nonetheless, inferences may be drawn for professionals working in other settings and applications made to nonbusiness professionals working within the culture of business, particularly those in leadership roles.

It is not necessary that research networks be in direct communication with one another in order to advance our understanding of the interwoven strands of performance. Those with interest in and varied responsibilities for sustaining the highest possible levels of performance (counselors, major employers and organizational leaders, continuing educators, professional associations, personnel specialists, state licensing and registration authorities, and professionals themselves) recognize performance in business and the professions as a promising field of research application. For these rich veins of scholarship to realize their full yield requires careful mining by persons best positioned to see the possible connections. Continuing educators who assess needs and develop and evaluate learning experiences for business persons and professionals are well placed to do so. Systematic culling of these fields is likely to provide a variety of versions of the performance model described in Chapter Three as well as applications to continuing education. The performance model clearly widens the field of vision required in the needs-assessment process. It demonstrates the need for a richer array of programs, that is, it addresses all the important developmental intersections of culture and individual, and it suggests evaluation strategies that measure impact on performance (see Chapters Five and Six). Since continuing educators have not been in touch with the research fields related to the performance model, the task of identifying the relevant existing research remains. Were continuing educators to undertake the challenge, perhaps through one of their professional associations, they might as a secondary consequence create a network of key parties concerned with performance in business and the professions. The organizational agenda of the performance model calls for collaboration among business, organizational, and professional-association leaders, members of the counselling professions, human-resource personnel and training specialists, and continuing educators in pursuing two objectives. First, such a network is essential for the dissemination of research findings appropriate to performance-related issues, including the role of continuing learning and, within it, continuing education. Second, collaboration among these key parties is necessary to insure educational experiences that are linked with human development through the organizational and psychological contexts in which professionals and business people make and find meaning (see Chapter Seven).

Even while the search and dissemination of existing research begins, however, the process of setting an agenda for new research and inquiry needs to go forward. The following lines of inquiry are intended only as suggestions.

Beyond Knowledge Mastery

A major focus of current continuing professional-education programs is the mastery of specialized knowledge. Indeed, a distinguishing mark of the professions is mastery of special bodies of knowledge expressed in a triple hierarchy. The world of certainty, rigor, and stability is expressed at the apex in basic science, theoretical knowledge, or general principles. Applied science or applied knowledge is one step down and the theoretical, translated by the applied, forms the third level: problem solving. As has been argued, this view of knowledge is based on the perception of a dichotomy between rigor and relevance, a distortion caused by the tri-focal lens of positivism (see Chapter One).

It is alleged that professionals perform best when a presenting stimulus virtually self-defines its way on to a decision grid formed by rigorous research and validated by practice. A common complaint is that professionals, particularly those new to the field, have serious problems in dealing with a stimulus that presents itself as uncertain, indeterminate, complex, unique, unstable, or fraught with values conflict. Furthermore, decision trees, grids, and maps may have a coercive effect on reality. Professional recommendations frequently coincide with professional solutions at which the person is specially skilled. "For the person who only has a hammer, the whole world is a nail." To be better at problem solving than at problem definition renders a professional troublesome or irrelevant much of the time.

These are assertions and hypotheses, richly supported by impressionistic and anecdotal evidence. They ring true, but remain unproven. An agenda of descriptive research clearly is required. The judgments of employers and clients should be subjected to survey research. A range of stimuli, appropriate to a given profession or professional specialty and reflecting a spectrum from self-defining and certain to indeterminate and complex, could be brought to life in simulations and games and used in practice-audits of assessment centers. The critical-incident technique and the behavioral-event interview could be used to augment surveys, simulations, and games (Flannigan, 1954; McClelland, 1978). The most productive emphasis this research could have flows from its centering upon those professionals who appear to deal most effectively with conditions of uncertainty, instability, values conflict, and the like. What knowledge, skills, experience, and educational patterns appear to be most influential in their success?

As the descriptive research goes forward, other research could be simultaneously testing related lines of inquiry. Piaget distinguishes between knowledge (cognitive or behavioral adaptation that allows the knower to hold something invariant in the changing flow of his experience, for example, professional knowledge such as decision trees) and intelligence (individualized and internalized adaptation that in its semiotic-operational form is a way of producing knowledge, for example, framing or defining presenting stimuli). Piaget further suggests that it is the equilibrium between meanings (semiotics) and operations that defines cognitive adaptation, the system for evolving mental structures (Brown, 1985). Perhaps it is the capacity for evolving new mental structures that distinguishes professionals who deal effectively with conditions of uncertainty, instability, and the like. Piaget suggests that it is assimilation and accommodation that are the part-functions of adaptation (1985, pp. 5–6). Assuming this to be the case, learning experiences that brought about increased skill in assimilation and accommodation and, therefore, equilibration and the capacity for evolving mental structures, would improve the way professionals represent a presenting stimulus that does not immediately correspond with the familiar structures of their professional knowledge. The several hypotheses of this construct merit investigation.

1. Professionals who deal effectively with conditions of
    a. uncertainty;
    b. instability;
    c. complexity;
    d. indeterminacy;
    e. uniqueness;
    f. values conflict

    demonstrate proficiency in evolving mental structures.

2. Learning experiences that strengthen the cognitive skills of assimilation and accommodation increase learners' proficiency in evolving mental structures.

3. It is necessary to use a medium familiar to the learner in teaching assimilation and accommodation.

Cognitive Complexity, Adult Development, and Performance

The principle of complementarity suggests that many phenomena can be understood only if several different perspectives are applied to them. Theories of cognitive complexity suggest that people who are more cognitively complex can perceive a number of dimensions in a stimulus and simultaneously can hold valid and make use of several different classification schemes or theories to describe the phenomena they observe. As a result, they are more capable than others in applying such multiple perspectives. Adult-development research indicates that cognitive complexity is integrally related to broader patterns of development such as the character and quality of moral reasoning, introspection and self-awareness, understanding others in interpersonal relationships, and pluralistic approaches to society and social issues. The orientation of persons with cognitive complexity includes emphathizing with persons holding conflicting views, accepting responsibility for the consequences of actions, acting on perceptions of mutual interdependence, and tolerating higher levels of stress and ambiguity. These qualities found at later or higher stages are consensually validated as descriptors of highly effective managers and, conversely, their absence represent limits on managerial effectiveness (Bartunek et al., 1983, pp. 273ff.).

This way of thinking about cognitive complexity and adult development also suggests criteria for designing teaching-learning experiences with increased cognitive complexity as one of the desired outcomes. The business issues addressed should be complex and interdependent problems requiring many persons' involvement and a substantial amount of time and energy in exploring alternative perspectives without any expectation of immediate results. The learning process should include mentors who take multiple perspectives themselves and are willing to use and support each others' different skills and perspectives. The right "developmental match" requires dealing with a business issue slightly more complex and demanding than learners' comfort level (Bartunek et al., 1983, p. 277). Participants who are less developmentally complex usually require a more structured approach, fewer perspectives and the like. Learners are likely to reject approaches that are too distant from their current level of cognitive complexity (Widick and Cowan, 1977, pp. 257–270).

As a result of this line of inquiry, several hypotheses are worthy of investigation. Hypotheses 2, 3, and 4 are suggested by Bartunek et al. (1983):

1. It is necessary to use a medium familiar to the learner in teaching toward cognitive complexity, that is, learning takes place indirectly, residually.
2. Educational programs that assist learners to use processes of differentiation and integration foster cognitive complexity and encourage learners' passage to more complex developmental stages.
3. The appropriateness of an instructional approach depends on its responsiveness to and developmental match with learner developmental complexity.
4. Teaching-learning designs that effectuate greater cognitive complexity
   a. deal with ill-structured but learner-important problems;
   b. create a complex learning environment;
   c. use mentors at high levels of development;
   d. are based on conscious assumptions that are congruent with the nature of developmental change in adulthood.

Technical Problem Solving versus Professional Artistry

As Donald A. Schon points out, there are large areas of professional practice that do not lend themselves to the application of basic science, even though the prevailing public view of the professions as well as the role concept of many professionals is of technical experts, applying basic science or first principles to the needs of their clients (1983, pp. 308–309; 1984, p. 30). Anomalous data, ambiguity, and confusion are often well handled by professionals who reveal their uneasiness in expressions such as "muddling through," "trial and error," and "sophisticated bumbling." Others lament that only under occasional circumstances (the well-formed problem, dealt with rigorously through applied science) do they seem to themselves to be acting as professionals. This latter sentiment is particularly dispiriting since it gnaws away at self-coherence. Still more unsettling, the psychic rewards seem more on the side of discovering the underlying pattern in a jumble of data than responding to a neatly self-defining problem with a confirming diagnosis and an obvious treatment or problem-solving strategy. The processes through which successful professionals address the daily jumble is either disturbingly unclear to them or, equally disturbing, appears to involve artistry, intuition, and prescience.

With this as the presenting phenomenon, Schon suggests four lines of inquiry (1983, pp. 309–323).

1. Frame analysis. This is the study of ways in which professionals frame their roles and, to some extent as a consequence of role framing, frame problems. Frame analysis is essential to professional self-insight, providing the professional with ample evidence of the extent to which practitioners play a major part in determining the shape of their practice. For example, among regional campuses of state universities that share a common mission, serve similar socioeconomic constituencies, and operate under similar or even identical financial constraints, significant differences in the character and range of continuing education offerings are observable. Differing sets of goals, priorities, and values appear to be at work. While these can sometimes be explained by the particular history of the continuing education unit in question, the differences are more easily and credibly explained by differences in the goals, priorities, and values of the continuing education professionals who direct the units, in short, by the ways in which these professionals frame their roles. A study of directors of conference programming indicated five major different orientations corresponding with significant differences in the way in which the same professional position is performed: client orientation; operations orientation; image orientation; institution orientation; and problem orientation.

2. Repertoire building. Sometimes, professionals find themselves "winging it" or "muddling through" in situations that fail to fit theories of action, models of problem solving, or techniques of control. They would be greatly aided if they could turn to a repertoire of such experiences particularly appropriate to their practice. What frame analyses were particularly useful in similar situations? What processes of reflection brought other professionals to successful decision making? Which problem-solving techniques yielded the surest or quickest results? Such a repertoire could yield precedents useful in individual situations, and taken as a whole, would lend itself to identifying promising ways of thinking about the difficulty of linking knowledge with situations of ambiguity, indeterminacy, apparent uniqueness, and the like. As Schon points out, while lawyers have case precedents for reference, these generally are confined to court decisions, while successful representation of a client often calls for informal negotiation with the other litigant's lawyer, leading one's own client to a more realistic view of matters or acting swiftly and surely to head off potentially unethical developments (1983, pp. 315, 316). There are few repertoires of lawyering that address precedents useful to ordinary activities that can consume professional time and energy.

3. *Methods and Theories.* Research describing the ways in which professionals represent situations to themselves so as to frame understandings and define problems (frame-analysis research) and research assembling performance case studies, particularly in situations that do not easily define themselves (repertoire research) are among the sources of methods and theories professionals use in making sense of situations, particularly those that don't fit into familiar decision trees and problem-solving grids.

4. *Reflection in Action.* Research describing the professional's interweaving of intuitive, logical, affective, and interpersonal processes in action is needed. Are there patterns to the leaps back and forth among these and other processes? Are some patterns more dependable or successful than others? Can skills in manipulating these patterns be identified and taught? The answers are to be learned from professionals in action thinking out loud, professionals who have worked together writing about one another's reflective processes, professionals who have broken out of unconsciously self-imposed protocols describing how it happened, and professionals who understand that they sometimes make decisions of certitude through processes that do not resemble inductive or deductive reasoning, recalling the paths followed.

Identification and Study of High-Performance-Related Cultures

Culture as defined here includes the full range of human behavioral expressions: thought, speech, action, systems of thought and values, institutions, artifacts, and nonverbal symbols, for example. Culture is taken here particularly to mean the combination of these expressions in the psychosocial environments, formal and informal, in which persons find, define, nourish, and develop themselves. This includes but is not limited to organizational or corporate cultures as Terry Deal and Allen Kennedy developed the concept in 1982. These contexts, networks, groups, holding environments, and formally structured organizations include the inescapable settings in which even the fast disappearing solopractitioner comes to terms with performance. Organizations taken formally as bureaucracies are but one expression, and a superficial one at that, of the psychosocial setting of performance. The profession, or a person's idealized concept of his or her profession, is another expression, and in a somewhat different way, so is a person's professional association. The small group of working colleagues that accounts for perhaps an average of three out of four daily contacts a person has is yet another. So also are those with whom a person serves on special assignment, a person's special network of mentors and business and professional friends, as well as trusted subordinates and mentees. Likewise, a person's religious identity and community, voluntary associations, circles of friends outside the business or professional practice, and, most particularly, his or her family unit(s). Each of these holding environments has its values and rhythms, its mix of interpersonal conflict and support, its career-related risks and advantages. All of them are psychologically present in a person, consciously or unconsciously, whether at a given moment the person is physically present in one of these cultures or not.

Each of these cultures, the small group on special assignment or the married couple, has standards of its own performance that, although for the most part unspecified, are brought sharply into focus when the standards are violated continuously over some period of time significant for the culture. Each person carries his or her own internal balance of self-standards and performance expectations of others into each of these cultural settings. It appears to be the common experience of those in business and the professions that the successful or unsuccessful performance of any of these cultures (quite apart from any issue of personal responsibility) influences the quality of the performance professionals contribute to other cultures. The alcoholic spouse who is drinking can for a while be kept in the closet, but the problem and effect of an alcoholic spouse is taken by other members of the family to work, to school, and to recreation. If the work of a special task force isn't going well, if the relationships of those on the task force are worsening, if its target date for recommendations isn't going to be met, and if there may be career implications for all concerned, many task-force members will find their concentration, their "embeddedness," in other cultures such as their own regular corporate setting or weekend MBA program or family dinner table, greatly weakened.

The reverse appears to be just as frequently experienced. The success of any one of the many cultures in which a person moves (again, without respect to personal responsibility) has a way of spilling over into other cultures, a kind of contact high related to greater self-esteem. A son or daughter's acceptance by one of the military academies, a stunning corporate promotion, or the governor's personal thanks to a special task force for its practical and realistic report will tend to benefit a person's performance in other cultural settings.

Here again, careful descriptive research is needed to identify persons who have been successful in business or the professions over long periods of time, that is, through more than one of the predictable passages or crises of life. Using approaches such as the behavioral-event interview and the critical-incident technique we may confirm that maintaining a developmental balance in major psychosocial cultures is critical to a person's performance in business and the professions (Flannigan, 1954; McClelland, 1978). Since all of the holding environments in which the professional is embedded challenge and rechallenge developmental balance, we need to identify the coping skills, values, and cognitive qualities that act as a kind of balance pole for high-performing persons. Professionals who have suffered mental illness, paralysis, or sight, speech, or hearing impairment during their professional careers, as well as those impaired from birth, merit close attention. Continuing educators will be particularly interested in understanding the role that formal learning experiences have played in developing and sustaining the qualities, values, and skills significant for balance and, therefore, performance.

The double helix of performance demands that the proper focus of inquiry be not only the high-performing individual who successfully maintains developmental balance but also the high-performing culture. Continuing efforts such as those of Peters and Waterman are a good beginning. In their work it is not the "zero-defect" bureaucracy with stability and predictability as its outstanding characteristics that turns out to be the high-performance culture. It is rather the organization with a culture that pays attention to its employees, has a bias for action, remains close to the client or customer, encourages autonomy and risk, recognizes persons' needs for belonging to successful groups as well as having individual recognition, has a hands-on, value-driven feeling, stays with its strengths, is organized simply with a lean staff, and has a mix of centralized and decentralized attributes. Peters and Waterman were surprised to find strong leadership guiding cultures with such characteristics (1982, pp. 8–26). Among the forces that hold such untidy cultures together appear to be the democratization of knowledge, the promotion and protection of shared values, and the sustaining of a distinctive identity.

Donald Schon emphasizes the professional's need for reflectivity in action as a key to lifelong professional growth and excellence in practice, and suggests qualities characteristic of cultures that both support individual reflectivity and act reflectively as a whole. Such cultures must be learning systems open to surprise and spontaneity in determining the boundaries and directions of organizational inquiry (1983, p. 328). Such a culture, in whatever organizational form, will be far from a bureaucracy's uniform procedures, objective measures of performance and center/periphery systems of control. It will place emphasis on flexible procedures, differentiated responses, qualitative appreciation of complex processes, and decentralized responsibility for judgment and action. It makes a place for attending to conflicting values and purposes (1983, p. 338). Schon maintains that for a culture to achieve and sustain high performance it must reexamine and may have to restructure its central principles and values from time to time. To do so requires that a learning system capable of sustaining tension and converting it to productive inquiry be in place.

Organization leaders as well as continuing educators need to develop and probe a much larger repertoire of high-performance cultures as case studies supporting or challenging the perspectives of scholars such as Peters and Waterman (1982), Schon (1983, 1984), and Edgar Schein (1980). This can be done at both the macrolevel (the business, hospital, or school) as well as the microlevel (the strategic-planning team, the hospital's accounts-receivables staff, or the curriculum-review committee for social studies).

In addition to looking respectively at high-performance cultures and individuals, we need to focus most particularly on the transactions between cultures and the individuals. In what ways do high-performance cultures intervene when individual performance flags? In what ways do individuals intervene when the culture's performance is declining? What elements are at work in individual or cultural performance turn-arounds? How do cultures help to prepare individuals for predictable life crises and support persons undergoing them? To the extent that individual developmental balance is one of the key determinants of sustained excellence, are there high-performing cultures that make personnel decisions, organize special group and individual assignments, and renegotiate the terms of individual-culture commitments with career-long performance in mind? What are the interactions of cultures, apart from the immediate work context, with respect to individual performance in business and professional life? Surveys of MIT alumni 15 years after graduation reveal three different career patterns in terms of background factors and current values. In engineering-based careers, for example, common values included the need for a challenging job; opportunities to advance and to exercise leadership; desires for high earnings; and the sense of making a contribution to the organization. In scientific-professionally based careers there was less concern about leadership, earnings, or contribution to the employing organization, and more of an orientation toward the intrinsic challenges of a task, the chances for creativity, a sense of accomplishment, and continued learning. Those in pure professional careers demonstrated a range of values spanning the engineering and scientific-professional categories. The implications of such descriptive research is that even within a fairly homogeneous occupation like engineering one will find many motivational patterns and degrees of work involvement, requiring different personal and organizational strategies for maintaining productive performance (Schein, 1980, pp. 789–81).

What are the contributions of families, professional associations, universities, and the counselling professions, for example, to sustaining and refining the ideals and motivations associated with persons' original professional commitment? "Leviticus" (Chapter 25) specifies a weekly sabbath for the Lord, rest for the land every seven years, and a period of national renewal every 50 years. Do some interactions of cultures and individuals take the shape of Sabbatical exercises in cultural and personal rethinking and renewal? Should they?

Career Performance, Liberal Education's Hidden Curriculum

Edward Wrapp, Emeritus Professor of the University of Chicago's Graduate School of Business, attacked the business school establishment for having done more to insure the success of the Japanese and West German invasion of America than any other single factor. Even the most talented of recent MBAs, according to Wrapp, ". . . run for cover when grubby operating decisions must be made and often fail miserably when they are charged with earning a profit, getting things done and moving an organization forward." Wrapp maintained that business schools' overemphasis on specialization and quantitative methodology had made it increasingly difficult for corporations to find candidates with the general qualities upon which business depended to fill its senior general manager positions (1980, pp. 82–88). Peters and Waterman refer to the growing sentiment that the last decade of MBAs lack the broader vision, the sense of history, and the perspectives of literature and art that are typically identified with a strong liberal arts background (1982, p. 35). The *Wall Street Journal* (Watkins, May 6, 1986) reports that among the reasons for a surge in business hires of liberal arts graduates is that after years of favoring applicants with technical degrees, employers are short on workers with more general analytical and writing skills, people who can take a variety of thoughts, from social to economic to political, and apply creative analysis to them. Joseph Johnston, Jr., argues the value of liberal education from the viewpoint of tomorrow's organizations and their needs. Many of his associates in "Educating Managers" argue the value from their experience as successful organization leaders (Johnston et al., 1986). Hardly an issue of *Mobius*, a journal of continuing education in the health professions, fails to report new and creative efforts to bridge professional education with liberal learning. Some of these efforts are predictably in the field of ethics, but others (for example, humanities-based inquiries into interpretation and related issues because interpretive skill makes up a good part of the art of medicine as it does of literature) are quite fresh. NYU's medical and dental center community enjoys a particularly rich program of classes and discussion groups. The health professions may feel a particular urgency since competitive entry compels many undergraduates to concentrate entirely on the physical and biological sciences, math, and statistics to the exclusion of the humanities and social sciences. The American Institute of Certified Public Accountants has offered interdisciplinary humanities programs for four years and in 42 of the states requiring continuing education for recertification, 10 hours of the 40 required may be earned through approved liberal education experiences.

AT&T's studies of its managers help to explain the growing consensus about the effects of liberal learning. The Management-Continuity Study, begun in 1977, was designed to examine differences and similarities between the current and former generations of college recruits. Two hundred and four college graduates from 13 AT&T operating companies have undergone the MCS, an assessment-center process. In the three dimensions of administrative skills assessed, organizing and planning, decision making and creativity in problem solving, nontechnical college majors such as humanities/social science were superior to technical majors such as math/science or engineering. Differences in interpersonal skills were even more pronounced. In leadership skills, oral communications, and forcefulness of personal impact, the humanities/social-science majors were significantly superior. Scores on the general information test showed nontechnical majors had broader interests. In verbal skills, the nontechnical and technical majors had comparable scores. Group differences on projective measures of need for achievement and advancement were significant with business majors clearly the highest scorers.

These general findings of the MCS are relatively stable over time, given AT&T's 25-year Management Progress Study. The MPS also points to the relationships of college majors with subsequent progress in the Bell System. Of the total MPS sample of 274 college graduates, 38% were liberal arts majors, only slightly fewer than in the MCS and heavily weighted toward humanities and social science majors. Humanities and social science majors turned in the best overall performance, scoring highly in all but the category of quantitative skills. On overall ratings of potential for middle management made by the assessors after reaching consensus on the ratings of the dimensions, there were highly significant group differences. Nearly half (46%) of the humanities and social science majors were considered to have potential for middle management, compared to only 30% of the business majors and 26% of the engineers. As a matter of record, engineering majors took about 18 months longer to be promoted than the humanities, social science, and business majors. Eight years following their first promotion, the average management level of the humanities and social science majors was highest, with the engineers still trailing well behind. After 20 years, the same trends were evident but differences were no longer statistically significant, though humanities and social science majors were still ahead. Among those who had achieved at least the midway point in the management hierarchy, a sign of considerable success, there were 43% of the humanities and social science majors, compared with 32% of the business majors and 23% of the engineering majors (Beck, 1986).

Liberal learning yields rich and diverse ingredients such as: critical thinking; cognitive complexity; the capacity to engage in dialectical thinking and to evolve mental structures; higher order skills in analysis, judgment, and choice; artistry, intuition and prescience; and the capacity to represent situations in pluralistic frameworks. Research describing widely varied careers has found a pattern of interpersonal skills, cognitive skills, and motivational characteristics to be chiefly related to successful performance (Klemp, 1977). Liberal education weaves just such a pattern (Chickering, 1981). Thomas B. Jones provides an excellent bibliographic essay in "Educating Managers: Executive Effectiveness Through Liberal Learning" (Johnston et al., 1986). Those interested in frameworks for research issues will want particularly to read "A New Case for the Liberal Arts" (Winter, McClelland, and Stewart, 1981); "Liberating Education" (Gamson et al., 1984); and "Beyond the Present and the Particular: A Theory of Liberal Education" (Bailey, 1984).

More conclusive and varied research efforts than Beck's AT&T studies are required. CBS has established a Corporate Council on the Liberal Arts at the American Academy of Arts and Sciences. CBS' gift of $750,000 will support a study of the relation of liberal arts to business leadership. Executives from other major U.S. corporations form an executive committee for the project. Ann Howard's "College Experience and Managerial Performance" builds on the AT&T studies. Should additional research validate the AT&T inferences, we must know more explicitly what the outcomes of liberal education are that contribute to high levels of success in the professions as well as in more general organization settings. Such occupationally related outcomes as may be identified are implicit but unintentional residuals of liberal learning, a curriculum domain needlessly hidden by ritualistic defenses of liberal arts as nonutilitarian. How can this domain become explicit and intentional in the substance of liberal education? What pedagogical and institutional strategies may be found or established to bridge the gulf between professional/technical learning and liberal learning?

Needed: Action-Research Centers for the Study of Performance in Business and the Professions

The constituencies with a serious stake in greater understanding of the key variables in the performance of individuals, groups, organizations, and cultures has reached a critical mass. Included are:

Leaders of business and industry;

Persons from business, industry, government, medical research, engineering, architecture, nuclear power, transportation, and environmental safety who understand the degree to which public health and safety depend upon sustaining exceptional standards of professional diligence;

State and national political leaders concerned with service and product cost and quality, productivity, and international competitiveness;

Professional associations as well as organizations heavily staffed by professionals such as universities, hospitals, and consulting firms;

Continuing educators who analyze needs, develop and evaluate programs for business and the professions;

Members of the helping professions, particularly those experienced in counselling business and professional persons, for example, psychiatrists, clinical psychologists, psychiatric social workers, milieu therapists, industrial psychologists, and personnel/human-resources specialists;

Scholars engaged in related research, particularly: human development, for example, constructive-developmental psychology and cognitive science; organizational behavior, for example, cultural anthropology, social psychology, sociology examining the interactions of professions working in the same occupational context, the client-professional interaction, and the professions-public interactions; descriptive survey research, for example, longitudinal career/organization studies seeking to identify variables significantly figuring into career/organization excellence; interdisciplinary studies of the professions as interpretive communities finding and making meaning and the roles of politics, economics, myths, rituals, and traditions as they do so; and the organized knowledge bases traditionally associated with business and the professions;

Individual business persons and practicing professionals committed to excellence but uncertain as to how to sustain it in themselves or lead cultures to foster it in others;

Increasingly sophisticated and organized consumers and clients concerned with both the need for greater professional and business accountability as well as the dangers inherent in allowing an adversarial climate to dominate the professional-client relationship.

In Pennsylvania, major figures representing many of these stakeholder groups have come together repeatedly to discuss issues related to professional competence and to encourage and collaborate in resulting research assisted by the W. K. Kellogg Foundation (see Chapter Two). There is no doubt that regional and national leadership concerned with the double helix of performance is sufficiently extensive, varied, and influential as to make possible the establishment of centers for the study of performance in business and the professions.

Such research centers could be located within universities, corporations, or clusters of professional associations known to one another through mastery of related knowledge bases and the sharing of practice settings. These potential research center locations offer such obviously distinctive strengths as to recommend at least one research center effort in each. In whatever settings the research centers are based, however, they must represent collaborative efforts of major employers, professional associations, scholars, continuing educators, the counselling professions, and representatives of client constituences. So constituted, the centers would be ideally configured to engage in what University of Chicago anthropologist Sol Tax called action research. Continuing educators in cooperation with employers and professional associations, or both, could be testing research assumptions and hypotheses about performance-significant variables by organizing learning experiences for individuals, groups, or organizations that intentionally taught toward such variables. To the extent that learners achieved the intended educational objective, the research centers would assess whether the learning had impact upon performance over a reasonable length of time.

These research centers would have the added value of providing a superb setting for the professional development of continuing educators who wish to specialize in the development, conduct, and evaluation of learning experiences for business or the professions. They might be expected to provide research-validated considerations for curriculum revision in professional schools, particularly with reference to the integration of liberal and professional learning. Finally, through the resulting books and papers, conferences, newsletters, and other vehicles of dissemination, the field of continuing education for business and the professions would communicate for the first time across boundaries of institutional, corporate, associational and professional cultures and do so over the issue that ultimately judges the quality of the field's programs: their impact upon performance.

References

ALDERFER, CLAYTON P. "Effect of Individual, Group and Intergroup Relations on Attitudes toward a Management Development Program," *Journal of Applied Psychology* 55, (1971): 302–311.

ARGYRIS, CHRIS. *Personality and Organization.* New York: Harper, 1957.

BAILEY, CHARLES. *Beyond the Present and the Particular: A Theory of Liberal Education.* Boston: Routledge and Kegan Paul, 1984.

BARTUNEK, JEAN M.; GORDON, JUDITH R.; AND WEATHERSBY, RITA P. "Developing 'Complicated' Understanding in Administrators," *Academy of Management Review* 8, no. 2 (1983): 273–284.

BASSECHES, MICHAEL. *Dialectical Thinking and Adult Development.* Norwood, N.J.: Ablex, 1984.

BECK, ROBERT E. *Career Patterns: The Liberal Arts Major in Bell System Management.* Washington, D.C.: Association of American Colleges, 1986.

BERLYNE, DANIEL E., AND MADSEN, KAJ BERG (EDS.). *Pleasure, Reward, Preference.* New York: Academic, 1973.

BLOOM, SAMUEL W. "Some Implications of Studies in the Professionalization of Physicians." In *Patients, Physicians, and Illness,* edited by E. Gartly Jaco. New York: Free Press, 1958.

BOTWINICK, JEAN *Cognitive Processes in Maturity and Old Age.* New York: Springer, 1967.

BOYATZIS, RICHARD *The Competent Manager.* New York: Wiley, 1982.

BROWN, TERRANCE. "Foreword." In *The Equilibration of Cognitive Structures,* edited by Jean Piaget. Chicago: University of Chicago Press, 1985.

BRUFFEE, KENNETH A. "The Structure of Knowledge and the Future of Liberal Education," *Liberal Education,* Fall 1981.

———. "Collaborative Learning and the 'Conversation of Mankind,' " *College English* 46, no. 7 (1984): 635–652.

CAMPBELL, DONALD T. "Science's Social System of Validity-Enhancing Collective Belief Change and the Problems of the Social Sciences." In *Potentialities for Knowledge in Social Science,* NIMH Conference, September 1983. Unpublished. Copies available: University of Chicago Office of Continuing Education.

CHICKERING, ARTHUR W. "Integrating Liberal Education, Work and Human Development," *AAHE Bulletin* 31, no. 7 (1981): 1–16.

CSIKSZENTMIHALYI, MIHALY. *Beyond Boredom and Anxiety*. San Francisco: Jossey-Bass, 1982.

DEPPE, DONALD A. "The Director of Conference Programming: Attitudes Toward Job Role." In *Continuing Education Report*, edited by Ann Litchfield. Chicago: University of Chicago Studies and Training Program in Continuing Education. Number 6, 1985.

DOWNEY, H. KIRK; HELLREIGEL, DON; AND SLOCUM, JOHN W. "Congruence Between Individual Needs, Organizational Climate, Job Satisfaction and Performance," *Academy of Management Journal* 18 (1975): 149–154.

EURICH, NELL P. *Corporate Classrooms*. Princeton, N.J.: The Carnegie Foundation for the Advancement of Teaching, 1985.

FITTS, W. H. *The Self-Concept and Performance*. Nashville, Tenn.: Dede Wallace Center, 1972.

FLANNIGAN, J. C. "The Critical Incident Technique," *Psychology Bulletin* 51, no. 4 (1954).

FORD, ROBERT *Motivation Through the Work Itself*. New York: American Management Association, 1969.

GAMSON, ZELDE F., BLACK, NANCY B. ET AL. *Liberating Education*. San Francisco: Jossey-Bass, 1984.

GEERTZ, CLIFFORD. *The Interpretation of Cultures*. New York: Basic Books, 1971.

GINZBERG, ELI. "Toward a Theory of Occupational Choice," *Vocational Guidance Quarterly* 20 (1972): 169–176.

GLASER, ROBERT. "Education and Thinking," *American Psychologist* 39, no. 2 (1984): 93–104.

HALL, DOUGLAS T. *Careers in Organizations*. Santa Monica, CA: Goodyear, 1976.

HAVIGHURST, ROBERT J., AND ORR, BETTY. *Adult Education and Adult Needs*. Chicago: Center for the Study of Liberal Education for Adults, 1956. (Available from Syracuse University, Publications in Continuing Education.)

HIRST, PAUL H. *Knowledge and the Curriculum*. International Library of the Philosophy of Education. Boston: Routledge and Kegan Paul, 1975.

HOWARD, ANN. *College Education and Managerial Performance*. New York: AT&T, 1985.

JOHNSTON, JOSEPH S., JR., ET AL. *Educating Managers: Executive Effectiveness Through Liberal Learning*. San Francisco: Jossey-Bass, 1986.

KLEMP, GEORGE O., JR. "Three Factors of Success." In *Relating Work and Education*, edited by Vermilye Duckman. San Francisco: Jossey-Bass, 1977.

KNOX, ALAN B. *Adult Development and Learning*. San Francisco: Jossey-Bass, 1977a.

———. "Current Research Needs Related to Systematic Learning by Adults," Occasional Paper no. 4, Office for the Study of Continuing Professional Education, College of Education, University of Illinois at Urbana-Champaign, 1977b.

LEHMAN, HARVEY C. *Age and Achievement.* Princeton: Princeton University Press, 1953.

LEVINSON, DANIEL J.; DARROW, C.; KLEIN, E.; LEVINSON, M.; AND MCKEE, B. "The Psychological Development of Men in Early Adulthood and the Mid-Life Transition." In *Life History Research in Psychopathology*, edited by D. F. Hicks, A. Thomas, and M. Roff. Vol. 3. Minneapolis: University of Minnesota Press, 1974.

LEWIN, KURT. "The Psychology of Success and Failure," *Occupations* 14 (1936): 926–930.

LOCKE, EDWIN A. "Toward a Theory of Task Motivation and Incentives," *Organizational Behavior and Human Performance* 3 (1968): 157–189.

LOWENTHAL, MARJORIE F.; THURNHER, MAJDA; CHIRIBOGA, DAVID; BEESON, DIANE; GIAY, LYNN; LURIE, ELINORE; PIERCE, ROBERT; SPENCE, DONALD; AND WEISS, LAWRENCE. *Four Stages of Life: A Comparative Study of Women and Men Facing Transitions.* San Francisco: Jossey-Bass, 1975.

LYNTON, ERNEST A. "Reexamining the Role of the University," *Change* 15, no. 7 (1983): 18–23, 53.

MCCLELLAND, DAVID C. *Guide to Behavioral Event Interviewing.* Boston: McBer and Company, 1978.

MCPECK, JOHN E. *Critical Thinking and Education.* New York: St. Martin's Press, 1981.

NEUGARTEN, BERNICE L., AND BERKOWITZ, HOWARD (EDS.). *Personality in Middle and Late Life.* New York: Atherton, 1964.

PASCAL, ANTHONY H. *An Evaluation of Policy Related Research on Programs for Mid-life Career Redirection.* Santa Monica, CA: Rand, 1975.

PETERS, THOMAS J., AND WATERMAN, ROBERT H., JR. *In Search of Excellence.* New York: Harper and Row, 1982.

PERRY, WILLIAM G. AND ASSOCIATES. "Cognitive and Ethical Growth: The Making of Meaning." In *The Modern American College*, edited by Arthur W. Chickering. San Francisco: Jossey-Bass, 1981.

PIAGET, JEAN. *Origins of Intelligence in Children.* New York: International Universities Press, 1952.

———. *The Language and Thought of the Child.* New York: Meridian Books, 1955.

———. *Development of Thought.* Oxford: Blackwell, 1978.

———. *The Equilibration of Cognitive Structures: The Central Problem of Intellectual Development.* Chicago: University of Chicago Press, 1985.

SCHEIN, EDGAR H. *Organization Psychology.* Englewood Cliffs, NJ: Prentice-Hall, 1980.

———. *Organizational Culture and Leadership.* San Francisco: Jossey-Bass, 1985.

SCHNEIDER, CAROL G. "Sources of Coherence in Liberal Learning: The Experiential Dimension." In *Field Based Experiential Learning* CAEL–NCHC Conference, June 1985. Unpublished. Copies available: University of Chicago Office of Continuing Education.

SCHNEIDER, CAROL G.; KLEMP, GEORGE D., JR.; AND KASTENDIEK, SUSAN. "The Balancing Act: Competencies of Effective Teachers and Mentors in Degree Programs for Adults." Chicago: Office of Continuing Education, The University of Chicago, 1981.

SCHON, DONALD A. *The Reflective Practitioner.* New York: Basic Books, 1983.

———. "The Crisis of Professional Knowledge and the Pursuit of a Epistemology of Practice." Paper presented on the occasion of the Harvard Business School's 75th Anniversary Colloquium on Teaching by the Case Method. The President and Fellows of Harvard College, 1984.

SMELSER, NEIL, AND ERIKSON, ERIK H. (EDS.). *Themes of Work and Love in Adulthood.* Cambridge: Harvard University Press, 1980.

STONER, JAMES A. F.; FERENCE, T. P.; WARREN, E. K.; AND CHRISTENSEN, H. K. "Patterns and Plateaus in Managerial Careers—An Exploratory Study." Research Paper no. 66, Graduate School of Business, Columbia University, 1974.

SUPER, DONALD E., AND JORDAAN, JEAN PIERRE. "Career Development Theory." Teachers College, Columbia University, undated.

VOSS, JAMES F.; GREENE, TERRY R.; POST, TIMOTHY A.; AND PENNER, BARBARA C. "Problem Solving Skill in the Social Sciences," *The Psychology of Learning and Motivation* 17 (1983): 165–213.

VYGOTSKY, LEV S. *Mind in Society: The Development of Higher Psychological Processes.* Cambridge: Harvard, University Press, 1978.

WATKINS, LINDA M. "Liberal Arts Graduates: Prospects and the Job Market Grow Brighter," in the *Wall Street Journal.* Boston: May 6, 1986.

WIDICK, C., AND COWAN, M. "How Developmental Theory Can Assist Facilitators to Select and Design Structured Experiences." In *Exploring Contemporary Male/Female Roles,* edited by C. G. Carney and S. L. McMahon. La Jolla, CA: University Associates, 1977.

WINTER, DAVID G.; MCCLELLAND, DAVID C.; AND STEWART, ABIGAIL J. *A New Case for the Liberal Arts.* San Francisco: Jossey-Bass, 1981.

WRAPP, EDWARD. "We Have Created a Monster," *Dun's Review,* September 1980.

FIVE

Program-Development Implications

By moving beyond the update and competence models to the double helix of performance, continuing educators' field of vision is enlarged and their scanning devices are multiplied. As a result, the programs developed will be far more varied, new program resources will be identified or developed, and program constituencies will be broadened to include organizations as routinely as individuals. Program evaluation criteria will be defined by performance specifics (see Chapter Six). New providers, discovering appropriate roles, will enter the field (see Chapter Seven). In the process, individuals and organizations will become more sophisticated about the variables critical to their performance and the characteristics of continuing education programs that form, support, or enhance them (see Chapter Eight).

For those working from a framework of updating professionals' knowledge and skills, the field of vision in which needs analysis and program development take place is defined by the profession's traditional knowledge and skill base. Often the vocabulary of the update model sharply limits its focus, for example, continuing legal education, continuing medical education, and so on. This is a curriculum driven rather than a performance driven way of thinking about professional needs, that is, continuing education for lawyers automatically admits a broader horizon than continuing legal education. The eye of the update model also scans the environment for profession-related developments in legislation and technology. In the last five years this field has been broadened to include the administrative needs of mid-career professionals who find themselves supervising other professionals, overseeing budgets and the like.

A considerably larger field of vision is enjoyed by those developing programs for professionals from a framework that includes any variables related to professional competence. As it has been described in Chapter Two, competence is related to any knowledge and skill required by whatever professionals really do for a living. This clearly enlarges the knowledge and skill windows considered appropriate for viewing professional needs by the update model. The competence model is not limited by idealized generalizations about what the professions are or prescriptive definitions of what the professions ought to be. In addition, the competence model adds new windows, for not just knowledge and skills are related to competence. The other windows through which program-development personnel need to look at professional life include motivation (sustained concern for goals, states and conditions that drive, select, and direct the behavior of professionals); self-schema (persons' self-image and their evaluation of that image); and traits (habits or consistent ways of responding to presenting stimuli).

The range of continuing education programs issuing from the competence model's field of vision are predictably more varied than those of the update model. Updates for business professionals look like business schools' curricula: marketing, accounting, finance, production management, and the management of technology. Competence model programs for business professionals include such curriculum areas but marshall them in a larger array addressing socioemotional maturity, entrepreneurial abilities, intellectual abilities, and interpersonal abilities. The University of Chicago's Management Development Seminar looks through these windows. Over three intensive weeks, it addresses the internal lives of executives, their interpersonal relationships in the small groups characteristic of corporate work settings, and their lives within larger corporate cultures and organizational structures.

Diverse as such continuing education programs are, the competence-model's program portfolio is limited. Most programs reflect needs analysis and development time spent in the knowledge and skill windows rather than in windows through which key motivations, self-schema, and traits that sustain and enhance competence can be identified and addressed. Positive regard, for example, is a key trait in successful teaching and counselling. It is essential to physicians in persuading patients to follow a regimen of medication, diet, or exercise. Positive regard is rarely a key element addressed by competence-based programs for persons in these fields, however. Among other variables within the competence model's field of vision are the management of personal affairs, particularly family life, and the skills to anticipate, avoid, or overcome emotional impairments, physical handicaps, chemical dependencies, and the like. Relatively few continuing education programs addressing these variables are to be found.

The major limitation in the competence model's vision, however, lies in its unrelenting focus upon job functions and individuals. It does not "see" the psychosocial cultures (the interrelated clusters of family and community members, patients or clients or customers, friends and enemies, peers and subordinates and bosses, organizations and institutions and professional associations, all with expectations and values and myths) that sculpt the personality and character of business and professional people, influencing their performance. By now, for example, many expected hundreds of thousands of people to be delivering business or professional services or at least interacting with their business and professional colleagues from their electronic cottages. The estimates of how many people are actually doing so ranges from The Office of Technology Assessment's 3,000 to 5,000 to a market-research firm's 30,000. Business and professional firms that educated people in the use of computer technology and, in many cases, supplied it, that is, matched new job functions with new competence, have been dismayed by the results. Why has home computer-based performance been so unsuccessful? Many people felt suddenly deprived of cultural support that had been unnoticed by them until they began to work at home. Coffee-klatch comradery, long-time friendships, personal recognition for their work, and even the intrigues of the office were missed. People became lonely, gained weight, and encountered much the same stress of too much sudden family togetherness that occurs in the recently retired. The performance of those still working at the office also suffered when they lost easy and informal access to face-to-face advice, and office-based executives found themselves uncomfortable with the challenge of supervising persons whom they rarely saw. Children encountered problems because Dad or Mom was home but not necessarily home for them. Mom or Dad reciprocated with guilt and anger (Noble, 1986).

The competence model's focus on individuals and their job functions also fails to draw attention to the collective or ensemble nature of performance as something other than the simple sum of individuals' competencies. Cultures, organizations, networks, and groups have performance profiles as distinctive as those of individuals. IBM is often described as robust and Chicago "still ain't ready for reform." Some money funds are "go-go" funds and some brokerage houses are relied on as prudent. Some physician groups have a reputation for aggressive patient management, others are conservative. Small local banks can consistently treat individual depositors arrogantly while at least one nation-wide banking system's services are praised for their personal touch by individual depositors. The rhythms and structures of these organizations, groups, and institutions, their ways of reaching decisions and taking actions, and their values expressed in information access and reward systems, determine whether or not individuals' efforts are orchestrated in collective performances that produce products or professional services of high quality and result in a favorable climate of patient, client, or customer satisfaction.

The update and competence models have appropriate roles and productive uses particularly if used within a more inclusive model. The performance model's field of vision is alert to signs that a professional's knowledge and skills need to be refreshed or updated, and that new research, technology, and societal developments need to be brought instructively to a professional's attention. The performance model sees the significance of any competence, taken as knowledge, skill, trait, self-schema and motive, which is shown to be *related* to effective or outstanding individual performance in a job. Nothing is lost by looking carefully at individuals and their job functions. The performance model is also sensitive to the role cultures have in equipping and motivating a person for business and the professions as well as for shaping the person's subsequent career performance. The performance model sees that it is not only the several cultures of the workplace (office friendships, formal and informal systems, networks of colleagues, client behavior and expectations, and affiliative, bureaucratic, participative, and entrepreneurial organizational values) that influence individual job performance but also the culture of the professional's home, neighborhood, friends, charitable activities, political involvements, and the like. These cultures are interwoven with the cultures of the workplace. Success or failure, contentment or unhappiness in one will influence performance in the others. Individual performance is defined by two interacting strands of personal and cultural variables. The performance model sees individuals but never without the many contexts in which they live, work, and find meaning.

Society requires excellence from its lawyers, physicians, teachers, and security price analysts. Society also requires excellence from its judicial system, hospitals, schools, and brokerages. This is not simply because a corrupt county court bench will have a corrupting influence on lawyers or because mismanaged hospitals will, over time, lose their best physicians. It is because clients, patients, and customers are served by both individuals and organizations.

The performance model brings into view the social dimension of individual performance. Of equal importance as a distinct but related subject of inquiry and continuing education, it addresses the performance of partners, groups, organizations, and institutions. Collective performance is as appropriate a constituency as individual performance for continuing education.

What are the implications for continuing educators? In *The Design of Education,* Cyril O. Houle provides a fundamental system of decision points and components of adult education (1972, pp. 46–58). As a widely used framework, continuing educators will be able to place the familiar cycles of needs analysis, program design, and evaluation within an overarching learning relationship with organizations as well as individuals.

1. A Possible Educational Activity Is Defined

The performance model raises questions about the frames of references used by continuing educators in identifying possible programs. When continuing educators speak with one another about identifying promising ideas, it is assumed that discovering promising ideas about possible *programs* for individuals in business or the professions is the key task. Popular ways of undertaking the search for possible programs include sampling current registrants about other desired learning experiences, scanning professional journals and business publications for new knowledge and skills persons ought to master or for new issues they will have to deal with, monitoring incoming telephone inquiries about whether a program in this or that topic is being offered, surveying what similar continuing education operations are offering, identifying the special strengths of the continuing education unit or its parent organization, and looking for patterns in what has worked well in the past. The needs-assessment process, only one of a number of formal procedures instrumental in generating, locating, selecting, or refining program ideas, usually is employed to test program ideas that have already emerged as a result of scanning the environment in the ways just indicated or as a result of continuing educators' intuition. Less frequently, continuing education staff will probe an event or trend significant to business or the professions to understand its complex economic, social, historical, and political structure with a view toward identifying what it reveals about business or the professions or what it is likely to mean to business and the professions. Emerging projections of performance issues, changes in societal esteem with possible public-policy consequences, the functions of organizations in which the profession in question works, and the like often provide the elements of a strategic plan for program development, within which identification of promising programs is more surely done. There are also continuing educators who find it more cost efficient simply to offer a new program and see if anyone comes.

The performance model suggests that discovering and tending promising *learning relationships* with organizations and individuals is a key task with potentially more promising results. Constructive-developmental psychology stresses the significance of our cultural imbeddedness in weighing critical factors in human development such as the balance between security and risk taking and the evolving nature of the terms of commitment. Culture and the individual are active agents in personal growth. Furthermore, the current critique of positivism by Kuhn, Schon, and others establishes that the formation and reformation of frames of reference and the growth of knowledge take place in interpretive communities marked by collaborative learning. While human thought may have its private side, it is also consummately social, a kind of internalized conversation involving the manipulation of objective materials. Therefore, as Kenneth Bruffee suggests,

> any effort to understand how we think requires us to understand the nature of conversation; and any effort to understand the nature of conversation requires us to understand the nature of the community life that generates and maintains conversation. . . . To think well as individuals we must learn to think well collectively, i.e., we must learn to converse well. [1984, p. 640].

The conversations to be joined are found in experienced communities of knowledgeable collaborators that have common interests, values, language, and paradigms of perception and thought (Bruffee, 1984, p. 646). Professional associations, scholarly societies, and organizations such as hospitals and accounting firms are examples of communities in which new knowledge is created, new conceptual frameworks emerge for knowledge, and continuous reflection in action takes place. Every survey of how learning actually occurs shows that it does not happen primarily through highly structured short-term courses for large-scale dissemination of information (for example, Goldfinger and Bennett, 1983). It takes place through an intensely active, yet informal network of individuals mentoring one another in the context of their practice and often through the very activity of their practice.

The learning relationships key for continuing educators in business or the professions, therefore, are those that place them as interlocutors within the ongoing conversations of interpretive cultures. These conversations can be seen through exchanges in the journals of medicine, law, and theology if continuing educators wish to interact with the culture of scholarship in those fields. For sampling conversations closer to the culture of practice, continuing educators can look to professional associations, associations representing certain contexts of practice settings, such as hospitals or—still more specific—emergency medicine, or publications representing certain kinds of industry, business service, or consumer products. Associations of professionals and employers are still at least a step removed from the actual contexts of practice. What is required is more than a version of advisory committee meetings or literature searches undertaken to identify promising program ideas. What is required is more than auditing someone else's conversation. What is required is that continuing educators identify and develop the relationships that permit them to join the conversations themselves, and in so doing, both to learn and to teach.

By way of illustration, a local Health Maintenance Organization (HMO) is a community of knowledgeable collaborators sharing interests, values, language, learning experiences, and paradigms of perception and thought. It is an interpretive community often engaged in collaborative learning. Its orientation is toward community and family medicine with emphasis on preventive care. It is a community that includes providers and consumers. Medical care is provided by professionals salaried by the HMO that is funded by a combination of employee and employer payroll contributions to insurance carriers that add incentives for keeping the patients well, so that hospital usage is reduced. Patient members of the HMO's health plan are often involved in discussing policy, representing unmet needs, and resolving disputes, since they are as concerned with health care cost and quality as are the HMO's salaried providers and staff. Questions of individual professional performance and of the HMO's collective performance in maintaining an appropriate balance between quality and cost are implicitly psychosocial issues and, eventually, explicitly cultural issues.

The continuing education agency that develops a two-way learning relationship with a local HMO is positioned to learn much. At one such HMO, the continuing educator would hear the conversation at monthly scheduled brown-bag luncheons to which all staff, including medical providers, are expected to come. These sessions are organized with a view toward working through treatment and administrative issues that cross professional boundaries. They are intended to reinforce policy or operational decisions in ways that invite feedback. These meetings also seek to identify new opportunities or problems and compare them with others at which the HMO is already at work. The major questions are unchanging: What can this HMO do to strengthen health care or lower the barriers to access, especially cost? Of the things that might be done, what is most doable in the shortest time and at the lowest cost with the greatest payoff to our patients? What resources are needed? If our judgment is correct, how can success be evidenced in terms of patient health and access? Questions are raised about the computer-based, patient record system. Someone comments on the increase of pediatric asthma among the population served by the HMO. Patient complaints about coordination of care issues are discussed. Everyone is concerned about the consequences of unplanned growth in the HMO's membership. The summer sun is coming and, the staff is reminded that the HMO's incidence of skin cancer is up sharply.

There is a continuing education and training budget. While it contains an amount in service of general professional development, it is largely allocated by priorities defined and redefined by the brown-bag staff luncheons: Can continuing education make a critical difference within the HMO's plans to improve community health as well as health care quality and access? The continuing education that follows frequently represents the inquiry or problem-solving mode rather than the more familiar instructional mode. A committee meets with a consultant on information systems and patient records, another with an authority on pediatric asthma and they report back. A task force, organized to select or design a planning methodology for estimating the impact on the HMO of adding 3,000 patient members in the next year, decides to attend an intensive short course on strategic planning and to adapt what it hopes to learn to the HMO setting. A staff dermatologist agrees to develop an article on skin cancer for the summer patient newsletter. The issue of continuity of care is somehow lost or else isn't regarded as a top priority by those present.

The observant continuing educator who is sensitive both to the role of the social in individual performance and to the characteristics special to group performance is able to develop working assumptions about the learning system already in place, for example, about the HMO staff who appear to be natural mentors or who are looked to for a kind of permission in the process of adapting innovations. The continuing educator can have some sense of the political nature of the HMO. The continuing educator can experience the common meaning that service in an HMO has for clerical workers, nutritionists, psychiatric social workers, administrators, physicians, nurse associates, lab technicians, and telephone operators as well as the special meaning it has for each group. In short, the continuing educator can see that the HMO is a community or culture with its own anthropological rites and sets of symbols, its own politics over issues and personalities, its own rhythm and process of adaptation, its values, hopes and fears, and its vulnerability to what happens in other cultures.

The continuing educator can see the disasters brought about by one or two professionals who are as superbly competent as they are immature, the positive impact on patient health that an elderly receptionist whose personal esteem for "her" patients is almost radiant, and the deeply depressed functioning of a nurse whose teenage son recently attempted suicide.

The HMO will also learn much from an interactive relationship with a continuing education agency and from inclusion of a proficient continuing educator in the organization's major conversations. (Few university-based continuing educators enjoy such a relationship at present. Few organization-based continuing educators or training and development personnel have such a relationship with their own parent organizations in which, more often than not, their role is confined to orientation of new employees, episodic training of blue collar workers and technical staff, facilitating of sales force meetings, and the like.) The continuing educator who is sensitive to the cultural forces that shape individual performance will be able to raise questions about how the HMO is prepared to address the performance challenge posed by even the most competent staff members' interpersonal problems, their inevitable passage through the transitions and crises of adulthood, the anxieties and sorrows of their parenting, marriages and friendships, the dulling effect on them of repetitive activity, the psychological problems some will encounter, the drug or alcohol dependencies a few will develop, the decline in energy some will experience as the result of illness or aging, and so on. What patterns of judgments has the HMO exercised with respect to the interaction of human development and performance and to what effect? Could individuals' performance be improved or at least better maintained by the HMO taking these influences on performance as seriously as it takes continuing education in radiology, inhalation therapy, or health-care systems planning?

The continuing educator sensitive to the distinct nature of ensemble or organizational performance will offer other instructive questions related to orchestration of the HMO's culture for enhancing collective performance. What are the HMO's patient care values? What are the HMO's economic realities? To what extent are its systems, procedures, protocols, search and hiring processes, performance-review instruments, and salary and wage incentives realistically supportive of its values? Are patients educated to expect the care valued by the HMO and therefore enabled and empowered to reinforce the HMO's efforts to maintain certain levels of excellence? How does the community perceive the HMO? Is the peer review mechanism designed with the HMO's objectives in mind? Is there an opportunity for those who work closely together but represent different professions to review their group performance? What are dependable proxies for the standards intended by the HMO, for example, what evidence generated by the HMO's activities can be relied upon to provide instructive feedback on the quality of care provided by various HMO family care, clinical specialties, and patient-education units as well as non-HMO resources, such as other physicians and laboratories, to which patients are referred? Who follows up, with what authority and resources? What is the organization-wide atmosphere with respect to aggressive versus conservative medical practices, the balance of financial risk and security, and critical expressions of loyalty? What is the organization culture with respect to individual development, for example, evolution in the terms of personal commitment and fulfillment, the balance of risk and security in accepting promotions and reversing the process when the promotion is a mistake, rotation of certain leadership positions, and the like? Does the physical environment, for example, the building's location, its traffic ways, the relations of units to one another within it, support patient care objectives and the formal and informal internal communication essential to the objectives? Which of these many considerations, if successfully addressed, would make the biggest positive difference to the HMO's mission and values? Which of the least costly issues to address would make the most substantive contribution? And so it might go, the continuing educator contributing a full palette of performance-related questions.

The HMO and the continuing education agency begin to develop carefully formed judgments about what each can best bring to a specific and long-term learning relationship. The HMO's learning agenda and the learning priorities of its individual staff members will reflect the widest possible view of factors influencing HMO and individual performance. The learning needs that cannot be addressed by either the HMO or the continuing education agency become, in turn, a specific shopping list with which HMO leaders and individual professional staff can turn to other potential providers. In the case of a university-based continuing education agency, such a learning relationship will help the agency identify appropriate existing resources as well as alternate ways of configuring them for HMO needs. New resource development may be necessary, involving not only the consideration of new degree programs and the design of innovative noncredit courses and course sequences but also the examination of promising new ways in which to provide access to current credit and degree programs. Furthermore, the continuing education agency will be able to generalize securely about the learning agendas of other HMOs and HMO-based professionals throughout the continuing education agency's service area. Valuable lessons gained in the continuing learning relationship with the original HMO will lower the costs of program development, the network effect will lower the marketing costs, and the experience is likely to improve the effectiveness of a generalized outreach to statewide or regional HMOs and their staff. In this sense, learning relationships do eventually lead to the identification of more traditional programs to be offered in the usual ways.

The once promising high-tech future held the hope of many new learning relationships, particularly between higher education, business, and the professions. Early steps in forging such relationships have been troubled by industry bringing detailed presentations of its educational needs, the result of a process often conducted entirely without contact with higher education, with the expectation of negotiating a prompt response. Higher education's inward focus during a decade of unusual financial stress and the deeply enculturated values that move its decision-making machinery, but only very slowly, have discouraged industry leaders. Higher education and industry could explore organization needs and educational resources simultaneously, with a better chance of identifying ways to nurture a lasting learning relationship.

Representatives of business, professional associations, and higher education have at times entertained the notion of developing internships through which continuing educators could exchange comparable positions within one another's organizations, providing each with windows on the other's culture, particularly the other's conceptual framework for examining needs, surveying resources, and the like. Such internships might greatly facilitate learning relationships among organizations and institutions if (1) they provided the interns with access to significant conversations about the other organization's performance-related strengths, problems, needs, and plans; (2) the interns were selected, in part, on their capacity to offer insight into the relationship between continuing education and performance; and (3) if all concerned understand the internship exchange is not a simple trade of the everyday duties of comparably salaried staff, but an investment strategy with a short-term net expense, since some guided and reflective roaming through the other culture is required. Such internships are bound to disappoint if (1) the internship is understood as primarily personal development rather than interorganizational development; (2) each culture is not thoroughly prepared to receive the intern as a part of ongoing conversations of importance; and (3) staff holding minor responsibilities or working in peripheral roles are selected as interns.

2. A Decision Is Made to Proceed

Among the HMO's carefully reasoned priorities for change and improvement, many performance goals will not require educational strategies for accomplishment. Sometimes prosaic and inexpensive changes, as in the way incoming telephone calls are handled, can bring about major changes in HMO-patient relationships. Nevertheless, there are likely to be far more possibilities for educational collaboration than can be pursued. Both sides will be looking to match learning needs related to highly desired individual, group, or organizational performance with available educational and financial resources. (The HMO also knows that it is important to build individual commitment and performance by supporting career planning and individual career-related learning experiences, even when these seem to have no direct benefit for the HMO and its patients.) When choosing among potential activities of this kind, both organizations will want to consider projects that are also likely to further the state and stage of their relationship. They will want to collaborate in something that will advance their understanding of one another and bring additional members of each organization into working contact with one another.

Organizations and continuing education agencies looking for their first collaborative activity will want to choose an activity of high priority and modest risk, perhaps one in which redundant or back up educational strategies can be designed or one that makes use of the mentoring and operational patterns of the HMO. They will want to select a collaborative effort in which the desired outcome permits close evaluation of the contributions of each with minimal chance that environmental factors outside the learning relationship might cloud project results with ambiguity. Organizations and continuing education agencies with some years of success in working together and with several projects in process are better positioned to take imaginative risks and learn significantly from their occasional failures without threatening the learning relationship.

3. Objectives Are Identified and Refined

An organization–continuing education agency learning relationship is one in which conversations about overall performance goals and the orchestration of the culture for sustained excellence include continuing educators as well as organizational representatives. Therefore, when the decision has been made to proceed with a collaborative educational activity, its goals are already specified and promising educational strategies have probably already been discussed. Learning objectives can be defined in support of each goal. Instructional objectives can be matched with each learning objective. When what is necessary for better performance is clearly identified to begin with, the requisite proficiencies for performance (knowledge, skills, traits, self-perceptions, motivations) can be defined. When proficiencies are defined, informed judgments can be made about the relative performance relatedness of informational and skill updating. In this way, the update and competence models are useful subsets of the performance model.

A strategic marriage of organization improvement and continuing education would serve specialized objectives, as for improving the quality and speed of on-site laboratory work, and general objectives, as for improving the capacity of HMO staff to anticipate and cope successfully with "personal" problems, thus reducing the frequency and length of performance impairment. As research progresses on the relationship between cognitive complexity and performance, technical problem solving and professional artistry, and liberal education and career performance, learning objectives related to cognitive complexity or professional artistry could be matrixed with the learning objectives specific to any particular educational vehicle.

Such educational activity is collaborative not simply because an organization and continuing education agency cooperate in the decision on what educational strategy is to be undertaken in service of certain performance goals. It is collaborative also in the sense that the HMO and the continuing education agency each have appropriate roles with respect to identifying those persons who are to be involved in various learning activities; defining, executing, and reinforcing each learning objective of those activities; and coordinating the activities for maximum effect. HMO identification of the measurable performance differences the educational strategy is expected to achieve is absolutely key to objective setting and educational design.

4. A Suitable Format Is Designed

4a. Resources. Seeing the utility of the update and competence models, but in the larger framework of the performance model, organizations and continuing education agencies in learning relationships will find themselves using more varied learning resources. The continuing education agency will have at its disposal an ongoing formal and informal learning system already in place, as in the natural mentoring typical of health care settings. The continuing education agency and the organization will have knowledge of the way in which the adaptation of innovation actually takes place within the context of everyday activity and at least partially on the basis of that knowledge will be able to design a format that the culture will own, endorse, and reinforce.

Organizations and individuals in business and the professions will have more varied resources at their disposal as they look for potential learning resources through the wider framework of the performance model. Beyond the obvious connections with business and professional schools' resources, the research and practice of continuing education, and a profession's literature, technology, and skills, the performance model shows the connectedness of anthropology, the behavioral sciences, the new geography, history, international studies, political science, sociology, urban studies, public-policy studies, medicine, psychiatry, public health, and the humanities—particularly the analysis of ideas and study of methods, language, composition and writing, logic, epistemology and ethics, the history of culture, and American studies. Aristotle, Augustine, and Shakespeare; Hamilton, Madison, and Jay; Freud, Mead, and Whitehead; Dostoevsky, Camus, and Gandhi have much to offer to persons who must deal with conditions of uncertainty, indeterminacy, values conflict, and ambiguity and to organizations led as much by friendships, politics, values, customs, rites and myths, imagination, emotions, and intuition as they are by econometric projections, decision trees, and strategic planning.

4b. Leaders. Familiar with the formal as well as informal leadership of the organization under various circumstances, the organization and the continuing educator can select persons who will take the initiative to guide, direct, instruct, question, demand, or interact in other ways directly related to the conduct of the collaborative learning project. Such leadership sometimes requires development, but most often is simply recognized during the period in which the continuing educator is learning to read the culture of the organization and the organization and continuing education agency are identifying promising educational strategies. Instruction in the specifics of the leaders' role in the activity selected, together with some coaching and early feedback, are often enough to make leaders drawn from the organization feel comfortable and perform effectively.

4c. Methods. The methods used in programs for business and the professions are often those common to schools the professionals attended. There are several reasons for this. The update and competence models have concentrated on extending the knowledge, skills, and issues represented in professional schools and have, therefore, drawn heavily on the academic resources of those schools. An update in mechanical engineering or international finance is likely to use instructional methodologies indistinguishable from the professional-school classroom. Those designing programs typically have had a homogeneous professional constituency in view such as radiologists, chemical engineers, or social service administrators. The low-risk, low-energy approach to program design opts for the familiar rather than the experimental. Finally, only the constituents' general profile is known during the program-design phase because in most cases, continuing educators do not know who will be participating until long after the program has been designed and marketed, that is, a few weeks before it is presented. By this time, not much can be done to alter methodologies even in the rare instances when a learning-styles inventory is administered.

In a learning relationship between an organization or professional group and a continuing education agency, a learning relationship characterized by the simultaneous pursuit of organizational and individual performance goals through multiple educational strategies, familiarity with the methodologies relatively more effective for individuals and working groups can be achieved and varied methodologies employed. The professionals' familiarity with the continuing education agency will increase their comfort when trying an innovative learning method for the first time. Professionals familiar with one another in a work setting may be embarrassed or repressed in certain methodologies, such as role-playing, behavior simulation, game situations and the like. When behavioral objectives are in view, professionals often give themselves more easily to methodological risks when they are in neutral settings with peers other than the persons with whom they work every day. These are not unusual challenges for the continuing educator but a learning relationship with an organization offers the continuing educator and the professionals and executives the time and opportunities necessary to respond with methodological design and referral processes.

4d. Schedule. Scheduling learning experiences for business and professional people is a vexing practical problem for continuing educators when they are designing programs to be offered to a general class of professionals and executives, such as physical therapists or brand managers. After eliminating the specter of scheduling a program at the time of year the state's physical therapists are attending their professional association's annual meeting or brand managers are all planning fall media campaigns, how can an optimal date for learning as well as attending be chosen? Religious holidays, K–12 spring breaks, and August family-vacation time are avoided, but continuing educators generally rely upon consumers to make the best possible match between perceived need, time of the year, and location. Continuing educators playing it on the safe side have peaks of programming intensity (and competition) in fall and late spring, and as a result, they have inefficient patterns of professional, technical, and clerical effort to manage.

The continuing education agency and organization in a long-term learning relationship will have a chance to grow flexibly toward one another in terms of the availability of educational resources as well as the work cycles of individuals and groups within the organization. If the relationship is mutually beneficial, there will be sufficient motivation to solve conflicts in scheduling in ways that serve individual learners and the organization's goals as well as further the relationship. The continuing educator is in direct contact with individual, group, and organizational goals, the decision-making process related to which priorities are best advanced by learning and education, and as a result, the willingness of the organization to commit resources including the diversion of professional energies from practice to formal learning. The relationship greatly reduces the risk of an accidental scheduling conflict occurring. Should an unforeseen conflict occur, the planned educational experience can be rescheduled without substantial loss to either the organization or the continuing education agency.

Maintaining a learning relationship with a number of organizations will also provide the continuing educator with an insider's view of the priorities and patterns of activity in HMOs, law firms, pharmaceutical companies, retail chains, and industrial manufacturing. This knowledge facilitates the design and scheduling of programs closer to organizational objectives and relatively less-costly diversion of executives and professionals for education. In this way, the learning relationship decreases the continuing education agency's risk in offering programs to general categories of professionals and business leaders. Programming designed in learning relationships with organizations also leads to a more even annual distribution of effort for continuing education agency staff.

4e. Sequence. The sequencing of events grows in importance as activities increase in complexity and length. In performance-oriented learning relationships, it may be useful to think of the organization or the group as the ongoing performance system and the educational strategies (and within them, the individual educational activities) as temporary systems. The organization and group also can be thought of as ongoing, informal learning systems with formal educational activities as their temporary systems.

When a complex series of educational activities are contemplated, sequencing must be considered before scheduling.

The sequence of events organization leaders are planning and the educational activities being designed will, in part, serve the same goals. The interplay between the two streams of activities may be as crucial as the order of events in either. Their interplay can be a conscious and creative embodiment of the double helix of performance: the orchestration of cultural variables by the organization (goal setting and planning, changes in organizational configurations, personnel promotion, recruitment and education, involvement of individuals in recommitment to organizational goals, identification of their role in bringing them about, and the like) and the tending of personal variables by the individual (assessing commitment to the organization and its goals, level of performance with respect to current roles and tasks, and proficiencies in undertaking new challenges; or planning for recommitment including considering the concept of self in relation to organization as well as other cultures, reducing impairments from circumstances in any culture, improving health and focus or energy, negotiating a learning agenda, and so forth). The general plan for the interplay between the ongoing operational system and its temporary educational system is established with the sociology and politics of organization culture and change in view, for example, identification and use of role models and change agents, incentives and the elimination of barriers. Sensitive collaboration also will uncover situations in the organization's life for creating or anticipating teachable moments with preplanned educational responses.

The intelligence gained in coordinating this interplay is useful in sequencing the individual events within each educational activity. The continuing educator will be better placed, for example, to understand whether or not professionals or executives have come to have a sense of ownership over their organization's goals and the part played by each educational experience in supporting their roles in organizational life. In some cases, little or no time at all need be spent in articulating how the educational activity fits with ongoing organizational patterns.

4f. Social Reinforcement. Feelings people have about one another and the activity that brings them together can enhance or limit learning within a single educational experience. This is the usual way in which social reinforcement is understood with respect to the design of individual programs. As has been noted with respect to other design issues such as methodologies, the continuing educator whose design work takes place within an institutionalized learning relationship is better positioned for informed design decisions, such as social reinforcement, than is the continuing educator who will know little about participating professionals and executives until shortly before the designed program begins. It may be useful for an interprofessional group to come together in a learning situation, for example. The continuing educator working with organizational leadership and the members of the group in question has an opportunity to help the individual members of different professions to decide for themselves that an interprofessional approach is correct. In the absence of a prior relationship with participating professionals, valuable learning time may need to be diverted to working the group through its discomfort in finding physicians, nurses, and technicians or principals, teachers, and school staff together as student peers. A temporary social contract may need to be negotiated for members of different professions to engage in collaborative learning, despite the extent to which an observer might conclude that the patient or student is best served by persons collaborating across professional boundaries.

When individuals are working to develop more successful behavioral patterns as coordinators of other professionals or directors of other executives or when they are learning how to use a wider range of alternatives in situations such as negotiation or conflict resolution, special social reinforcement may be appropriate. For example, executives working on their interpersonal skills may be more highly motivated to master new sets of behavior if they know that they will be returning to different assignments, that is, those in which their new behavior is likely to be more credible. On the other hand, if such executives are returning to the same assignments, those with whom they have daily contact (bosses, peers, and those supervised) need to encourage the new or different behavior because they judge it will ultimately serve the organization and themselves better. The informal culture within any office or setting of practice will develop apprehensions and anxieties in the absence of preparation for new behavior by a familiar figure. Negative feedback will not promote the repeated practice required for the executive to continue to feel comfortable in exercising new skills and soon things will be back to normal, often with a judgment that the continuing education program failed. The collaboration of the employing organization is required in such matters. Even outside a regular learning relationship, individuals who enroll in a program shortly before it is held can be counselled that upon returning to their regular employment they should negotiate either a change in assignments or the support of their daily colleagues if the educational experience is to have any lasting value. Naturally, they also can explore the possibility of changing organizations.

These examples of social reinforcement for specific learning experiences speak to the need for organizations to monitor the quality of the social reinforcement that they provide for the learning relationship itself. Are the culture's values supportive? Do they maintain a climate that rewards rather than punishes self-assessment, group performance evaluation, and acknowledgment of depressed levels of performance? Is there help for persons with insight into their performance problems? Is loyalty critical and strong because it is reciprocated? Has the culture and its individual members reached an understanding about the ways in which organizational development and human development serve one another? Do professionals and executives and the leaders of their organizations see continuing education as one of the vehicles through which organizational and human development stimulate one another? Are the same messages about these issues sent and received at different levels within the organization?

There is no shortcut to accomplishing the social reinforcement necessary for both the overall learning relationship and the individual educational experience to succeed. The continuing educator and the adult student, the educational agency and the organization can make many mistakes and still achieve their joint goals if they have created and maintained supportive social reinforcement.

4g. Individualization. Continuing educators can offer help to individuals whose learning agendas are not specifically organization related. The organization that operates on the basis of valuing human and organizational development as serving one another will support the identification of personal, career-related needs if not actually finance pursuit of some of them, some of the time. A little time spent counselling the individual may identify the places where individual needs and ambitions intersect with organizational objectives, a happy marriage likely to be fully supported by the organization. In organizations striving for individual–organizational links with respect to performance, the in-house, human-resources staff can offer professional guidance. Many professionals and executives are uncomfortable with discussing personal career objectives with organization-based resource persons, however. A mid-career institute located in an external continuing education agency but supported as a feature of the overall learning relationship can provide a needed alternative system. The return for this individualized learning service is a strong social-reinforcement base for the learning relationship, in which individuals are willing to have learning styles and preferences surveyed, to participate in private, work-group, and organization discussions of performance issues, and the like. Another important return is information significant for individualizing educational activities directly serving organization performance goals.

Highly individualized sequences of formal and informal, other-directed and self-directed, group and solo learning activities can be designed if continuing educators, organizational leaders and the professional or executive in question all contribute to the process. Realistic personal goals can be linked with organization needs and the resulting agenda translated into an individual educational plan. A sample plan spanning 18 months might include opportunities to work with figures who display desired strengths and skills and have a reputation for successful mentoring, to participate in a mid-life support group, to follow lists of suggested readings and discuss them in special seminars designed for persons with similar agendas, to attend a particular sequence of credit courses at a local campus or by means of interactive video or computer linkage with a distant university, to experiment with new orientations and skills or to practice new proficiencies in special assignments and projects, and to have the opportunity for increased feedback on performance.

Professionals and executives pursue complex educational goals. Experience suggests that adults at any given moment are pursuing as many as five or six lines of learning simultaneously. One or two are work related, another is likely to be related to a family physical or mental health problem, another represents puzzling over societal role changes and at least one is probably related to leisure activities. Professionals and executives are self-directed learners who occasionally are engaged in guided independent study or formal teaching-learning relationships. Experience suggests that the majority do not have much sophistication as self-directed learners nor do they consult with educators or human resources staff when developing an educational agenda. It would be relatively easy for any learning relationship to lead to increased sophistication in self-directed learning. Organization-based individuals who participate in goal setting, needs analysis, consultation about program-design issues, and evaluation need only to be led to reflect on the process as they might conduct it on their own behalf. In addition, formally organized opportunities for gaining knowledge and skill related to self-directed learning could be regularly offered within the organization–continuing education learning relationship. Many individuals have a learning relationship with continuing education agencies in virtue of their episodic registration in a variety of programs. These frequent registrants are excellent candidates for increased sophistication in self-directed learning.

4h. Roles and Relationships. In the National University Continuing Education Association - American Society of Association Executives survey of 110 responding professional associations and 136 responding universities that had engaged in cooperative continuing education activities, Lillian Hohmann found that 47% of the associations and 43% of the universities experienced difficulty in defining the roles of the collaborating organizations and individuals. Only 17% of the associations predicted that problems experienced with role definition would inhibit them from future cooperation but 25% of the universities reported that role definition was a serious inhibitor of future cooperation (Nowlen and Stern, 1981). In most cases, these role and relational difficulties were encountered over the development of a series of intensive short courses or the preparation and administration of a single major conference and there had been no prior relationship. Nonetheless, the warning in this data is instructive.

Clarifying the roles and relationships of the organizations and agencies, the executives, professionals, and continuing educators in a learning relationship is particularly important. The difficulty professional associations and universities have had over single projects suggests the wisdom of undertaking no specific educational activity until the organization and continuing agency have: identified the special values, self-interests, advantages, and constraints that each brings to the relationship; specified organizational performance and human development goals and the ways in which continuing education strategies might serve them; and defined respective roles and responsibilities likely to facilitate the goals. Periodic review of the relationship (as a separate matter from evaluation of the educational strategies) should lead to reforms, improvements, and recommitment or a winding down of collaborative educational activities. A strong relationship has room for program failures; in fact, if there aren't any failures it is possible that reasonable risks aren't being taken. Successful educational activities, however, will not survive a relationship tortured by the high psychic costs of misunderstandings and unresolved conflicts.

If relational roles are clear and routinely reviewed, a wholesome climate will exist for sorting out roles and responsibilities in individual educational activities. There are more issues to clarify than the organization–continuing education relationship. Professionals and executives of the same organization bring their ongoing work relationships to educational experiences. When senior partners, chiefs of medical sections, or managers are involved with their staff in a learning activity, everyone must understand whether they are participating "in role," that is, engaging in teaching or learning while remaining authoritative representatives of the organization, or temporarily "out of role" as peers in the learning process. Continuing educators and organization leaders will already have decided whether "out of role" participation for the individuals in question will have functional credibility among their temporary learning peers.

Roles must be both well defined and believable. The role of every person participating or auditing needs to be made clear. One person in the rear of the room who is not introduced, whose purpose in being there is not explained, who doesn't participate interactively, and takes copious notes is a distracting annoyance.

4i. Criteria of Evaluation. Evaluation issues are addressed in Chapter Six.

4j. Clarity of Design. The general design of the learning relationship has to be made clear to all involved whether they have a specific role in designing, shepherding, and evaluating it or a general role participating in emerging educational activities and evaluating them. The design should be congruent with the culture of the organization. In high-process style organizations, for example, most employees will have a role in setting goals, measuring progress, and suggesting strategy and tactics, from the assembly line to the board room, from hospital admissions to discharge. Professionals and executives in such settings will expect to participate in decisions about how temporary educational systems and ongoing operations will interact for maximum effect.

Organization leaders and continuing educators are both responsible for making the design of individual activities clear to all participants, defining roles and expectations. It is a great help when the activities themselves are derived from the prior reflection of individuals and groups who are defining their learning agendas with specific organization goals and career ambitions in mind. Even when this has been done, however, the relationship of parts of a program to the whole, of panel members to one another, of individual learning to collaborative learning must be made clear.

5. The Format Is Fitted into Larger Patterns of Life

5a. Guidance. Typically, professionals are guided toward or away from educational programs through advice by peers whose evaluations of the program may be on record or by consulting directly with the program provider. The frame of reference in which such guidance is provided is narrow and neither assumes the existence of a larger learning agenda in which the program in question represents only one step in a sequence nor raises questions related to the performance of inquirers in their organizations. Guidance for persons who have access to learning and development resources is likely to raise the issue of fit with a larger agenda as well as question whether that larger agenda includes an appropriate mix of objectives that address both organizational and personal-performance variables. Educational counsellors in this situation are likely to have access to information about inquirers' learning priorities, preferred learning style, methodologies found to have been particularly congenial, and the like. Upon inquirers' reflection or the counsellor's pointed observation, the experience of this mode of guidance with its broader frame of reference is likely to sharpen the critical apparatus brought to bear on future educational decisions and contribute especially to the quality of individuals' self-directed learning.

Guidance may also include suggestion of social reinforcement, for example, lateral transfers or special assignments where wanted skills can be practiced at lowered risk, or therapeutic evaluation in cases in which performance appears to be diminished by depression or other disorienting characteristics.

5b. Special Arrangements. For an individual, group, or organization to undertake educational strategies represents a diversion of operational and professional resources that is potentially far more costly than the expense immediately related to educational activities. The responsibilities of individuals and groups can never be simply deferred. Patterns of life will be temporarily altered. The organization's functioning will follow special temporary procedures. Work will have to be delegated, reporting lines rearranged, and some people may have to be relocated, if only for a while.

When the question is what to do while someone is away at a three-day seminar, special arrangements are negotiated by would-be students with their editors, managing partners, or chief engineers. When the question is what to do during the 18 months in which a professional will be pursuing educational activities that will involve the equivalent of one day a week, deciding what to do is more complex and negotiating special arrangements is more time consuming. Cost-benefit analysis doesn't always yield clear support for the longer, more complex educational plan, particularly when there is no overall organizational strategy within which an individual's learning agenda has a clear role.

On a larger scale, special arrangements need to be made in order to position and nurture a learning relationship of organizations and continuing education agencies. In the case of an HMO with 80 staff members or a group practice of clinical psychologists with 12 partners, the challenge is straightforward. Complex organizations employing attorneys, accountants, highly trained business specialists, engineers, chemists, and industrial psychologists, for example, and offering services or producing goods at widely scattered sites, pose a dramatically different problem. What are the corporate conversations or accounting firm decision-making processes or correctional authority situations that are important for a continuing educator to join? How many levels of responsibility, how many discrete functions, how many financial and communications paths does the continuing educator need to understand in order to be a contributing interlocutor? What characteristics are crucial to the chief collaborators in such a relationship? What special performance variables characterize continuing educators who have learned new cultures and see in them the varied strategic roles that educational experiences might play? Turning the question the other way, what special proficiencies are typical of persons who are deeply knowledgeable about their own organizations and cultures, who perceive the organizations as learning systems and who see the potentially strategic leverages that continuing education might provide for performance? What is important for that person to know about the culture of the continuing educator's agency? These are but a few of the interesting questions to which the research activities of centers for the study of performance in business and the professions might be devoted.

5c. Finance. The investment of the time and effort of senior personnel in initiating a genuinely collaborative learning relationship with one or more continuing education agency, the articulation of an organization-wide learning strategy, and its careful coordination with operational goals and strategies should be assessed in a variety of ways, including cost. Few organizations have thoroughly audited their continuing education expenditures. Most refer to training budget dollars when surveyed. Continuing education for professionals and executives is often funded by contingency and travel accounts or from the accounts of projects that the education is expected to facilitate or to which the professional is temporarily assigned. The cost of professionals' lost billable time and the dislocation and delay of salaried executives' work while attending continuing education programs is rarely factored in although these are real costs. However, the start-up costs of an organizational learning relationship could not possibly exceed the funds expended by organizations on the inchoate miscellaney of context blind, culture denying "technology transfers" and "knowledge updates" that so uncertainly address performance, particularly when lost professional billings and the dislocation and delay of work are estimated.

For continuing education agencies, the costs of initiating and sustaining learning relationships are offset in several ways. Probing for possible relationships, carrying on the extensive conversations required to decide the nature and utility of a relationship, and understanding significant dimensions of the other organization's culture are start-up costs for the continuing education agency. Once a decision has been made to proceed, it is reasonable to expect the costs to be shared. The organization is beginning to benefit. The continuing education agency has an opportunity to study the culture of a particular organizational learning system with a view toward collaborative design of an organizational learning strategy, within which the agency can reasonably expect to provide at least some of the learning experiences desired. In this way, the cost of finding and securing the relationship is offset by the elimination of marketing costs. Furthermore, the continuing education agency will be gaining a competitive edge. It will be identifying compelling performance issues for business and other types of organizations employing professionals, working with new analytical frameworks, gaining collaborative experience at orchestrating the occupational culture for improved performance and, in so doing, discovering continuing education strategies of demonstrable success for organizations as well as individuals. It also will assemble a diverse portfolio of programs that can be offered even outside formal organizational learning relationships. If the continuing education agency has a research center for the study of the performance–continuing education relationship, its data base will be extended and complemented, new questions and issues will be identified, and the likelihood increased that organizational funding for such research will be secured.

5d. Interpretation. Both the learning relationship and individual teaching and learning experiences undertaken in its behalf need interpretation for related constituencies. Persons who are to gain a set of proficiencies, engage in an inquiry process, or address the turmoil of mid-life transitions must understand how these activities serve them and their organizations. Time spent away from significant interpersonal relationships and a person's network of civic, charitable, or leisure-time acquaintances must be explained. Others, not immediately involved, assume additional burdens while colleagues are participating in formal learning experiences and must be helped to see how their own interests are served by an overall strategy that occasionally brings them additional grief. Understanding and assent build commitment.

The learning relationship and its many possible configurations should be interpreted to wider constituencies such as associations of professionals and employers facing analogous challenges, to the field of continuing education research and practice, to human resources and personnel specialists, to those in the helping professions who counsel or treat professionals and executives, and the like. If this is done in ways that welcome critical examination of both the theoretical frameworks underpinning the performance model described here and the educational strategies followed in its name, the many constituencies vitally interested in the nature of individual and organizational performance will have been well served.

6. The Plan Is Put into Effect

The leaders who design and execute the structure and processes of the learning relationship, the collaborators who make use of the organization's culture as a natural learning system, and the specialists who develop formal learning strategies are engaged in a dialectical enterprise with considerable tension. Plans must be designed and executed with the certainty that builds confidence and the adaptability that expects surprise and occasional failure. Houle's fundamental system for educational design suggests that it is wise to have periodic reinspection of the purpose and format of individual activities, and the same is true of the larger learning relationship. Since both consistency and fresh perspectives are desirable, it may be well to have an organization–continuing education agency committee, its composition changing slightly each year, overseeing the relationship.

7. The Results of the Activity Are Measured and Appraised

The relationship and its activities deserve formative as well as summative evaluation at points mutually determined by the organization and continuing education agency. (Evaluation is addressed in Chapter Six).

8. The Situation Is Examined in Terms of the Possibility of New Educational Activity

The seeds of many new programs are to be found in examination of activities coming to a close. Often new constituencies for the same programs are to be discovered in the same process. For example, in the discussions concluding an intensive residential workshop on death and dying that had been attended by members of hospital-based helping professions, the participants began an animated conversation about the special problems of dealing with the death of children. It was the participants' view that unique issues are raised by the death of children and special knowledge and skills are required to deal with them—a possible new program. Listening to the same conversation, a continuing educator heard a person lament the absence from the participant roster of K–12 school teachers who, it was alleged, needed help in handling the classroom effects of deaths in students' families—a possible new constituency. Each activity shepherded by a long-term learning relationship will contain possibilities of the same kind.

The same careful listening process at periodic evaluations of the health and productivity of the learning relationship leads to the revitalization of priorities, discovery of other organizational constituencies that might benefit from particular strategies or programs, and identification of new ways in which organizational processes and educational programs can reinforce one another. Unnecessary or ineffective strategies and marginally effective activities can be abandoned.

Individuals, considered as patients, clients, consumers, investors, and citizens, as well as institutions are served by professionals and executives and the organizations they have formed. The strength or weakness of individual performance stems from the interaction of deeply personal variables (many of which are not usually associated with business and the professions) and cultural influences (including the opportunity and encouragement from organizations and institutions to be excellent). The strength or weakness of organizational performance stems from the quality of individuals' performance *and* the effectiveness of leaders in orchestrating ensemble performance through understanding organizational values, renewing the terms of reciprocal organization-individual commitments, sensitive managing of the organization development–human development relationship, and by the extent to which the organization's structures, systems and processes, and formal and informal learning activities consistently reflect shared goals.

Educational activity, as a strategy or temporary system undertaken for reasons of performance, is likely to achieve the result desired when organizations' and individuals' learning agendas are carefully interwoven in patterns sensitive to the ways in which occupational and other cultures enhance or diminish organizational and individual performance. The interlacing of the strands of variables key to performance occurs most favorably when the organization as a learning system, individuals whose selfhood is never fully distinguishable from the organizations and other cultures in which they are imbedded, and continuing education agencies become students of one another's cultures and collaborators in synergizing the resources each brings to performance. Teaching-learning relationships of this kind lead to the selection of particular strategies and the design of specific educational activities in their execution. Some of the educational activities employed will retain a high level of effectiveness outside such special teaching-learning relationships. In this way, the performance model is a framework for forging learning relationships as well as for identifying continuing education programs for individuals in business and the professions.

The performance model also is a critical theory, that is, a reflective theory that gives agents a kind of knowledge inherently productive of enlightenment and emancipation (Geuss, 1981, p. 2). Currently organizations, individuals, and continuing education agencies (even those within some large corporations), have a relationship with more of the characteristics of vendor–contractor arrangements than collaborator arrangements. Indeed, when an organization or individual is looking for updating in knowledge and skills or a continuing education agency is offering such programs, the interaction need only cover whether what is wanted is being offered.

Providers and consumers are sometimes punished for failing to bring larger frames of reference to bear. For example, one state's correctional authority was severely critical of a continuing education provider, alleging that a program for prison guards in various helping modalities such as behavior modification had been a failure, "A year later, there wasn't a single guard functioning in a positive way toward the inmates." An independent observer reported that the state appeared to have received exactly what it contracted for, a series of programs explaining in some detail to guards in state correctional facilities the theory and practice of major behavioral change strategies. Furthermore, a concluding exam indicated reasonable success in that most guards appeared to have learned what they were supposed to learn. Nevertheless, the state organization and the continuing education agency have not worked together since the experience of that program.

The performance model, used as a critical theory by either the state or the continuing education agency would have urged questions about the difference the desired program was intended to make for the guards, prisons, and prisoners. It would have urged that the performance objectives be shared in a collaborative, reflective way. It would have demanded understanding of whether the guards saw it as in their self-interest to become "more positive toward the inmates" and whether the correctional system was prepared to deal with the larger self-conceptual difficulties inherent in any attempt to move career-long paramilitary persons into helping roles. It would have asked what social reinforcements had been prepared, how success or failure would be identified and rewarded or punished. It would have raised serious issues about client benefits and reactions, for example, would the prison population find the change credible? It would have chanced the prediction that in the absence of any coherent strategy to change the way in which the largest single occupational group in the prisons thought about themselves and their clients, guards would dutifully undergo the educational experiences and return to their correctional settings with no noticeable change in attitude or behavior. When the guards themselves were interviewed, one remarked, "Look, the only reason anybody still gets fired around here is if they lose somebody, besides they (the inmate population) ain't worth shit."

On a more positive note, the performance model used as a critical theory can offer continuing educators a way to consider a contractor's presentation of a request for a vendor's program through such a variety of probing questions that the vendor–contractor relationship will shift toward a genuinely collaborative learning relationship, much to the long-term performance improvement of the continuing education agency, the organization, and their professionals and executives.

References

Bruffee, Kenneth A. "Collaborative Learning and the Conversation of Mankind," *College English* 46 (7), 1984.

Eurich, Nell P. *Corporate Classrooms, The Learning Business.* Princeton: Carnegie Foundation for the Advancement of Teaching, 1985.

Goldfinger, Stephen E., and Bennett, Nancy L. "Sub Rosa Continuing Medical Education: The Personal Network System," *Mobius,* 3 (4), 1983.

Geuss, Raymond. *The Idea of a Critical Theory.* London: Cambridge University, 1981.

Houle, Cyril O. *The Design of Education.* San Francisco: Jossey-Bass, 1972.

Kuhn, Thomas. *The Structure of Scientific Revolution.* 2d edition. International Encyclopedia of Unified Science, 2(2). Chicago: University of Chicago Press, 1970.

Larkin, Jill H.; Heller, Joan I.; and Greeno, James G. "Instructional Implications of Research on Problem Solving," *New Directions for Teaching and Learning.* No. 2. San Francisco: Jossey-Bass, 1980.

Noble, Kenneth B. "Commuting by Computer: The Workplace Isn't Ready," *The International Herald Tribune,* May 23, 1986.

Nowlen, Philip M. "Program Origins." In *Developing, Administering and Evaluating Adult Education,* Edited by Alan B. Knox. San Francisco: Jossey-Bass, 1980.

Nowlen, Philip M., and Stern, Milton R. "Partnerships in Continuing Education for the Professions." In *Partnerships with Business and the Professions,* 1981 Current Issues in Higher Education. Washington, D.C.: American Association for Higher Education, 1981.

Schon, Donald A. *The Reflective Practitioner.* New York: Basic Books, 1983.

Szilagyi, Andrew D., Jr., and Wallace, Marc J., Jr. *Organizational Behavior and Performance.* Santa Monica, CA: Goodyear, 1980.

SIX
Implications for Evaluation

EVALUATION OF CONTINUING EDUCATION for business and the professions has a kind of mythic quality about it. "Mythic" is not meant here to suggest that evaluation is fiction or illusion. Evaluation is mythic in the sense that it connotes the sacred and manifests itself in ritual commemoration. It is also somehow inaccessible and vaguely disturbing. Evaluation in any form is not a subject about which continuing education practitioners can be expected to be dispassionate. It is part of the field's constitutive mythology, and however questionable the worth of a given practice may be, criticism often is taken as questioning the continuing educator's worth, his or her professional selfhood. A questionnaire soliciting opinions about an educational program's worth is frequently administered at the conclusion of a program. It is the most typical expression of evaluation.

> What did you like best/least about the program? What were the strengths/weaknesses of the instructor/materials/format? Rank relevance and effectiveness of each topic. Will this improve your performance? (And the prayer for a final blessing:) Would you recommend this program to a colleague in your field?

Teasing meaning from these questionnaires is a hazardous process. Physicians' favorable opinions of changes in their performance resulting from continuing medical education do not track with audits of quality of care such as chart-review measurements (Mazmanian, 1984). Criminal justice system executives had disdain for one program's utility to their performance, but six months later the program-related changes in their performance and in that of their organizations were well evidenced (Nowlen, 1973). Yet, these questionnaires can have a powerful effect on the future of a continuing education program.

Continuing education's evaluation rites are like sudden breakthroughs of the sacred. They are not instrumental so much as they are expressive. They are not unlike the "cargo cults" of Oceania which, in turn, help explicate the meaning of this phenomenon. Some "cargo cults" are millennialist and persons and activities are evaluated in terms of their faithfulness in awaiting the arrival of Christ or America (!) on a loaded freighter or in a C–47 air-cargo plane. Other cults are orgiastic, and persons and activities are judged by their prefiguring of that day when the dead return with unimaginable quantities of stores and provisions, the day when taboos and traditions will be succeeded by absolute freedom (Eliade, 1963, pp. 1–20). The "cargo cults" are an expression of the need for external validation, a theme more acceptably expressed by Goedel's argument that even mathematics cannot validate itself.

The need for external validation may be continuing education's way of acknowledging the impossibility of assessing the impact of its ubiquitous updates upon individual and organizational performance, so little does their origin have to do with performance analysis. For these updates, the sacred realm of academic knowledge and research offers validation through the trappings of science: the program-ending survey, its quantitative and qualitative analysis and subsequent interpretation, for example. Yet at the core of its evaluative activity is faith—faith that persons will perform competently when their knowledge and skills are up to date and faith that the more the program resembles an academic course, the better it is. Take, for example, the growth of the nationwide Program on Noncollegiate Sponsored Instruction (PONSI), a project of the American Council on Education. PONSI evaluates corporate courses and recommends academic credit at appropriate levels. Some believe PONSI evaluation is the best yardstick of quality that exists for corporate classrooms and they maintain that the quality of corporate-based instruction may be measured by comparing it directly with the same subject being taught in a regular collegiate institution (Eurich, 1985, pp. 80–82). The rational processes of corporate-classroom evaluation are thus oddly grounded in a deferential faith: faith that colleges regularly and carefully examine the quality of individual courses; faith that academic instructional objectives and criteria for excellence are appropriately transferrable to the corporate classroom; faith that collegiate-input measurements (faculty research, library facilities, science laboratories, admissions standards, etc.) have some causal relationship to corporate-output expectations (better management of technology, more productive research and development units, a wider range of options from more critical minds). This grounding of reason in faith ultimately fails to justify the educational program or its evaluation.

There are excellent justifications for evaluation. The most common use of evaluation outside the field of continuing education is in diagnostic, formative, and summative judgments of learning: assessing students' knowledge and skill before setting learning goals or undertaking learning activities; providing feedback on student progress; and, measuring gains and certifying achievement (Bloom, et al., 1971, pp. 91–92). This use is deservedly widespread, occupying a place of respect within American schools. Within continuing education, the most common form of evaluation is the appraisal of teaching, that is, monitoring an activity in progress to assess the extent to which its elements facilitate learning, require modification while still in progress, or must be changed or eliminated before representation. Occasionally continuing education evaluation will move beyond questions of teaching and learning to the issue of impact, that is: Did the learning make the difference it was intended to make? (See Knox, 1979, pp. 1–28.) Almost never does evaluation focus on the quality of the original judgment by which an individual, professional association, or corporation concluded that a particular educational activity or sequence would achieve the goal desired.

Evaluation in the Update Model

Most current programs of continuing education for business and the professions are designed to keep persons up to date. There is an obvious demand that such programs satisfy. Many providers and consumers believe that the fully up-to-date professional is a person who functions effectively. It is rare for these activities to be preceded by a continuing educator's assessment of learner knowledge and skills because it is assumed that the decision to participate flows from learner self-assessment or the suggestion of the learner's boss. Evaluation of knowledge or skill gained from updates is indirect, for example, a survey of opinions about the extent to which programs meet participants' expectations. Evaluation of program design and arrangements is much more extensively done, for example, a survey of judgments about the degree to which the instructors, group leaders, and materials successfully addressed the program's general objectives: Did instructor "A" hold the participants' attention? Did group leader "B" stimulate useful discussions? Did materials contribute to learning during the program? Was the conference room comfortable? Were the preprogram instructions clear? Evaluation of this kind occurs during the concluding moments of a program at a time when those who are still present are already in transition, feeling a sense of release, achievement, or survival, estimating when they should be in the shuttle bus or taxi for the airport and whether there's a later flight, and the problems left at the office are returning to consciousness. There is growing evidence that participants are not good predictors of the value of educational experiences, even under more reflective circumstances (Chambers and Hamilton, 1981, pp. 28–34; Mazmanian, 1984, pp. 62–65; Nowlen, 1973, pp. 33–54; 119–152).

Some improvements in the use of evaluation within the update model can be achieved with modest effort and expense. The same concluding questionnaire can be mailed to program participants several months later. Marked differences between the profiles of participant opinions will invite selected follow-up.

Small groups of randomly selected program participants meeting with continuing educators during a break in program schedule can provide descriptions of the decision-making process that resulted in their attendance at the program. Borrowing the techniques of leading focus groups from the field of marketing, continuing educators can probe for whether intuition, personal career strategy, a colleague or senior partner's suggestion, or the organization's educational priorities or environmental challenges brought the executive or professional to consider attending the program. Under sensitive leadership, the group will say whether the decision involved selecting among many possible ways to update knowledge and skills and, if so, why this alternative seemed to have relatively greater value. Ultimately the process can bring into view the personal needs or dimensions of performance that the program was perceived to address. Six months following the program, the persons who participated in the focus group can be questioned about the extent to which they believe the program met its objectives. Six months is a period of time in which the quality of opinion about the utility of a program is likely to be experience based, and therefore of substantially greater value than program-ending predictions of its utility. Judgments about the "active half-life" of program materials, skill-building sessions, lectures, and the like are less likely to be based on factors such as entertainment and prestige. Finally, participants can assess the quality of the decision-making process that led them to select the update or provide useful feedback on educational strategy to their organizations. With the permission of those involved in the focus group, participants' superiors and colleagues can also be surveyed six months later with respect to whether their interactions with the program participants have evidenced the outcomes for which the program was selected.

Improvements such as these hold many surprises for continuing educators. Some programs, to be abandoned because of low exit ratings, deserve a second look, since their value appears to grow. By carefully examining shifts in judgment, the continuing educator can discover more precisely the intersection of participant need with program resources, a discovery that leads to greater specificity in program redesign. Other programs might be reoffered without modification following high exit ratings were it not for a jarring decline in participant satisfaction. Suspending such programs until the decline can be understood can halt a slide in the provider's reputation, damage all the more dangerous for not having been perceived. The case of a negative shift in judgment can be instructive for everyone concerned. In the case of one popular seminar in accounting for executives not primarily involved in corporate finance, the decline in judgment was owing to an inadequate command of mathematics, hidden so long as the instructor was performing illustrative equations, and a lack of sufficient accounting activity to reinforce what had been well learned about accounting frameworks. Without this discovery, the instructor would have been replaced or the program canceled. With the discovery of the reasons for misplaced judgment of the program's effectiveness, a new program was designed to sharpen nonfinancial executives' math skills and offered as an introduction to the accounting program, and participants in both programs were counseled about the need for regular exercise of their math and accounting skills.

With respect to performance, however, the most that can be concluded is that there is a correlation between relatively more effective performance and relatively more frequent participation in continuing education, including subscriptions to journals in one's field. It may be that persons who are relatively more competent engage more frequently in continuing education and not that more frequent participation in the most popular forms of continuing education increases effectiveness (McCloskey, 1981, pp. 139–141). The update model offers a narrow field of vision in which to address performance variables. As such, evaluation of teaching and learning inspired by the update model is confronted by the model's structural weaknesses when causal links with performance are sought. It is a little like looking at a sunset through a keyhole. Even the most rigorously validated evaluation favoring the quality of the view fails to persuade.

Evaluation in the Competence Model

The competence model presents thoroughly researched baseline descriptors of actual practice, including data about crucial practice interfaces, tasks and their interrelationship and interdependency, and variability among practitioners and their practice settings. Pharmacists, for example, must dispense drugs within a professional context shaped by legal requirements and limits. Pharmacists also have a role in providing information and monitoring services to the patient and members of the health care team, including the physician, in order to optimize the therapeutic process. Pharmacists have a practice process of interrelated and interdependent tasks. No two pharmacists experience the process in exactly the same fashion or context. The pharmacists' crucial interfaces include situations in which the pharmacist receives, analyzes, and imparts specialized information and services. These situations include wholesalers, pharmacists, physicians, nurses, and patients (Kalman, 1981, pp. 77–80).

Given the actual demands of everyday practice, particularly in crucial interfaces, the competence model goes on to identify the knowledge and skills required for the duties, responsibilities, and tasks involved. In the competence model for pharmacy, the knowledge and skills required by competent pharmacists are defined jointly by practicing pharmacists and subject-matter authorities. These include skills in the interpersonal, communicative, analytical, and decision-making realms.

Individuals assess themselves, sometimes with the help of independently developed assessment inventories, or are assessed by independent agencies in terms of knowledge and skills with demonstrated relationships to the demands of actual practice. Generally, assessment materials are confidential and nonthreatening but reasonably rigorous and engaging so as to provide a reliable assessment of the relationship between practice and competence. Deficiencies, if any, call for remedial action to be taken on the part of the concerned practitioner. According to Kalman, the aim in pharmacy is to have assessment and development materials that are based on how pharmacists actually use knowledge in their practice, rather than on retention of knowledge (1981, pp. 80–81). In addition, Kalman holds,

> the assessment and development effort must be individualized so that the pharmacist is not expected to demonstrate competency in areas for which he does not have responsibility. Assessment should be as realistic and meaningful as possible in keeping with the actual situations encountered in the work environment. [1981, p. 81]

Not just prior learning is being assessed, then. Assessment of the professional in the competence model involves examining both knowledge and skills and the ways in which they are brought into play. Assessment takes many forms including paper and pencil self-assessment batteries, interactive computer-based practice simulations and gaming, the formal processes of an assessment center that may combine several modalities including simulation of decision making under practice-like conditions of stress, and attentive peer review or performance evaluation. The American Pharmaceutical Association's self-assessment program, "Measuring Up," includes units devoted to monitoring and counselling the diabetic patient, providing pharmacy services to the diabetic/hypertensive patient in an ambulatory-care setting, and managing an admixture service.

Minimalists and maximalists continue a lively disagreement over whether the construct of ineffectiveness, that is, faults or weaknesses, is easier to identify, more useful to practitioners, and easier to assess than the construct of effectiveness, that is, competencies related to high performance. Kim Cameron refers to the work of Hirschman and Lindblom, Cangelosi and Dill, and concludes that *institutional* change and improvement are motivated more by knowledge of problems than by knowledge of successes, that is, negative feedback is more conducive to advancement than positive feedback (Cameron, 1984, pp. 67–83). Studies of effective teachers and mentors (Schneider, Klemp, and Kastendiek, 1981) positively associate high student self-esteem, high teacher/mentor positive regard, and frequent positive feedback with significant *individual* learning gains. These are not irreconcilable positions and, taken together, may act as helpful correctives.

Once the quality of the relationship between competence and practice requirements has been assessed, an inventory of weaknesses to be remedied or higher levels of excellence to be pursued emerges. The knowledge and skills related to items on this inventory become the learning objectives for reflection and consultation leading to either self-directed activity, the identification of educational programs addressing the learning objectives or, when needed, the collaborative design of a new program with those objectives in view. Continuing educators can be provided with the generalized results of self-assessment-based learning needs, for example, through individuals' voluntary mailing of a second copy of the assessment to a professional association pooling the data and publishing the generalized profile. In this way, educators can respond by making appropriate revisions in current offerings or by designing new programs.

Resulting continuing education programs can evaluate whether participants' learning objectives were met and, by recourse to the assessment processes mentioned above, determine whether learning has been translated successfully into practice-related competence. The distinct contribution to competence sustained or gained through each program content area, methodological approach, and related arrangements such as reinforcement can be evaluated as well.

Links between competence gains and actual performance can be suggested by constructing hypotheses about continuing education-related shifts in performance proxies, that is, measureable signs of quality of performance such as patient-chart data, the prescribing patterns of hospital-based physicians, insurance-carrier data, auditable variations in practice, adaptation of certain innovations in protocols, technology, cost reduction, productivity enhancements, organization structure, and the like. Scenarios can be sketched that portray reasonably probable shifts in performance proxy data if the continuing education program is effective. Proxy data that moves toward the scenarios hypothesized, however, would yield only inferential evidence of a performance linkage.

Evaluation in the Performance Model

No such performance proxies need to be guessed at in evaluating performance-model continuing education. More often than not, the organizational learning agenda and that of individual professionals spring directly from reliable measures of performance, and positive changes in those reliable measures will be the expected educational outcomes. For example, Department of Defense (DOD) hospital-discharge abstracts are used as a source for detecting potential problems in the care delivered within military treatment facilities.

Screening the data, DOD has identified potential quality of care problems, postoperative surgical complications and mortality, and obstetrical care issues (Health Data Institute, 1985, pp. i–vii). Specifically related continuing education activity has resulted and the discharge abstract is being modified so that an enriched analytic package can be developed. More elaborate measures of hospital performance are being developed that are insurance carrier, hospital, staff, and group derived. Comparisons can be made based on key fields and diagnostic groups. Measurements can be adjusted for number, percent of admissions, number of deaths, age and sex, mortality rate by group, length of stay, and the like. The data includes performance ranking on 38 defined criteria including hospital responsiveness to utilization-review suggestions. The process yields important information on the relative performance of internal units, for example, the emergency room, radiology, pathology, etc. While it is premature to jump from such performance proxies to performance standards, the current descriptive research is a step toward identifying realistic standards.

In the performance model, formative evaluation of learning and of teaching (or in complex educational sequences, of the major decisions in educational design and the effectiveness with which they were carried out) and summative evaluation of learning occur within a framework that has already specified the ultimate summative criteria of evaluation, the difference the learning activity or sequence of activities is expected to make. The performance objectives of the organization or the individual are, thus, the origins as well as goals of learning activities. As such, evaluation functions intrinsically to the process. There is no need to look to comparisons with university courses or to input criteria as sources of external validation.

The criteria of validity are present from the moment a decision has been reached that an educational strategy has a reasonable probability of achieving a specific impact. Sometimes the educational strategy itself, carefully coordinated for reinforcement and for integration with current and future responsibilities, is considered sufficient. For organizations, an educational strategy can also be orchestrated with other strategies such as changes in policy, modifications in structure, reallocation of resources, transfers of personnel, and the like. For individuals, an educational strategy usually is coordinated with personal strategies such as self-renewal or new positioning for career advancement in a highly competitive environment. Whether it stands alone as an organizational or personal strategy or is combined with other strategies in each, the educational strategy either makes the intended difference in performance or it does not. If it does not, it may be the result of poor educational design (for example, the learning format was confusing or learning was not connected with ongoing patterns of life) or poor learning performance. If it does not, it may be a more fundamental error about the probability that an educational strategy, by itself or in coordination with other moves, was an appropriate means. Thus evaluation in the performance model can inevitably lead to more sophisticated educational decision making as well as better educational design.

The origin and evaluation of continuing education programs within the ensemble performance model is the life and culture of the business or professional firm and the relationship of its leaders to a continuing education agency, internal or external to itself. The firm, viewing itself as an ongoing learning system, may have a partially articulated plan in which individual career paths are intentionally exposed to assignments that serve the firm's immediate needs, represent significant personal learning and development opportunities, and are investments likely to produce valuable future returns for both firm and individual. The firm sets in motion or takes note of: a new strategic plan, annual performance targets, a new international opportunity, and greater absenteeism and stress in persons 50 to 60 years of age. These events enter the conversations of organization leaders and then, through them, are discussed with wider circles including continuing educators, staff members, consultants, and perhaps members of the helping professions. The events are ultimately analyzed in terms of the firm's culture and priorities. The leaders want to know more about the benefits of addressing some and the cost of failing to address others.

The firm decides that the new international opportunity could be a major advantage and sets a task force in motion to assess the risk, with particular attention to any special financial, structural, or cultural problems envisioned. The firm has studied the stress and absenteeism among its more senior professionals and executives and has established several facts: (1) there has been a 150% increase in the number of staff caring for aged parents; (2) 50% are providing care in their own homes, 15% in nursing homes; (3) 33% of those caring for parents with Alzheimer's disease are using prescription drugs to cope with their depressions; (4) 8% devoted 35 or more hours each week to parental care; and, (5) only 2% have sought counselling or participate in community support groups.

The firm concludes that its prevailing culture punishes rather than encourages professionals who enter counselling relationships and does little or nothing to help its personnel anticipate life's predictable stress points with their consequent impact on performance. At least two sequences of learning activities emerge from these decisions and conclusions.

As the task force dealing with the international opportunity begins to assess the risk, it develops questions about the other country's political stability, the volatility of several of its ethnic and religious minorities, and the hidden costs of dealing with the network of families that appears to control important segments of the economy from government purchasing to construction. A continuing educator, the vice-president for finance, and the vice-president for operations are asked to work together to identify the academic resource persons, financial institutions, and state and commerce department officials who might help the firm address these questions. A search for related commercial and government data is also begun. The continuing educator's role is identification of academic resources and consultation on the process by which all resources, including written data, can best be brought together to facilitate the firm's decision. The role will be formatively evaluated in terms of its facilitation of a collaborative effort; the criteria with which academic resource persons were chosen (for example, are they actual experts as well as consensually perceived as experts; can they communicate data and analyses generated in an academic culture to a culture in which meaning is mediated by business executives, or practicing engineers and geologists?); the extent to which all resource persons were appropriately briefed on the question and were guided by the time available in which to address them and the learning style of the senior leadership that will hear them; the correspondence between the sequence of the whole learning process designed and appropriate cues from past experiences of senior leadership's interactions; and the drive with which the learning project goes forward balanced by flexibility in pursuit of unanticipated turns of interest. The continuing education role will be summatively evaluated, first, by opinion: whether the sharpest and critical minds among the leadership group served perceive that they have been well prepared for reaching a decision. The more crucial summative evaluation belongs to succeeding history. For example, the firm may decide to take the international opportunity presented, and encounter no major problems that were not factored into the risk assessment process, or the firm may decide against taking the risk, and subsequent events foreseen by the assessment process with some degree of probability may confirm the decision's wisdom. If the firm decides to venture the risk, several streams of other continuing education activities will have begun, for example, the preparation of key personnel in the languages, values, role of elites, formal political structure, and economic climate of the culture the firm has chosen to enter. Some of the activities such as language studies will be pursued through already-existing programs, while others may need to be freshly designed. Evaluation of activity-based learning will be made, but ultimately evaluation will hinge upon the performance of those who complete the activities and are placed in roles directly related to the new venture.

Meanwhile, a second task force, including the firm's senior personnel officer, continuing education staff, and a special assistant to the firm's CEO, begins to examine the perception that the firm may be depressing its performance by failing to help personnel prepare for the stress of life's anticipatable passages and for the disorientation of statistically probable marital crises, eventual parental dependency and personal physical and psychological problems. The task force also wants to examine the possibility that the firm's culture may provide disincentives for seeking help when personnel find themselves faced with difficulties that will ultimately threaten performance. A continuing educator is asked to organize several briefings that will illustrate the major frameworks within which the firm might best consider these questions. The continuing educator does so following a process, including evaluation, much as in the international risk analysis illustrated above. As a consequence of this process, the firm's leadership commits itself to a culture that will encourage personnel to seek appropriate counselling, support, and treatment. The leadership authorizes identification of community-based resources, including educational programs. Where the helping professions or range of educational programs seem inadequate, the firm will consider providing them or assisting in their development.

The continuing educator is asked to assist the director of human resources to organize leadership briefings on the orchestration of corporate culture in support of human development. The briefings are expected to lead to recommendations on reconfiguring fringe benefits; establishing guidelines covering performance review, salary increases, leaves of absence, promotion and reassignment of persons undergoing counselling or therapy; the employment of a professional staff to monitor related firm policies, hiring, and administrative practices.

The human resources staff surveys existing educational resources available in the firm's employment area and makes information about them available to the firm's personnel. Those identified include programs in stress management, career-planning workshops, parenting seminars dealing with children's chemical dependencies, and programs devoted to values clarification at mid-career. None are found anticipating mid-life crisis, none provide divorcing parents with ways to help their children through the transition, none address the stress, guilt, and financial burden of caring for aged parents. The continuing educator designs learning experiences addressing these and other issues. The firm now has a reasonably complete set of learning resources addressing human development proficiencies and strategies intended to encourage personnel to anticipate specific periods of stress and difficulty and to seek help as problems arise.

While the value of individual continuing education programs can be assessed, it is the entire strategy that should be evaluated and, within it, the relative contribution of each distinctive continuing education activity. The entire strategy may be evaluated by comparing quantitative indices of productivity in firm divisions that have initiated the program with the performance of divisions where the strategy has not yet been implemented. It can be evaluated by similarly comparing negative data: absenteeism, abuse of sick leave, and evidence of alcohol and drug abuse. The strategy may be evaluated by qualitative evidence of changes in the firm's informal culture, for example, before-and-after observations and surveys of the frequency and ease with which staff discuss personal- or family-development issues among themselves, bring newly found, community-based resources to the attention of the firm's human resources office, and so on.

Within the personal-performance model, the origin and evaluation of continuing education programs lies in the interaction of individuals with the cultures that shaped them; the cultures in which they now live, work, and find meaning; and the cultures they find inviting. Past cultures remain alive in them, limiting in one way, empowering in another, but always expressing themselves in professionals' characters and self-schema.

The culture of work includes the workplace as a network of peers and daily contacts as well as the culture of the larger organization in which the workplace is located. The culture of work often includes the distinctive cultures of persons' professions as well as those of the settings of practice. Individuals scan the many cultures of their work environments for opportunity and danger. Key actors in the workplace, organization, and profession provide a range of feedback from daily memos and informal signs of acceptance to the advancements and honors that signal recognition of outstanding performance. The periodic formal performance-review process offers critically important information if both parties work hard to make it meaningful. Interactions with patients, customers, and clients are also revealing.

Learning tasks may be easy to identify for lawyers who have been told that their skills in statistical analysis need improvement or for social workers who realize that their uneasiness in supervising other professionals is well deserved. Selected educational strategies are evaluated by feedback on subsequent performance. On the other hand, an MBA in marketing who experiences great difficulty in pursuading oil-company decision makers of the validity of his or her research may not know what educational move to make until someone explains that engineers have a controlling influence on the corporate culture in question, particularly on the architecture of conceptualization and judgment. The MBA's performance will improve if he or she can locate and cross an educational bridge to the culture of engineering. Engineer–executives can be counted on for evidence of educational success, such as fewer requests "to sketch that idea on the board," and will otherwise note improved communications. The marketing MBA might also have decided, however, to find an organizational setting in which managing across cultures wasn't as critical to performance.

The origin and evaluation of continuing education programs lies in interactions with nonemployment cultures as well. Many choose educational sequences that address interpersonal skills, or competencies associated with personal finance or parenthood because they conclude that proficiency in these areas increases the energy and focus required for successful career performance.

It is quite conceivable for persons to misdiagnose their performance problems, however, and improve their management of personal financial affairs, for example, with no observable change in day-to-day professional or executive performance. Apart from minor headaches, colds, and irritations, executives and professionals do not diagnose their own medical problems, prescribe medicine, or ask their secretaries to make an appointment for surgery the following Tuesday morning. Misinterpretations of performance issues and failure to engage in any consultation before selection of an educational remedy, even when such services are readily available, are sometimes the culprits when educational strategies seem to fail.

Alternative future cultures can also powerfully generate continuing education activity. The culture of retirement can cause anxiety as well as anticipation. Preretirement education can, therefore, have a beneficial effect on current performance as well as achieve its goal of preparation for a different period of life. Midcareer reassessment can lead to selection of a new path within the same organization or a more dramatic change of direction. In either case, both the individual and the organization benefit.

In continuing education efforts originating from either form of the performance model, it will be important to critique the quality of thinking that led to framing a situation and, subsequently, to selection of an educational strategy. The judgment of probable success needs careful review. The relative effectiveness of resources, methods, schedule, sequence, social reinforcement, individualization, delineation of roles and relationships, overall design clarity, and arrangements for fitting the experience into larger patterns of life and work, needs to be assessed. The success with which the design was carried out requires evaluation.

In performance-model evaluation, it is not difficult to determine whether a desired level of performance has been achieved. It can be somewhat more difficult to establish whether continuing education played the intended instrumental role. In organizations that are learning cultures, the distinction between formal continuing education programs and related administrative actions, protocols, computer-generated reinforcements, and the like is often somewhat artificial. Furthermore, it is frequently desirable for continuing education to be perceived as simply part of the learning flow. Using control groups and scanning the organizational and personal environments for distinctive and formal continuing education influences on performance are among the effective approaches for isolating continuing education as an instrumental cause. In efforts that meet with mixed results or appear to have failed, formative evaluation and summative evaluation of learning will identify crucial breakdowns in learning or flaws in design. Having found no major problem within the design, the evaluator should stand outside the design to consider whether, gem though it was, its *little* gem-like quality rendered the teaching/learning process inadequate to its intended performance impact. Douglas D. Sjogren describes this factor as "the power of treatment" and observes that expectations are unrealistically high, especially with short-term programs (1979, p. 112). Continuing educators, experienced in the field, should be able to compare the power of treatment of the program in question with successful programs addressing similar objectives.

Among the variables to be compared are: rigor, depth of content, use of a range of methodologies appropriate to a range of learning styles, development of a sense of participant "ownership" of the experience, opportunities for reinforcement, close collaboration of organizational leadership in prior demonstration of the ways the educational strategy serves the organizational strategy, and the like. The issue of adequacy or power of treatment is one of the more important reasons for continuing educators to be involved in any discussions that may lead to decisions about educational strategies to influence performance. Continuing educators ought to know whether other strategic salients (policy changes, new incentives and personnel performance criteria, and organizational reconfigurations, for example) will be marching supportively on the flanks or that they are leading a small patrol through a mine field.

When the educational strategy's power of treatment compares favorably with that of similar programs with favorable performance results, organization leadership should evaluate the quality and inclusiveness of parallel noneducational strategies, particularly the process of identifying and eliminating barriers to the desired impact. A major teaching hospital embarked on a program of continuing medical education for area physicians associated with small community hospitals. The impact intended was intentionally instrumental, that is, it was expected that as a result of these periodic updates, the teaching hospital would experience sustained increase of patient referrals from the community hospital-based physicians involved in the continuing medical education relationships. Six months later, the opinion was widely held that the continuing medical education strategy had failed. However, for a brief period of time, patient referrals did increase from community hospitals with continuing medical education relationships to the teaching hospital. Then referrals dropped back to prior levels of experience. The educational strategy had, in fact, worked. However, the uniform experience of referring physicians was that they "lost" their patients. The teaching hospital-based physicians regarded the referral physicians as bumpkins and made no attempt to keep the referring physicians informed about their patients' progress. Referring physicians' telephone calls were routinely left unreturned. The lesson learned was that failure to anticipate the consequences of a successful educational strategy reversed all the hard-won gains.

When continuing education emerges from actual performance circumstances and is designed intentionally to modify those circumstances, the culture is stirred in many ways, some anticipated, others unanticipated. Continuing educators must be cautious and, in turn, caution organization leaders about unanticipated consequences. The very process by which some persons have access to an educational experience and others do not, to say nothing of the way in which this comes to be known, can inflate the program's cost in terms of the time and energy required to manage the resultant anxiety or disaffection. Noting such unanticipated consequences is the first step in controlling for them when reviewing or redesigning a program.

It is not necessary to evaluate each learning experience in the same way, at the same depth, and in similar detail in order to maintain or increase program effectiveness. Doing so can quickly exhaust the patience of participants and render the learning experience prohibitively expensive as well. It may be desirable, instead, to select a small, isolated but representative group and to do a substantial formative and summative evaluation of learning and performance outcomes as a type of pilot test of effectiveness. Assuming the effort is reasonably promising, this pilot test will provide the continuing educator with cues as to which variables merit continuous or occasional monitoring, which assessment and evaluation interventions are both valuable in triangulation or cross validation as well as minimally intrusive on learning and achievement, the capacity of representative groups of learners to participate in formative evaluation, and the like.

Many thorough evaluation reports of continuing education impact are available. Twenty-five or 30 are addressed, some at length, in Alan Knox's "Assessing the Impact of Continuing Education." They stand up well in Knox's view when compared with the few impact evaluations of preparatory education and compare favorably with studies of the impact of practitioners in the helping professions on the people they intend to benefit (1979, p. 119).

References

ABRAHAMSON, STEPHEN. "Research in Continuing Medical Education," *Mobius* 4 (4), 1984.

BAILIT, HOWARD L. "Identification of Practice Problems in Dentistry," *Mobius* 3 (2), 1983.

BLOOM, BENJAMIN S.; HASTINGS, J. THOMAS; AND MADAUS, GEORGE F. *Handbook on Formative and Summative Evaluation of Student Learning.* New York: McGraw-Hill, 1971.

CAMERON, KIM S. "Assessing Institutional Effectiveness: A Strategy for Improvement." In *Determining the Effectiveness of Campus Services,* edited by R. A. Scott (New Directions for Institutional Research, no. 41). San Francisco: Jossey-Bass, 1984.

Cangelosi, Vincent E., and Dill, William R. "Organizational Learning: Observations Toward a Theory," *Administrative Science Quarterly* 19, 1965.

Chambers, David W., and Hamilton, Douglas L. "Continuing Dental Education, Reasonable Answers to Unreasonable Questions," *Mobius* 1 (2), 1981.

Davis, David A. "A Critical Analysis of the Literature Evaluating Continuing Medical Education," *Mobius* 4 (4), 1984.

Eliade, Mircea. *Myth and Reality*. New York: Harper and Row, 1963.

Eurich, Nell P. *Corporate Classrooms*. Princeton, NJ: The Carnegie Foundation for the Advancement of Teaching, 1985.

Fidler, Judith, and Loughran, David R. "A Systems Approach." In *Assessing Educational Needs of Adults*, edited by Floyd C. Pennington (New Directions for Continuing Education, no. 7). San Francisco: Jossey-Bass, 1980.

Fox, Robert D. "Discrepancy Analysis in Continuing Medical Education, A Conceptual Model," *Mobius* 3 (3), 1983.

Green, Joseph S. "Evaluation of Continuing Education in the Health Professions," *Mobius* 4 (4), 1984.

Green, Joseph S., and Walsh, Patrick I. "Impact Evaluation in Continuing Medical Education—the Missing Link." In *Assessing the Impact of Continuing Education*, edited by Alan B. Knox (New Directions for Continuing Education, no. 3). San Francisco: Jossey-Bass, 1979.

Hallawell, A. *Instrument Catalog*. Kalamazoo, MI: Western Michigan University, 1980.

The Health Data Institute. *Quality of Care: Pilot Demonstration Project*. Department of Defense Contract MDA 903–83–C–0291. Newton, MA: The Health Data Institute, 1985.

Hirschman, Albert O., and Lindblom, Charles E. "Economic Development, Research and Development, Policy Making: Some Converging Views," *Behavioral Sciences* 4, 1962.

Kalman, Samuel H. "Professional Competence and the Pharmacist." In *To Assure Continuing Competence*, edited by D. S. Falk; N. Weisfeld; and P. J. McCarberg. Washington, D.C.: National Commission for Health Certifying Agencies, DHHS No. (HRA) 81–5, 1981.

Knox, Alan B. "What Difference Does it Make?" and "Conclusions About Impact Evaluation." In *Assessing the Impact of Continuing Education*, edited by Alan B. Knox (New Directions for Continuing Education, no. 3). San Francisco: Jossey-Bass, 1979.

Lashof, Joyce C. "Risk and Healthy People," *Mobius* 4 (3), 1984.

Mazmanian, Paul E. "Developing an Alternative Approach to Evaluation," *Mobius* 4 (4), 1984.

McCloskey, Joanne Comi. "Toward An Educational Model of Nursing Effectiveness." Unpublished Ph.D. Dissertation, University of Chicago, Department of Education, 1981.

MILLER, JUDITH R., AND PENNINGTON, FLOYD A. "Of Horses' Mouths and Toothpick Houses," *Mobius* 4 (4), 1984.

NOWLEN, PHILIP. *Institute for Criminal Justice Executives: Final Report*. Chicago: University of Chicago, Center for Continuing Education, 1973.

SCHNEIDER, CAROL; KLEMP, GEORGE O., JR.; AND KASTENDIEK, SUSAN. *The Balancing Act: Competencies of Effective Teachers and Mentors in Degree Programs for Adults*. Chicago: Office of Continuing Education, The University of Chicago, 1981.

SJOGREN, DOUGLAS D. "Issues in Assessing Educational Impact." In *Assessing the Impact of Continuing Education*, edited by Alan B. Knox (New Directions for Continuing Education, no. 3). San Francisco: Jossey-Bass, 1979.

STEELE, S. M., AND BRACK, R. E. *Evaluating the Attainment of Objectives in Adult Education: Process, Properties, Problems, Prospects*. Syracuse, NY: Syracuse University Publications in Continuing Education and the ERIC Clearinghouse on Adult Education, 1973.

SEVEN
Vendors, Providers, and Collaborators

THE MAJOR PROVIDERS OF CONTINUING EDUCATION for executives and professionals are commonly taken to be: the organizations that employ them; universities and colleges; professional associations; and firms in the business of offering continuing education programs. Each provider works with a unique mix of advantages and constraints. Each faces questions of mission and constituency, competition and collaboration, accreditation and evaluation. Each is concerned with financial equilibrium.

Organizations Employing Executives and Professionals

From small law partnerships and medical group practices, real estate brokerages and independent weekly newspapers to federal agencies and computer manufacturers, pharmaceutical companies and the major accounting firms, organizations form the single largest continuing education–provider category. Former Director of the American Society for Training and Development Robert Craig finds the generally accepted figures credible but rough: In 1980, 16.8% of the workforce and 38% of executives and professionals in the United States were provided with formally organized education by their employers. This represents an investment of some $60 billion.

IBM is representative of corporations with major commitments to continuing education and identifies continuous learning with every IBM job. IBM employs over 400,000 persons. Among them are 103,000 professionals. The company spends $1 billion annually on education and training, currently supporting 4,000 employee MA and MS candidates. IBM maintains several residential campuses that are equipped with state-of-the-art technology including the capacity for conducting interactive multisite educational experiences. Many factors in the history of the organization and the personality and values of its early leadership have shaped this commitment. IBM's commitment continues as today's leadership periodically reexamines the corporation as a learning system that addresses the intersection of organizational, professional, and human development. Aetna, Motorola, Texas Instrument, and Xerox are among the business corporations with similar commitments. According to the Carnegie Foundation's special report, "Corporate Classrooms," there are 250,000 educators and trainers who are full-time faculty and another 500,000 who are considered adjunct faculty in efforts such as these (Eurich, 1985, p. 52).

Organizations reflecting industrywide concerns, in textiles, insurance, and banking, for example, have founded or supported continuing education agencies such as the American Institute of Banking or the recently organized National Technological University. Among professional, research, and consulting organizations alone, there were six accredited degree-granting agencies by 1985 (Eurich, 1985, p. 85).

Organizations provide for learning in a variety of ways. Learning opportunities can be

- pursued in executive development, technical and professional education, as well as liberal education;
- centrally coordinated by organization leadership, negotiated with the person to whom someone reports, or self-selected;
- designed by the organization, by outside consultants, by other providers, or by some collaborative configuration of these;
- conducted by the organization, a university or college, a consulting firm, a professional or trade association, or resources drawn from them;
- led by an on-site resource person and/or mediated by television, telephone, computer, laser discs, or audio and video tapes;
- supported by extremely varied and experimental teaching methods;

- pursued alone or in groups of executives or professionals related to a single organization, or in groups composed of non-organization personnel as well;
- scheduled as a part of the regular working day, during several evenings each week, on weekends, in short intensive residential experiences that provide the isolation occasionally required, or in a work–study combination;
- expressed in academic credit, certification, or degrees granted by traditional higher education or by corporations' fully accredited colleges, institutes, or centers;
- evaluated in terms of assessing knowledge or skill gained, quality of design and instruction, impact on individual performance and that of the working group to which an individual returns, or unevaluated except in informal or quite accidental ways;
- financed entirely or partially by the employing organization.

Organizations have some obvious advantages as providers. Customers, patients, and clients, stockholders, officers, directors, and regents make performance demands on organizations all the time. Organizations, in turn, have fairly explicit performance expectations for their subunits and individuals. Organizations are capable of orchestrating their cultures to achieve the best possible individual and group performances. Organizations are the contexts for most individual professional development decisions, including the selection of educational experiences. Organizations can coordinate educational strategies with day-to-day operations, ensuring mutual reinforcement. Organizations don't have to guess about an educational strategy's intended impact. Organizations are in continuous touch with their executives and professionals as learners and thereby have a unique research window, following executive and professional cohorts through multiyear learning sequences, comparing educational profiles of persons demonstrating career-long excellence with those of career-long adequacy and developing diagnostic tools. However, the same factors that position organizations so favorably as direct or indirect providers of continuing education can work against them.

There is no reason to assume that the quality of educational decision making will be more sophisticated than decision making in other organizational spheres. An organization's strategic educational planning (if any) is likely to be less proficient than its strategic planning in its primary arena: hospital-based health care, state revenue estimation and collection, petroleum exploration, consumer-goods manufacturing, or the like. Many major employers of executives and professionals do not have a senior, corporate-level, executive or partner in charge of education. Most organizations associate the role of education and training with personnel or human-resources management, which is perceived as a world of relatively modest advancement opportunities and financial rewards dealing largely with government paper work and clerical, technical, and blue-collar employees. Strategic organizational discussions rarely involve a highly placed educator, much less one who is sensitive to continuing education's uses as well as its limitations as a strategic instrumentality. Consequently organization leaders frequently select strategies involving education without second guessing the quality of their judgments. Planning goes forward and, at some considerable remove, educational-resource persons inside or outside the organization are approached as if they were pharmacists whose apothecary jars contained the elements of all remedies, triple strength and tamper proof. An implicit diagnostic process has taken place and now a prescription must be filled. The educational agency is placed in the position of either dispensing the prescription or making a referral. It is of little use at this point for the educational agency to warn that the dosage is suboptimal, instant relief is unlikely, or that there are risky side effects. Collaboration is a problematic issue between organizational leaders and in-house or external educational resources.

While organizational cultures can be orchestrated for optimum performance, they can also be orchestrated to serve leaders' limited vision, propping up outmoded frames of reference and resisting change and "alien" ideas (the "not invented here" syndrome). Strategic educational planning gives organizations a powerful instrumentality without assuring that it will be wisely and effectively used. If an organization's self-designed, in-house provision of education isn't balanced by learning opportunities external to itself, for example, the educational strategy can become as incestuous and self-deceptive as the organizational culture that developed it.

Organizations usually have a range of educational relationships reflecting the major professional constituencies they employ. A hospital's schedule for the day might include a state nursing association sponsored program for nursing supervisors of its own and neighboring hospitals, a medical school sponsored workshop for cytotechnologists, and a seminar on malpractice issues for the medical staff by the hospital's legal counsel. Meanwhile, the hospital administrator is away attending a hospital association sponsored program on returning the emergency room to financial viability.

Programs and relationships like these are frequently episodic, random, even accidental. They correspond with interests and needs, but are not steps in ongoing learning sequences designed on the basis of organizational objectives or individual performance goals. Although such programs and the relationships they represent are commonly viewed as collaborative, most simply involve cooperation and a few involve no more interaction than determining a seminar's time, place, and cost.

To be intentional, discriminating providers of continuing education, organizations need genuinely collaborative, long-range relationships with educational partners. Both need to understand the interplay of organizations and individuals in determining performance as well as the strategic uses of education. Both need to teach as well as to learn. This mutuality is fundamental to designing and maintaining a comprehensive educational strategy within which organizational, professional, and human development are pursued (see Chapter Three). To achieve it an organization can collaborate with its internal corporate- or professional-development unit or with an external resource such as a university's division of continuing education. An organization can also create a new educational partner reflecting the special strengths of several potential collaborators: in-house education and training units, professional associations, counsellors experienced in helping professionals and executives, and so on. Once an organization and its chief educational collaborator identify a promising strategic design, tactical educational salients develop, some mounted by in-house units, others by educational allies, or mercenaries, each understanding its link to the others within the strategy in which they are grounded. Units as well as individuals across the organization will understand how the educational experiences in which they are involved are related to one another and to performance goals.

Currently, however, there is as much competition as cooperation among organizations' potential educational partners. Organization leaders deciding whether to work with an existing educational resource or to form a new collaborative arrangement need to examine carefully the climate of relationships among specific potential collaborators. Reading the signs is particularly hazardous because several categories of providers speak with more than a single voice. Senior corporate leaders (and state governors) are pressing for a significant increase in collaboration with higher education in continuing education usually in the name of high tech and higher employment. Corporate-based educators and trainers view this as "a euphemism for a series of short-term programs and projects aimed . . . at income replacement for institutions of education that are feeling the pinch of lower enrollments and the decreased tax-based funding" (Zemke, 1985, p. 21). They see collaboration as a cover for entrepreneurial fervor by technical schools, community colleges, and universities. These in-house educational resources believe the underlying trend is running toward vendor competition for clients, and feel undervalued and undercut by organizational leadership. Higher education has sent mixed signals to organizations. In an official position paper on continuing professional education, the National University Continuing Education Association asserts that "the development of programs with clearer and greater impact on performance will require the sensitive collaboration of many groups including professional associations, employers, universities, government agencies and foundations" (Nowlen and Queeney, 1984). The College Board, on the other hand, has offered a popular workshop entitled, "Making Business and Industry Your New Clientele," and representatives of many community colleges favor tax incentives for training that Patricia Galagan, in the *Training and Development Journal,* concludes could make community colleges a cost-beneficial alternative to in-house human-resources development units (Zemke, 1985, p. 22). The two voices of Carnegie's *Corporate Classrooms* leave distinctly different impressions: "The 'unexpected breadth' of general education at GMI (the General Motors Institute) stands out when compared to technical degree programs at traditional institutions" (Eurich quoting Baker, 1985, pp. 82–83) and "Corporate classrooms are not likely to achieve the kind of insight and understanding that can result when students and teachers meet together, not only to acquire information and develop skills, but also to weigh alternatives and reflect upon deeper meanings" (Boyer, 1985, p. xiv). For both organization-based educators and continuing higher education, Milton Stern's question in *Power and Conflict in Continuing Professional Education,* "Who shall develop, organize, provide for, control and profit from the continuing education of professionals in our society?" suggests it is a win–lose game. Business schools take the question very seriously. However, in the only chapter specifically devoted to universities in *Power and Conflict,* Lawrence Berlin contends that the cultural distance of most professional schools from professional practice means there is little self-interest for them in entering the game.

Collaboration is also troubled because neither business and professional firms nor higher education are in control of their own resources. With the exception of a handful of major corporations, most organizations have neither coherent educational strategies nor ways to monitor how organizational funds are actually being spent on continuing education, particularly the learning experiences chosen by professionals and executives. Higher education does not control the involvement of its faculty in nonuniversity educational programs or in consulting. Some organizations, including government agencies, collaborate with higher education in developing a sequence of programs but contract directly with faculty, as private consultants, for subsequent presentation of the same programs. Indeed, some faculty operate private consulting firms that compete for continuing education dollars with their own universities and professional associations as well as with in-house professional development units. There is cooperation and competition among universities and colleges. There are also rare occasions in which a business school, a school of public administration and a continuing education division of the same university find themselves offering competing programs or needlessly duplicating support systems for outreach efforts.

The same volatility characterizes the relationships of professional associations. Associations find themselves cooperating with other professional associations, organizations, colleges and universities as well as competing with them. The mix of cooperation and competition characterizes association-sponsored programs as well as association use of academic and organization-based resources. Adding a degree of soap-opera complexity to the plot, many professional associations "accredit" other providers or their programs and on their accrediting committees sit members of other provider organizations, that is, the faculty of university professional schools and leaders of organizations that represent the chief contexts of practice. Associations representing the common interests of certain types of organizations, banks, hospitals, and real estate brokers, for example, have a cooperative relationship with the organizations they serve. Some, such as the savings and loan field, have developed comprehensive educational strategies for the continued development of their professionals.

The private sector includes seminar vendors, program franchisors, training companies, and proprietary schools. Competition within the for-profit education industry is intense. The mixed pattern of competition and collaboration, typical of the rest of the field, characterizes the for-profit sector's relationship with organizations, higher education, and professional associations.

Many forces are plausibly associated with this roiling environment. The deep and perennial suspicion that the tribe in the next valley is cannibalistic surfaces in the negative regard educators and trainers have for one another and in the uneasiness with which for-profit and not-for-profit sectors work together. It is also true that the prevailing update model doesn't demand the collaboration of the more complex competence model or the still more inclusive performance model. That performance is an organizational matter as well as a personal affair, that performance is a function of the interaction of organizational, professional, and human development, and that executives and professionals are embedded in multiple cultures (organization, profession, family, and community, for example) which influence behavior across their largely imaginary psychological boundaries presents organizations and individuals with a manageable framework for reaching strategic educational decisions based on all the variables critical to performance. There is more than enough work here for organizations, higher education, professional associations, profit-making educational firms, and individual executives and professionals. The performance model has room for all the provider groups and, in fact, depends upon their collective strengths.

Organizations themselves are living learning systems with enormous potential for intelligent selection and reinforcement of educational experiences. Organizations' internal educational personnel are undervalued resources with unique windows on the intersection of organizational and individual performance issues. The associations of organizations provide a communications network for strategic educational planning and the adaptation of innovation. Higher education has

> ways for organizations and individuals to step outside the boundaries of their immediate context and experience, in order to inquire how that context works, what its values are, the gains and costs of participation within a system, and alternative ways of construing the purposes of that system. [Schneider, 1985, pp. 20–22]

Higher education also offers the research tools of the social sciences that can probe the many cultures of business and the professions and their interaction with personal and group performance. The idealization of profession, and by extension, the related professional association, is closer to a person's self-identity than is the particular context of the profession. ("I *am* an engineer. I am *with* the city's department of water and power.") The profession and its associations are connected to deep fonts of personal values and commitment and serve as communities of interpretation for the specialized body of knowledge and skill essential to professional practice. The for-profit sector maintains large inventories of tested educational vehicles that are readily accessible and often can be tailored for special organizational needs and constraints.

Organizations are likely to continue to find a mixture of cooperation, competition, and autonomous markets among providers, according to Patricia Cross. However, to the extent that the update and competence models are subsumed by the performance model, collaboration is likely to grow.

Higher Education

Annual registrations in university- and college-sponsored continuing education for business and the professions range from several hundred at small colleges to 30,000 to 40,000 persons at major universities. These efforts represent an equally wide range of commitments, from a program here and there, coordinated by part-time staff and budgeted at $30,000 to $40,000, to ranges of diverse program series, directed by 25 to 35 full-time staff and budgeted at $2 million to $4 million per year. Some major efforts are staffed by 50 or more and operate budgets of from $13 million to $17 million per year (Nowlen, 1987). A few are budgeted at over $25 million. The resulting programs may be sponsored by continuing education divisions, professional schools, or by one or more professional schools working in cooperation with a division of continuing education.

Programs differ from one institution to another not merely in content and format, rigor and intensity, but also at the deeper level of assumptions made about the nature of a given enterprise. With respect to management, for example, there are mini-MBA approaches like Harvard's Professional Management Development Program or the Virginia Executive Program. There are classical programs for which the integrating principle is the process of formulating policy (Dartmouth's Executive Program, for example) or the process by which organizations plan, implement, coordinate, and control (Cornell's Executive Development Program). Other schools focus on managers' personal proficiencies rather than on the functions of the organization or the development of organization policy, encouraging executives toward situational styles, the use of temporary systems such as task forces, and high interpersonal skills. There are sharply different models based on diverse assumptions about how similar public management and business management are. There is a Kennedy School and a School of Business at Harvard. Yale's School of Organization and Management, on the other hand, believes its students to be equally qualified in government and business. Some institutions assume the profession of law to be about the study of precedents, legal reasoning, and the techniques of argumentation. Others emphasize the nature of law as a learned profession addressing fundamental issues of justice in relation to economics, government, and society. A vocal minority holds that legal doctrine is indeterminant, that is, unable to lead to an inevitable conclusion because it is not value free or "above" political, economic, and social considerations. The indeterminist position regards law as one of the ways in which, as a society, we deal with our life together, one of the ways we decide conflicts. These deep and significant differences about the nature of management and law suggest that programs with similar titles ("Management Development Program," "Product Liability," or "Current Problems in Federal Jurisdiction") may not be at all like one another.

The publics served appear appropriate to the providers. At Harvard, 73% of the students in extension already have bachelor's degrees and 22% have graduate degrees. Similarly, at Berkeley, 78% have first degrees and 50% have graduate or professional degrees (Cross, 1983). Like the organizations they serve, many institutions cannot fully identify the staff, funds, or programs through which they address learning needs in business and the professions.

Higher education honors many of its own values offering continuing education to business and the professions. Through continuing education, colleges and universities

- continue to serve the same constituencies with which they already have graduate or collegiate ties;
- address the needs of the population most likely to look to higher education for continued learning;
- fulfill these public service and lifelong learning roles in a highly visible way;

- place those who teach in professional schools and graduate divisions in regular educational contact with practitioners in corresponding professional fields;
- pursue an indirect strategy for strengthening the quality of teaching, that is, practicing professionals are relatively more stimulating and demanding than professional school and graduate students and are frequently best addressed through methodologies with which faculty are unpracticed;
- discover individual professionals with potential for making contributions to curricula as guest lecturers, practica directors, etc.;
- conduct programs that implicitly, and sometimes explicitly, validate or question professional-school curricula;
- expose professional-school graduates to academic resources outside their professional schools;
- discover opportunities for supported research into significant issues of some immediacy to the professions (for example, nutrition and behavior, compensation and motivation); or into questions of professional life itself (for example, patterns of adaptation of innovation, the role of constitutive myths, assessment of performance, and the like);
- enhance the placement opportunities of graduates;
- nurture a development network of persons of higher-than-average income, influence, and inclination to be supportive of higher education (Nowlen, 1987).

It is of no small importance that these values can be served at no net expense to the institutions, even when continuing professional education is fully costed.

A professional school does not have an exclusive teaching relationship with any constituency. Architects, engineers, and accountants have intellectual needs far broader than the resources of their professional schools. Successful journalists need to keep apace of developments in libel law. Business people increasingly need cross-cultural skills. K–12 educators in social studies must reintegrate their approach within a global perspective. Health administrators want to move easily in the worlds of public-policy development and insurance and technological innovation. Higher education has many constituencies that identify themselves as professional and yet do not correspond with any particular professional school: psychologists, hospital administrators, human-resources managers, probation officers, and the like.

Unresolved internal questions of turf and the companion problem, the failure to distinguish among the continuing education strengths and missions of graduate divisions, professional schools, and continuing education units, are residuals of continuing education's exponential growth. Higher education's planning, policy, and control systems are only beginning to react to these and other issues such as implications for institutional integrity and the university ideal, establishment of appropriate academic governance, accountability, structure (particularly, centralization versus decentralization of the continuing education function), compensation of faculty for continuing education activities, and financial accountability (Nowlen, 1987). Left unresolved, these issues have plagued higher education's relationships with significant constituencies. The National Research Council's Committee on the Education and Utilization of the Engineer created a special panel to examine continuing education for engineers. That panel's report includes the following "overriding recommendation":

> The National Science Foundation (NSF) or other appropriate organization should undertake a program designed to establish the spectrum of values and objectives of continuing education for individual engineers, industry, and academia and to describe how continuing education could or should operate in the engineering world of tomorrow. Because most universities do not have the resources (and most faculty lack the incentives) to produce quality continuing education programs, the NSF project should examine the impact of industry's assumption of this responsibility. [1985, p. 3]

In a chapter of the panel's report devoted to the role of the university, the panel concludes that the disincentives outweigh the incentives in higher education's provision of continuing education for engineers. The panel specifically mentions: continuing education is placed outside the regular teaching load at most institutions; financial compensation for continuing education teaching is relatively lower (sometimes as the result of an institutional ceiling on extra-service or overload compensation) than for regular teaching or outside consulting; the majority of continuing education courses are not at the cutting edge; and involvement in the continuing education of engineers carries no weight for advancement in the evaluation of the faculty member's performance (1985, pp. 49–55). In future, the panel sees a brighter prospect in coalitions that include universities and colleges but that are industry led.

Issues such as those that have frustrated higher education's relationships with the engineering community cannot be successfully resolved unless the underlying question is addressed: How can continuing education for business and the professions become a genuine part of the intellectual life of a university? To some extent, the question is simply a new expression of the uneasiness with which professional education participates in the life of the university. Some professional schools are criticized by members of the academic community for their stagnant and dismal emphasis on practical training. Other professional schools are taken to account by the professions for their distance from the major concerns of the practice (Freidson, 1986, p. 212). It is a kind of Americanism, according to Edward H. Levi, that professional education somehow forced its way into university education. Professional education in law, theology, and medicine was the reason for the medieval university. Liberal education was viewed as training for the profession of citizenship. Nevertheless, continuing education for business and the professions suffers by extension from the particularly American perception that professional schools don't quite belong in the way graduate research belongs, for example. Unfortunately the behavior of powerful isolates such as medical and business schools has reinforced the perception. Nonetheless, as Levi suggests, it is no compelling argument against the inclusion of subject matter within a university to say that the approach is professional. But what are reasons for including subject matter dealt with in a professional mode? Once included, how can integration rather than parallel development be fostered? It is difficult to find underlying coherence in the lifeforms professional schools have taken within universities. Universities run medical clinics and hospitals, sometimes sustain operations of theater and the arts, but never run the court system. Edward H. Levi's 1971 address on the place of professional education in the life of the university offers considerations that might equally apply to integrating continuing education in the intellectual life of an institution.

Assuming that higher education has a primary concern for the kind of doing and understanding believed to be helpful to the individual who is going to handle important problems, which doing and understanding should be addressed by an institution? What can an institution do well, and what is the effect of the doing on the quality of other activities of the enterprise? Of these, which can have quality of their own and, more significantly, be sufficiently related to the ways of thought and to the particular and appropriate standards of excellence for the entire institution, so that inclusion is mutually helpful? Does the interrelationship have qualitative advantages both to the institution as a whole and to the separate disciplines? Ultimately, are both the profession and the life of the university well served (Levi, 1971, pp. 230–233)?

By implication, university-based continuing education for business and the professions can neither be simply responsive to what organizations and individuals want nor insist simply on what they ought to have. Continuing education can neither be market driven nor product driven. Medieval universities recognized the tension between responsiveness and questioning and embraced it in the motto "To be in the world and yet not of the world." No one maintains that higher education ever gets the balance just right, but higher education has never lost sight of the value of the tension.

Continuing education leaders need to position the function within that same tension. Organizations, professional associations, and individuals often want recipes and formulas to make things easier or clearer or more rewarding—and on Monday morning if possible—or want programs reflecting issues celebrated by the media or having the aura of organizational status, like strategic planning. Higher education encourages questions more than it provides answers, and indeed learning has much to do with asking the right questions. Each continuing education program is unlikely to balance these differences perfectly but the continuing education relationship between higher education and business or the professions should combine the characteristics of responsiveness and questioning. "Yes . . . but . . ."

When a university or college functions as a collaborator in a teaching and learning relationship with organizations, or with individuals for that matter, there is opportunity for ongoing dialogue about the nature and purpose of the enterprise. This invites the "Yes . . . but . . ." exchanges that are at the heart of higher education's strength and culture. When a university or college is invited to design a single response to a particular need, the degree of healthy tension and genuine collaboration may be reduced, but remains present in discussions of individual program-design decisions. When higher education is approached as a vendor, there is only room for a "Yes" or "No."

Continuing education is already integrated in the intellectual life of many institutions through its connections with research bases such as adult education, organizational psychology, and the disciplines characteristic of various professional schools. New connections are being forged with constructive-developmental psychology, cognitive science, and cultural anthropology. Establishment of centers for the study of performance in business and the professions would bring much of this research to focus, add a research dimension to present teaching relationships with business and the professions, and in so doing add value to higher education's "Yes . . . but . . ."

Professional Associations

There is no official count of professional associations. Of the more than 13,000 *national* associations listed by the *Encyclopedia of Associations,* at least 3,000 appear to be associations of professionals. The membership of some, such as the American Medical Association, is confined to a single profession, across all its specialties and contexts of practice. Some associations reflect the trend toward double professions, the American Association of Attorney–Certified Public Accountants, for example. Others reflect a single special context of practice for many different professions, for example, the National Association of Counties includes lawyers, public administrators and planners, public health and education specialists, engineers, environmental experts, and so on. Associations represent professionals in the scholarly disciplines, for example, the Modern Language Association of America, and those in a particular industry, for example, the American Society of Heating, Refrigerating, and Airconditioning Engineers. There is an Association of Black Elected Officials, an Association of the Graduates of Italian Medical Schools and a Chinese Institute of Engineering. Some, like the American Medical Association and the American Bar Association are over a century old while others are in their infancy. There are approximately 140 national associations in the field of engineering, over 1,000 in medicine and health-related fields and 6 or more addressing university-based, continuing education scholarship and practice.

There are professional associations with only a national structure while others have chapters in each region or state. A few have major structures in regions, states, and metropolitan areas. Many associations of professionals exist only here or there on the state or local level, but can be quite energetic. There are state councils of association-based continuing educators and some metropolitan areas have ecumenical associations of clergy.

Most associations are supported by small staffs and depend

heavily upon work contributed by their membership. While associations often are managed with a view toward assuring continuity (board terms can be staggered and promising members hold a succession of important committee assignments, serve on the board, and pass through senior offices to the presidency), they remain voluntary organizations with highly political processes. As such, associations experience shifts in values, priorities, and interests as membership sentiment evolves and board composition changes.

Professional associations are not coterminous with the professions. Only about 45% of American physicians (and only 27% of women physicians) belong to the AMA. In 1962, 75% of American physicians were AMA members. Specialty associations, such as the American College of Surgeons, the American College of Obstetricians and Gynecologists, and the Radiological Society of North America, appear to be more attractive to physicians today. Professionals routinely hold multiple associational memberships reflecting the range of their concerns about their specialty or subspecialty fields; the settings of their practice; the other professions with which they practice; issues of public policy, such as legislation, regulation, and accountability; the need for maintaining networks of supportive colleagues; and their financial self-interest and that of the organizations they serve.

Professional associations are involved in continuing education in ways as diverse as their distinctive missions, history, structures, interests, and current leadership and membership would suggest. Some are energetic providers of continuing education experiences at national- or state-level annual meetings. Others offer or, with employers, universities, colleges, other associations, or private companies, cosponsor a variety of learning experiences throughout the year. These include conferences, institutes, seminars, and workshops in typical conference or classroom settings. There are also laboratory-based instruction and interactive television, telephone, and/or computer-assisted learning. Associations provide confidential self-administered inventories of professional proficiencies and support for self-directed learning agendas such as directories of relevant programs from all providers, audio and video tapes, computer-based instruction, journals and occasional papers. Some associations help professionals in isolated practice settings to participate in distant continuing education programs by putting them in touch with others who have volunteered to fill in for colleagues in just such circumstances. There are other imaginative strategies through which associations have supported continuing education and continuing learning. In one state, cooperation between an association, a major employer, and a university resulted in establishment of two regional learning-resource centers for practitioners in rural communities (Hodapp, 1982, pp. 220–230). In British Columbia, a regional network of professionals acting as coordinators of continuing education was established to increase the accessibility of programs and to help professionals develop their own learning experiences. In 10 years, a fivefold increase in programs, a twofold increase in contact hours, and a sixfold increase in registrations was experienced (Fielding and Dinning, 1984, pp. 5–11).

Associations have been able to respond quickly to member needs for informational and technological updates, particularly through traditional didactic methods. It has been more difficult for associations to sustain the commitment across many years (and many boards of directors) required for developing a long-range strategy related to professional performance. The work of Sam Kalman in pharmacy is a shining exception (see Chapters Two and Six).

Centrifugal forces within associations such as the multiplication of professional specialties and subspecialties, the proliferation of context-specific professional and administrative roles, members' loss of a sense of personal identification and ownership as associations grow large and unwieldy, and the failure of leadership to provide associational recognition to new professional contexts such as group medical practices have led to the rise of more specialized associations and vigorous competition for membership. As a result professional association–provided continuing education has become more specialized. Another result of association proliferation has been decline in general revenues available to any one association for support of national- and state-based continuing education staff and for risking on the development of new programs and materials. The increase in association–university cooperation may be seen, in part, as an association wish to offer as well as to be perceived to offer continuing education programs of utility to members of the profession who are not members of the association.

Associations hold diverse positions on the issue of continuing education as a mandatory condition of relicensure or good standing. Many associations believe they are moving desirably toward mandatory continuing education by accrediting either providers or individual programs toward some specified minimal number of contact hours per year. (The hours specified as minimal often vary widely from state to state for the same profession.) Other associations are opposed to mandatory continuing education and choose to accredit either providers or individual programs and quantify professional participation as a member service or as a demonstration that voluntary mechanisms are helping professionals enhance or sustain their competence. Within any given association there is likely to be a wide spectrum of opinions on mandatory continuing education and accrediting. The American Nurses' Association has a national system for continuing education and state associations follow the national pattern. Medicine first had a single system, then adopted parallel programs at the national level. Currently the Accreditation Council for Continuing Medical Education has succeeded the AMA program and the Liaison Committee on Continuing Medical Education. Pharmacy uses the widely respected American Council on Pharmaceutical Education program and has developed a provider-approval system. (See Chapter One for the status of mandatory continuing education for selected professions.)

Several factors at work, such as accreditation, turf building, and other centripetal forces, raise difficulties for associations that might wish to provide interdisciplinary or interprofessional learning experiences. There is a political base within associations for using associational resources to address members of the profession outside the association. There is little political base for using associational resources to address other professions. When an interdisciplinary or interprofessional program is mounted, the consequent problems are at least as difficult. As William Blockstein reported in *Mobius,* the necessity to negotiate multiple approaches to accreditation so that practitioners from different professions and states can get credit for shared learning activities provides serious disincentives to the provider. With respect to a course entitled, "Emergency Care: the First 90 Minutes," the University of Kansas announced that the Division of Continuing Education

> has been accredited by the American Medical Association and certifies that this offering meets the criteria for 13 hours of Category 1 for the Physician's Recognition Award and is acceptable for 13 hours of Continuing Education Credit (non-academic) or 1.38 CEU's and is acceptable for 13 hours of Prescribed Continuing Education Credit by the AAFP. Also this program has been awarded 15 points in category 4 for continuing education by the National Registry of EMT's, 9 continuing education hours by the Kansas Registry of EMT's and 9 continuing education hours by the Kansas Registry of EMICT's. [Blockstein, 1983, pp. 69–70]

After the brochure was printed, Blockstein relates that the Kansas State Nurses' Association also approved the course for credit. (For even deeper factors working against interdisciplinary and interprofessional approaches, see Chapter 8, "Caution, Professionalization at Work.")

Thus, professional associations have many reasons to find it easier to operate in the update model rather than the competence model, which inevitably involves the interprofessional context of work, or the performance model that takes into account the social dimension of individual performance, specifically addresses the interprofessional when it is a factor of ensemble performance, insists on the collaboration of organization leaders, and demonstrates that persons with superb professional proficiency, practicing in excellent contexts, will still malfunction seriously without a similar degree of attention to their human development.

For-Profit Vendors, Providers, and Collaborators

There are companies that are in the full-time business of selling learning experiences directly to organizations or individuals. The sale is made on the basis of the provider's reputation, the satisfactory experience of an organization member or colleague who has participated in a prior offering of the program, the reputation of the instructor, or the perceived utility and timeliness of the title and curriculum description. A program package contains the instructor, all supporting written materials, audio–visual aids, games, simulations, and exercises. Programs are approximately two and one-half days in length, on the average. There is usually only one instructor per program, although for the more popular offerings such as "Electronic Data Processing for the Non-EDP Executive," and "Finance for the Non-Financial Executive," there may be a cadre of 8 or 10 different instructors who present the program at one time or another throughout the year. In 35% to 40% of the direct-mail brochures received over a period of six months by the University of Chicago's Office of Continuing Education, the instructors were described as holding regular academic appointments. Any program offered by a for-profit company 10 to 12 times each year will have been praised by the usual concluding evaluation questionnaires. There is little data available about participants' evaluation of the experience six months to a year later, but then there isn't similar data available for organization, university, or professional-association provided programs. These providers believe themselves to be at a disadvantage in competing with the nonprofit sector and its special mailing rates.

There are also firms whose sole business is offering to local entrepreneurs, colleges, or universities exclusive regional or local rights to the for-profit company's programs. This relationship has some of the qualities of franchise about it, including restrictions on competition outside the area consigned to the local provider, provision of predesigned brochure graphics and copy for direct-mail campaigns, and cost-beneficial access to mailing lists because of efficiencies of scale. The exit evaluations of courses being offered to the local provider are usually available and quite positive. The wholesaler or franchiser usually wants a percentage of the gross. In this model, the favorable mailing rates of the nonprofit sector can be turned to the for-profit program developer's advantage.

The programs resulting from either the direct or indirect models need to be high-volume cash cows. Thirty to 75 registrants for each presentation, with 12 or more presentations a year, and 13% to 18% nets after indirect costs and before taxes is favorable. The programs must be positioned, therefore, in the generic center of business and professional responsibilities. This positioning is achieved through programs for executives and professionals who have organizational responsibilities, such as supervision, negotiation, performance appraisal, motivation, time management, and quality circles. The pattern for professional groups often involves a core module that is then modified for distinct professions, for example, "Teleconferencing: A New Approach to the Educational Needs of Social Service Professionals," or Lawyers, or Nurses, or. . . . This reflects a cost-effective approach to product development and marketing, multiplying the applications and markets of a single core module.

There is another quite distinctive category of for-profit vendor, however. Many companies have moved into continuing education as a somewhat logical extension of their other involvements as well as a marketing tool serving those other goods or services. Trade and textbook publishers, consulting firms, cable television producers, high-tech manufacturers, pharmaceutical houses, clinical psychology partnerships, and for-profit hospitals are also continuing education vendors. In the case of publishers and professional partnerships in the helping professions, the continuing education experiences themselves may generate profits. For others such as pharmaceutical houses, high-tech manufacturers, and for-profit hospitals, there may not even be a fee charged, let alone profit generated from the continuing education program itself. The profits come from the prescriptions written and filled, the computers and software purchased and the hospital beds and services used as a result of contacts made through continuing education. For these reasons, the continuing education programs offered tends to be target-market specific, for example, "Data Base Management for Hospital Receivables," rather than generic, for example, "Performance Appraisal Techniques." This is also the reason that this category of vendor is more likely to be in direct competition with higher education and professional associations.

Employer cooperation with the for-profits involves no insurmountable difficulties. Professional association or higher education cooperation often raises a tangle of issues. Should pharmaceutical firms join associations or universities in providing continuing education to psychiatrists, gynecologists, or pharmacists? Should textbook publishers co-offer learning experiences with associations representing teachers or school boards? Are there appearances of impropriety? Are there genuine dangers of impropriety? Can a middle ground be found, for example, through the for-profits creating foundations exercising independent judgments about worthwhile educational programs to fund? Would the for-profits reap sufficient rewards from a more distant relationship? As this category of vendor/collaborator continues to grow, the questions become more urgent.

Individual Learners

The individual learner is rarely included in lists of major providers but, in truth, the individual learner is the chief provider of informal learning and one of the major providers of formally structured education. Everyone is a self-directed learner on an almost continuous basis. Especially for the best educated people, every situation in life has something to offer. The many cultures in which people are embedded and make meaning, and with which people associate their very identities, offer reciprocal teaching-learning experiences. This is as true in interactive situations of conflict or collaboration, direction or execution as it is in solitary situations of accounting, architectural design, sermon writing, or class preparation. Informally, professionals and executives can reflect on the dazzling performance of another professional or, themselves, offer mentoring to an associate through their own performance. They can decide that another professional really has something to offer and deliberately understudy their new model, whether or not the model is conscious of the process. Executives are always scanning the environments inside and outside their organization, interpreting what they see, and testing their judgments. More deliberately they can set up formal means to study and interpret their environment.

Professionals and executives who have an orientation to learning frequently find themselves pursuing five or six learning agendas at the same time. One of the learning agendas may appear to be addressed formally through organized educational programs and another may appear to be entirely informal, almost intuitive. There is always a good deal of each in the other. Most formal educational programs, provided by others, are chosen because they suit a larger learning strategy under an individual's own direction. No formal program will leave an independent self-directed learner without fresh learning desires. Persons alive to learning never have a sense of closure and never stop providing for their learning needs. Only a small portion of these needs are addressed by the so-called major providers: employer organizations, professional associations, higher education, and the for-profit vendors.

Individual executives and professionals are ultimately as influential providers of learning experiences as the organizations that seek to coordinate and enhance their collective performance. If the quality of judgment they exercise in providing learning for themselves is shaped by an understanding that performance is a function of professional, organizational, and human development, a secure relationship will have been established between continuing learning and performance.

References

BAEHR, MELANY E. "The Empirical Link Between Program Development and the Performance Needs of Professionals and Executives," *Continuum* 48 (3), 1984.

BALDERSTON, FREDERICK E. *Managing Today's University.* San Francisco: Jossey-Bass, 1978.

BERLIN, LAWRENCE "A Contrary View," in *Power and Conflict in Continuing Professional Education,* edited by M. R. Stern. Belmont, CA: Wadsworth, 1983.

BLOCKSTEIN, WILLIAM L. "Interdisciplinary Continuing Education," *Mobius* 3 (3), 1983.

BOYER, ERNEST L. "Foreword." In *Corporate Classrooms,* edited by N. P. Eurich. Princeton, NJ: The Carnegie Foundation for the Advancement of Teaching, 1985.

CROSS, K. PATRICIA. "The Changing Role of Continuing Education." In *Proceedings of the 45th Annual Meeting of the Association for Continuing Higher Education,* edited by Jack L. Huff. Athens, GA: University of Georgia, 1983.

EURICH, NELL P. *Corporate Classrooms.* Princeton, NJ: The Carnegie Foundation for the Advancement of Teaching, 1985.

FIELDING, DAVID W., AND DINNING, BEVERLY C.A. "Regional Coordinators of Continuing Pharmacy Education," *Mobius* 4 (2), 1984.

FREEDMAN, MORRIS. "The Hodgepodge of Professional Education," *Chronicle of Higher Education,* March 18, 1985.

FREIDSON, ELIOT. *Professional Powers: A Study of the Institutionalization of Formal Knowledge.* Chicago: University of Chicago, 1986.

HODAPP, WILLIAM J., AND CLINE, ROBERTA S. "Components of a Successful Learning Resource Center for Health Professionals," *Mobius* 2 (1), 1982.

HOFSTADER, ROBERT. "Continuing Education for Engineering Productivity." Paper presented at the National University Continuing Education Association Annual Meeting, 1985. Washington, DC: NUCEA, 1985.

LEVI, EDWARD H. "The Place of Professional Education in the Life of the University," *Ohio State Law Journal* 32 (2), 1971.

NATIONAL RESEARCH COUNCIL. *Continuing Education of Engineers.* Report of the Panel on Continuing Education, M. A. Steinberg, Chairman. Washington, D.C.: National Academy Press, 1985.

NOWLEN, PHILIP M. "Continuing Education for the Professions." In *Handbook on Continuing Education,* edited by Q. Gessner. New York: Macmillan, 1987.

NOWLEN, PHILIP M. AND QUEENEY, DONNA S. *The Role of Colleges and Universities in Continuing Professional Education.* National University Continuing Education Association Occasional Paper. Washington, D.C.: NUCEA, 1984.

SCHNEIDER, CAROL G. "Power and Conflict in Continuing Education Reviewed," *American Journal of Education* 92 (4), 1984.

———. "Sources of Coherence in Liberal Learning," *Forum for Honors* 16 (1), 1985.

STERN, MILTON R. (ED.). *Power and Conflict in Continuing Professional Education.* Belmont CA: Wadsworth, 1983.

VEBLEN, THORSTEIN. *The Higher Learning in America.* Reprint of 1918 edition. New York: Hill and Wang, 1957.

ZEMKE, RON. "Industry-Education Cooperation: Old Phrase With a Strange New Meaning," *Training* 22 (7), 1985.

EIGHT
Consumers

THE INDIVIDUAL ALONE MAY CHOOSE an educational opportunity and finance it personally, acting as *the* consumer, indeed the only person interested in the educational program's effect. Usually, however, a set of persons is involved in the selection of continuing education experiences. The life of organizations and professions sets broad learning agendas. Within these parameters, organizations may have general policies and specific priorities with respect to continuing education. In addition, persons conducting performance or peer reviews stimulate professionals and business people to consider personal learning needs. Organization leaders are inclined to favor requests for continuing education experiences that are linked with the organization's learning needs or with formal and informal performance-review processes. Leaders also initiate the process, designating someone to pursue a learning agenda in behalf of the organization or directing someone to chart a personal learning path as the result of a performance review. The professional or executive is provided with the time required. Part or all of the tuition is paid by the organization. Travel and per diem are sometimes furnished. The managing partner, supervisor of nursing, or vice-president for operations sees that work is redistributed. In situations of extended learning, pursuing a second professional degree, for example, the organization may require a commitment of professionals' continued employment in return for the employer's substantial development investment. The organization and the boss are significant co-consumers.

Other sign-offs are required. A week-long seminar out of town, or a weekend MBA program, involves rearrangements of family, civic, and religious commitments. Others must fill in for the absent spouse, school-board member, Sunday-school teacher, or Little-League umpire. Pursuing an educational agenda requires negotiation skills at many levels. Family members or nonoccupational colleagues may need to understand how the educational opportunity fits into the larger patterns of life. A spouse who makes significant sacrifices in order to permit a partner to pursue an extended learning agenda will develop a justifiable sense of personal investment.

Another set of persons has an investment in the outcome of educational agendas. The 10 or 15 persons whose work ties them most closely to the persons continuing their education are co-consumers, stakeholders in the inevitably interactive quality of someone else's learning. The larger organization has, by encouraging a specific learning agenda, intervened in the immediate occupational culture of the learner. The persons in closest contact with the learner develop concerns, expectations, and apprehensions. If innovation or change becomes a desirable outcome of the learning agenda, these co-consumers become facilitators or saboteurs.

The individual professional or business person, nonetheless, has the most point-of-purchase leverage in continuing education decision making within the range of possibilities brought into focus by organizational and professional life and encouraged or allowed by a framework of policies, priorities, and practices. Organizational leaders frequently encourage individual executives and professionals to exercise intuition and imagination in discerning the personal learning links required by the firm's strategic plan or their own development.

The educational decisions reached by individual professionals and executives and supported by their employer organizations are the primary consumer demands that heavily influence what higher education, professional associations, the training and education industry, and organizations themselves provide. Consumers and their employers pay for continuing education. The information-heavy marathons characteristic of the update model are what individual and organizational consumers have wanted and what providers have furnished. The massive, flexible, and varied response of providers is convincing evidence of the dominance of consumer specifications in the design of continuing education.

If the professionals and the executives, as well as their key co-consumers, demand continuing education activities that seriously deal with performance issues, there is no reason to believe that providers would fail to respond. In Milton Stern's disorderly market place, only a new consumer consensus will integrate the uses of the update and competence models in the larger perspective of the performance model. First, however, some of the obstacles to a performance-oriented consumer consensus must be addressed.

Caution: Professionalization at Work

> The most problematic of all these human aspirations is how to define the limits of comradeship. This, indeed, is where humanity's myth-making and myth-destroying capacity comes elementally and directly into play by defining the boundary between "us" and "them." Broadly inclusive public identities, if believed and acted on, tend to relax tensions among strangers and can allow people of diverse habits and outlook to coexist more or less peacefully. Narrower in-group loyalties, on the other hand, divide humanity into potentially or actually hostile groupings. [McNeill, 1986]

The characteristics associated with the professionalizing process address the nature *and limits* of professional comradeship (Houle, 1980, pp. 34–75). Novices enter professional life with certain views of the central mission of their professions. These views, often romantic and idealized, reflect the power of professions' constitutive myths in binding together those who belong and, by so doing, marking others apart. Deeply influenced by these views, novice professionals encounter the rhythms of day-to-day professional life as little related to the professional mission that motivated their years of preparation. Time and effort expended seem inversely related to professional mission and priorities. The personal process of questioning the profession's mission and the individual's commitment begins. It is repeated by the lawyer after time spent as a public defender, FBI agent, corporate counsel, federal marshal, or specialist in product liability litigation. It is repeated by the teacher after several school years of fifth-grade math, curriculum-review meetings, union contract negotiations, or assistant-principal tasks. It is repeated by the clergy after the first 100 weddings, 200 funerals, 300 sermons, 400 coffee hours, or 500 confessions. Just as in the cultures of athletics, married life, or religion, periodic reexamination and restatement of the terms of commitment is indispensable to persons in the professions. The process is characteristic of the lifespan of the professions themselves. Dentistry has evolved from a physiological perspective to a complex biopsychosocial framework, from remedial to preventive patient encounters. Several different missions coexist for the several different settings of pharmacy. Architecture is divided between a specific focus on design of buildings and a broad claim to judgment over spatial relationships of any scale. Sharply different public views of corrections do not permit that profession a clear choice between rehabilitation and punishment as its mission. This concern with mission is regarded by Houle as the first and most dominant characteristic, the conceptual characteristic, in fact, of professionalizing vocations. It has a powerful inward, reflexive orientation.

Mastery of distinctive theoretical knowledge bases, their problem-solving approaches, decision trees, and protocols of practice are characteristic sources of intraprofessional communication and collegiality. These languages of thought and action are mastered in the formal training provided by professional schools, cultural islands that combine the exhilaration of coming of age with the humiliation of boot-camp discipline—powerful bonding agents. University of Chicago Professor Joseph M. Williams, who teaches writing to young professionals, recalls one young lawyer's response: "I spent $50,000 over three years learning to sound like this and you—you want me to sound like everyone else." As a particular profession's next generation is formed, so also is its distance from other professions. The professions' distinctive theoretical knowledge bases, decision trees, and protocols are the paradigms of unique languages that make interprofessional communication and collegiality difficult. Furthermore, there are few interprofessional experiences to balance the intensive bonding of formal intraprofessional training.

Until quite recently formal credentialing, another professionalizing characteristic, was a process entirely internal to a profession, either through admission of graduates from an accredited curriculum to the licensure process, through candidates meeting the requirements of an association or qualifying for an official registry, or by automatic approval of graduates from designated institutions. While relying heavily on committees representing each profession, state governments have begun to involve citizens representing the public interest in accrediting boards and licensing committees. There is no similar trend toward opening the credentialing process to members of those other professions with which candidates for licensure can expect to be routinely interacting in ordinary practice.

Legal reinforcement and public support are characteristically sought by professions with respect to the protections and privileges asserted to be essential to their missions and functions. These functions are the shaping of public policies, laws, and regulations that touch upon issues of practice, reimbursement for services, funding of research and education, and limitations on liability and related insurance costs. Legal reinforcement is usually pursued by state or national professional associations. In some of the professions, associations represent the mission of a profession as well as their members' narrower self-interests. In other professions, the higher virtues are represented by one association, and trade or guild issues such as economics and turf are pursued by a separate association. At times legal action is taken in the name of protecting the public, to reserve an activity to a profession's exclusive use, or to restrain the activity of other professions. Projects in behalf of legal reinforcement and public support are often the largest budget categories of associations and may represent the single largest category of contributed effort by members. Projects undertaken to strengthen a profession can have an obvious connection with the performance of professionals, for example, protecting confidentiality in psychiatry and journalism, assuring the special powers of attorneys, and defining licensure standards for the allied health professions. For the most part, however, there is no necessary connection between the power, prestige, and influence of a profession and the performance of professionals in specific contexts of practice. Legal reinforcement and public acceptance for one profession can be at the expense of another profession, whereas effective performance frequently rests upon members of several professions working effectively together.

Similarly, the praiseworthy concern of professions for ethical practice is centered upon the development of profession-specific standards, codes, and rules, and upon the misconduct of individual members. These frames of reference are important. They keep the focus of activity relentlessly within the profession.

The professionalizing characteristics (constitutive missions and myths; distinctive knowledge bases, problem-solving approaches, decision trees, and formal training; admissions, licensure, and credentialling processes; the drive for legal reinforcement and public support; and the concern for ethical practice) are among the strongest bonds of the unique professional cultures that they form. As with the many cultures in which persons move, the reciprocity between culture and individual makes it impossible fully to distinguish the two. In fact, professionals affirm the extent to which their very identities are bound up with the culture of their professions. "I am a chemical engineer." "I am a lawyer." "I am a rabbi."

Professions and professionals are greatly enhanced by these ties that bind. There is less understanding of the ways in which they and their clients are disadvantaged by the same ties (Friedson, 1986, pp. 209–230). Examples from the field of health care include the tendency to build fences (if not walls) around areas of practice that are silently declared one or another group's turf, a practice that makes task sharing more difficult at a time when the comprehensive, relatively nontechnical nature of care includes more and more tasks that must be shared across occupational and professional groups (Blockstein, 1983, p. 61).

Continuing education consumers should take caution. Consumer perceptions of performance issues and, particularly, the relationship of continuing education to performance can be seriously distorted by some characteristics of professionalization.

- There is more to performance than the professional "I." The professional "I" coexists with "I," the spouse, parent, sibling, son, or daughter. The professional "I" resides in a person who is also a partner, employee, organization leader, colleague, or mentor. The professional "I" is just one of the identities involved in the developmental balancing act, for example, self-regard versus self-criticism; commitment versus critical distance; stability versus risk. "I" the professional has no immunity from the distraction felt by the 50-year-old son of dependent parents, from the impairment of the risk-averter's alcohol dependence, from the inadequate interpersonal skills of the partner, from the numbing effect of too many years at the same tasks, or from the paralysis of an incompetent organization.
- The mission of a profession corresponds to only some of the many day-to-day functions of professionals. Most professionals count themselves fortunate if they can make direct use of their specialized knowledge, decision trees, and protocols as often as 40% of the time. Yet, professionals and their clients suffer when there is inattention to functions outside the range recognized as "professional."
- Professionalization is a relatively decontextualizing process, distancing the professional from the unique and immediate culture that enhances or frustrates personal performance or, in turn, whose performance is enhanced or frustrated by the professional.

- Professionalization emphasizes individuals in the face of the social nature of performance.
- Professionalization emphasizes the exclusive comradeship of the guild, sharpening the boundaries between "us" and "them"; while performance often demands spirited interpersonal, interoccupational and interorganizational collaboration.
- Professionalization narrows what some continuing education providers offer.

The continuing education staff of professional associations do not have a mandate to address professional performance issues that fall outside the traditional framework of knowledge and skills. One medical association's continuing education committee endured an exercise in defining the physician proficiencies desired in any member specialist they would want to treat their spouses. When confronted with the distance between the proficiencies they desired and those actually addressed by the continuing medical education programs they directed, no conflict was perceived between the quite different physician profiles. "Physicians ought to be all those other things too, but we're a professional association. We have no competence or mandate to address the other proficiencies and probably couldn't accredit programs that did."

What university professional schools provide depends upon the research and teaching interests of the faculty that, in turn, are heavily influenced by the professionalization of the professoriate and the strength of the positivist paradigm. The scholarly professions have their own constitutive myths, demands, and rewards. It is in the culture of scholarship, not of professional practice, that professional-school faculty are embedded. Ernest Lynton comments that a professional label on a curriculum does not make it any more useful than any arts and sciences label makes a curriculum liberal. "Particularly at the graduate level, the programs in many of our professional schools have moved away from the issues of the profession to the pursuit of disciplinary goals and the training of academic specialists" (Lynton, 1983, p. 21). The culture of professional schools is also distant from the rest of the university. The inward, reflexive qualities of professionalization limit the capacity of professional-school faculty to collaborate imaginatively with members of different scholarly professions. In addition, the positivist paradigm is honored in professional schools while its critique is elsewhere quite lively (Lynton, 1983; Reingold, 1976; Rudolph, 1984). Finally, universities need to maintain the tension between being in the world, if not quite of the world—a position of helpful distance, it is hoped.

- Professionalization narrows what consumer-professionals desire in continuing education. The power of the professional "I" is so strong that consumers sometimes limit their search for appropriate continuing education to the narrowest examples of the update model. Among consumers who try to take stock of their strengths and weaknesses in order to define their educational needs more carefully, professionals who are inadvertently "in role" as they do so will reflect on how they measure up to the generalized ideal for their profession or specialty or they will turn to a professional association's self-inventory instruments to chart their educational agenda. If the professional "I" dominates this process, the frame of reference will be the profession, not performance in the context of practice. Therefore the consumers' shopping list is not likely to address issues of human development, interpersonal skills, organizational behavior, higher-order reasoning, or the uses of art, intuition, and wisdom.

- Professionalization disinclines consumer–professionals to participate in interprofessional continuing education. The pattern is set early. One medical school found that medical students' overall reaction to a one-week obstetrics–gynecology–pediatrics orientation involving both nursing and medical students was negative to joint-learning situations, was strongly negative to joint conferences between medical students and other health professionals, and was supportive of the view that less contact with nursing students would be a positive benefit (Blockstein, 1983, p. 61). While it is hard to imagine a patient-centered or clinically focused interprofessional continuing education program without the presence of physicians, getting them to come is extremely difficult. As a colleague remarked to William Blockstein, professor of pharmacy and preventive medicine at the University of Wisconsin–Madison,

> My guess is that one might get less than ten M.D.'s to attend if we went to extraordinary efforts. That handful of M.D.'s would be subtly disruptive of the conference—mainly because they will be fairly vocal with their early questions of the instructor and their questions

> will be physiopathological/technical. [The instructor] will deal with them without difficulty, but by that time the major part of the audience will be intimidated and reluctant to ask their questions, so the majority will go home dissatisfied. [Blockstein, 1983, p. 67]

It is ironic that the processes of professionalization that inspire a career-long zest for learning propel professionals toward such myopic educational agendas.

Auguries of a Performance-Oriented Consumer Consensus

> Most professionals and executives, most of the time, are self-directed learners. Most learning in business and the professions occurs outside the *formal* arrangements of providers. Formal education experiences are positioned within larger self-directed frameworks. Self-directed learners comprise the single most powerful influence in the field.

Allen Tough's summary of more than a decade of research concluded that the adults he had studied undertook a median number of eight study projects a year. Some of them were pursued in parallel. Most of them were self-planned. The average effort involved 100 hours and it was, therefore, common for adults to spend 700 or more hours a year in self-directed learning activities. Forty-two percent of these learning efforts were undertaken to improve the practitioner's job, volunteer, or recreational competence (Tough, 1978). Subsequent studies across a number of cultures and countries have confirmed Tough's conclusion that among the educated and professional classes, self-directed learning has become the norm. As consumers, self-directed learners look to providers for educational experiences that are, in effect, temporary systems stemming from, as well as advancing, one or another of the several self-directed learning strategies the professional or executive is pursuing.

Self-directed learners make whatever sense is to be made of the range of providers and programs by selecting, coordinating, and integrating what is available in service of their educational aims. Self-directed learners are not isolates. Stephen Brookfield calls them gregarious because they are so thoroughly involved in networks of information exchange and problem solving. It is the pattern of such networks that Brookfield suggests must be understood by providers in order to identify learners' needs and questions as the learners perceive them (Brookfield, 1984).

> Most professionals and executives are only partially aware of their role as self-directed learners. Having no explicit preparation for the role, they rely upon intuition and personal experience, and do not challenge the merits of one undertaking relative to competing or alternative possibilities. They find the results disappointing.

The most commonly self-directed learning is a seamless, reflective conversation of the professional or executive with the practice situation. It is so much a piece of each professional act that it is virtually impossible to distinguish action from reflection. The reflective act of practice is the elemental, atomic structure of self-directed learning in business and the professions. Each reflective act is a teaching–learning situation. The professional or executive enters a situation of practice (either to create something or to understand something, objectives that eventually merge) as Schon puts it,

> to impose a frame on it, to follow the implications of the discipline thus established, and yet to remain open to the situation's back-talk. Reflecting on the surprising consequences of his efforts to shape the situation in conformity with his initially chosen frame, the inquirer frames new questions and new ends in view. . . . Faced with some phenomenon that he finds unique, the inquirer nevertheless draws on some element of his familiar repertoire which he treats as exemplar or as generative metaphor for the new phenomenon. . . . Further, as the inquirer reflects on the similarities he has perceived, he formulates new hypotheses. But he tests these hypotheses by experimental actions which also function as moves for shaping the situation and as probes for exploring it. [Schon, 1983, p. 269]

A step above the reflective act in terms of the consciousness with which professionals and executives engage in self-directed learning is the inner voice that, in the manner of some dictation equipment, "marks" certain ideas, events, exchanges, texts, meetings, strategies, tactics, and exemplars for subsequent reflection even as, Woody Allen style, the practitioner's other voice continues to interact directly in the situation at play. Sometimes the "mark" is a flash of insight or the briefest of mental judgments. "This jerk has just taken the meeting away from me—how did it happen?" "Absolutely brilliant memo." "Her intuition about this patient has been on target again and again." These marks do not trigger major educational efforts. They prompt, in these three examples: a quick conversation with an ally about how the inquirer lost control of a meeting process; quiet reflection on the elegant strategy underlying a particularly effective memo; and an instinct formed to track the physician as a possible mentor.

More conscious than these barely liminal inner voices are deliberate but simple acts, such as purchasing a trade publication related to a practitioner's work, subscribing to a journal in the field, or registering for the next annual meeting of a professional association. At a level of considerable intentionality are complex learning projects undertaken with personal and organizational outcomes in view and typically mixing self-managed learning experiences with provider-directed programs in an over-arching framework that is, itself, largely self-designed.

These categories of self-directed learning, distinct in complexity and degree of self-consciousness, are not stages of increasing sophistication through which self-directed learners progress. They are coexisting, often interrelated, and thoroughly appropriate expressions of self-directed learning.

Professionals and executives exhibit widely varying degrees of competence in engaging in self-directed learning, from each act of reflective practice to the design and management of a complex curriculum. There are domain-specific criteria for excellence that reside in both the range and quality of instrumentalities that practitioners bring to reflective acts. They include

- media, languages, and repertoires used in describing reality and conducting experiments;
- appreciative systems brought to problem setting, evaluation of inquiry, and reflective conversation;
- role frames that expand as well as limit the intended scope of activity (Schon, 1983, pp. 270–275).

There are also criteria for excellence that reside in the skill with which these instrumentalities are wielded. They include skills in

- setting objectives, particularly those describing the difference the learning is intended to make for personal or organizational performance;
- identifying resources;
- learning design;
- self-instructional techniques;
- formative evaluation (mid-course corrections) and summative evaluation (outcome analysis).

These are the skills typically associated with self-directed learning. They are important but, considered in themselves, are quite ambiguous when it comes to linking self-directed learning with performance. The proficiencies of some self-directed learners simply make them more dangerous to have around—loose cannons within their organization or profession who "operate within fixed and uncritically assimilated frameworks of knowledge . . . and are unable to question the validity or worthwhileness of one intellectual pursuit as compared to competing, alternative possibilities" (Brookfield, 1986, p. 57).

The skills of critical thinking, analysis and choice, expressed in domain-specific media, vocabulary, grammar, and repertoires; appreciative systems; and role frames make self-directed learning genuinely adult. As Brookfield puts it, "The most fully adult form of self-directed learning . . . is one in which critical reflection on the contingent aspects of reality, the exploration of alternative perspectives and meaning systems and the alteration of personal and social circumstances are all present." The reflective instruments and educational skills come together "when adults come to appreciate the culturally constructed nature of knowledge and values and when they act on the basis of that appreciation to reinterpret and recreate their personal and social worlds" (1986, pp. 58–59).

From the foregoing, it can be safely concluded that fostering adult self-directed learning is only partially a matter of mastery of the principles and skills of educational design. The literature of cognitive and affective development, particularly that of constructive-developmental psychology, strongly suggests that the ability to generate and manage one's own learning agenda is an advanced and hard-won developmental achievement. The field of continuing education must understand how to account for the processes that foster this ability if it is to assist individuals to develop it.

> Many people are growing irritated by what seems to them to be a mindless proliferation of courses and conferences, each of which may be valuable but which are not collectively undergirded by any unifying conception of how education can be used in a mature, complex and continuing way to achieve excellence of service throughout the lifespan. [Houle, 1980]

The prosperity of the update model has been particularly vulnerable to drafts and chills in the business cycle. A slowdown in some sectors of the nation's economy from 1979 through early 1981 resulted in decreased enrollments in higher-education-sponsored programs for business and the professions. Two major for-profit providers declared bankruptcy during this period and professional association leaders complained of the same phenomenon, although enrollment data across professional associations are unavailable. The rueful story going the rounds at the time was that enrollment patterns in continuing education for business and the professions provided earlier warning of economic recessions than boxcar loadings. It is the common perception of providers that business as well as other major employers of professionals cut the continuing education budget at the first hint of economic problems. The evidence is impressionistic and anecdotal that hard times trigger diminished support for continuing education because doing so appears to have no adverse effect on performance or profit! When the economy improves, however, support for continuing education reappears in the haze of faith, "No one believes that continuing education is just a fringe benefit even though its relationship with performance is pretty soft." Providers have a powerful incentive to develop programs with a demonstrable impact on performance. In so doing, they may be able to avoid pneumonia whenever the economy sneezes.

Fifteen years ago, the idea of flying to another city for a week-long seminar was a novel and reassuring experience for most professionals and executives. For many it was the first time they had been separated from their spouses for that length of time. Not everyone else in the office attended two or more such programs a year. It was a confidence-building event that represented recognition by a person's organization. It might even have meant that someone was on a fast track, being groomed for larger responsibilities. For persons who lacked feedback on their performance, requesting approval to participate in continuing education was a low-risk way to test where they stood with their bosses. In other words, no matter what the quality of the continuing education program might have been, the experience was already surrounded by a favorable aura before it began.

Today there is neither quiet celebrity nor glamour attached to continuing education for business and the professions. It is pervasive. Airline deregulation, making connecting flights at O'Hare or Atlanta, and the dubious comforts of most hotels reduce travel to an endurance contest. Program registrants arrive cranky. The willing suspension of disbelief has given way to "This better be useful and entertaining." Thanks to the growth of continuing education, consumers now have ways to express dissatisfaction and do so. Registrants threaten suit under truth-in-advertising precedents. When they have paid the same tuition and fees as more traditional students, they demand equal access to the library and other facilities during the hours they are on campus. When registrants request their tuition refunded, they sometimes threaten to have the program or provider "blacklisted" by their employer if the provider fails to comply. Professionals and executives are much more demanding, if not always in very educationally sophisticated ways.

The number of organizations in which continuing education dollars are audited and policies developed linking educational support to organization and individual needs is growing. When organizations begin to monitor continuing education experiences, individual consumers gain strength through the third party-payer influence of their employers. Program registrants routinely file opinions of the educational experience, and other organization personnel considering a program have recourse to the resulting consumers' guide.

> Growing consumer and third party-payer irritation with the miscellaneous and random quality of continuing education for business and the professions helps energize promising innovations based on actual professional practice or business requirements. These often involve collaboration among providers and employer organizations. The competence model represented by some of these innovations is spreading.

The competence-based approaches illustrated in Chapter Two represent a model that is rapidly gaining acceptance as an alternative to the update model. Alverno College has used it imaginatively on the undergraduate level. The University of Minnesota's College of Pharmacy has used it. A variety of Pennsylvania professional associations have collaborated with the Pennsylvania State University in experimenting with the model. Continuing educators at the University of Chicago have used the model with reference to effective teaching and mentoring of adults. The American Association of Colleges of Pharmacy have made a serious national commitment to it. The American Society for Training and Development finds it works effectively for its membership. The American Management Association, supported by the Fund for the Improvement of Postsecondary Education, has developed a competence framework for management, and, as a result, the Association has restructured its whole approach to continuing education in management. The U.S. Navy and the State Department have found the model effective and it is well known in banking and the savings and loan field.

Those who advance the competence model are not in agreement about whether its baselines should be drawn on the basis of adequacy or excellence, the one providing minimal but measurable thresholds of absolutely necessary proficiency, the other providing the relative distances of persons from highly desirable proficiency.

The very quality of the controversy is a contribution of the competence model.

> The achievement of the competence model lies in its pointing beyond itself to elements of a unifying conception of how education can be used in a mature, complex way to achieve and maintain performance excellence. Within this broader, more complex model, the competence and update models can play useful roles.

Professionals, executives, and continuing education providers who have been exposed to the competence model, especially those who have participated in conducting related research activities or in designing competence-based educational programs, found it to be their first experience with a coherent, overarching frame of reference for performance-related learning. Competence frameworks make it possible to choose rationally among the educational alternatives of the update model. Since the mid-1970s, the model has been used in increasingly imaginative ways. The model has identified key proficiencies that, heretofore, had not been isolated or taught toward, for example, managing or practicing across cultures. It has greatly simplified the task of evaluating the impact of continuing education.

Ultimately, however, it is found to be a reductionist model that cannot easily address the cultural strand of performance's double helix, for example, the ensemble characteristics of performance itself and the social determinants of individual performance that include organization culture, relationships with clients, the other environments in which the person is simultaneously embedded, and the social nature of knowledge and its contingent relationship with communities of interpretation and belief. The competence model has also skirted issues related to the individual strand of performance's double helix, for example, the relationship of appropriate human development to performance in domains such as commitment, maturity, and values, and questions of physical and psychological impairment. Nonetheless, the competence model makes possible the very insights that demonstrate its limitations:

- five fully competent individuals are not necessarily the equivalent of one adequately performing group;
- most persons who are fully competent with respect to their job descriptions have significantly elevated or depressed performance levels from organization culture to culture, from one human development stage to another, from feeling committed

to feeling trapped, from role freeze to pluralistic cognitive qualities.

The streams of scholarly research related to performance are coming together in a flood of popular articles and trade publications.

The critique of positivism and the role of communities of belief and interpretation in meaning making has reached the coffee tables of executives and professionals. The celebrity of the "superstring theory" (that the world at its simplest level is not composed of subatomic particles, but of one-dimensional elongations of energy called superstrings) is the latest shock to those still trying to emulate the rigor of hard sciences such as physics. The theory has the potential to incorporate gravity mathematically with other fundamental forces in nature and eliminates the infinities generated by previous attempts at an overarching theory. Because in size, a superstring is to an atom as an atom is to the universe, no accelerator within modern technological imagination can be constructed to validate the theory experimentally. There can be no "proof" therefore that the theory is related to the real world and no consistent connections have been established with known experiments. Nonetheless, the elegance of the theory has captured a strong position among theoretical physicists. Dissenters warn that so many graduate students are working exclusively on the theory that a generation of physicists is at stake if the theory is discarded but concede that "Superstring" has taken physics off in a new direction. Physicists do not perceive themselves as stepping out of role or functioning outside their competence as members of a profession when they use intuition and art (some would say, faith) to reach a new conceptual framework that, thereby, redirects the profession.

Research has identified a pattern of interpersonal skills, cognitive skills, and motivational characteristics to be chiefly related to successful performance. That this is the pattern classically woven by liberal education is more and more widely observed, not only in the literature of training, development, and continuing education, but in professional and business publications and the op-ed pages of newspapers as well. Employers planned to increase their hiring of liberal-arts graduates by about 20% in 1986 while hiring of new college graduates in other areas of concentration was predicted to rise less than 1% (Wyman, 1986).

The impossibility of keeping the "I" who is a professional or executive completely free of the depressing influence of the "I" who is a partner in a failing marriage has destroyed the myth of airtight life compartments. The powerful influence of culture on high-performing organizations and individuals is better known thanks to several best-selling trade publications. The relationship of technical problem solving to professional artistry; the limitations of knowledge mastery; and the advantage of holding valid and using several different frames of reference, classification schemes, and theories for understanding or probing the layers of reality are issues that have been addressed on talk shows or in magazines popularizing the social sciences.

> Professional schools are, here and there, beginning to introduce curriculum experiments which acknowledge the influential role culture, interpersonal skills, art and intuition play in performance.

We still have a system of medical education that some believe produces a few superbly qualified medical researchers, but that prepares them inadequately for effectiveness as general practitioners or internists. Business schools provide experts in the analysis of security prices and multivariate approaches to marketing but otherwise bright MBAs have little sense of history or of shifts in the societal balance (Lynton, 1983, p. 22). There are promising experiments, however. One medical school has a behavioral medicine section that studies the interaction between physician and patient with a view toward identifying patterns of supportive as well as dysfunctional physician behavior with respect to patient health. At least one business school now has a curricular relationship with its university's international studies programs that can lead students to several kinds of cultural concentrations in combination with various MBA paths. Another business school is looking to add anthropological frames of reference to traditional business school approaches. A medical school has a compulsory liberal arts program and uses patient surrogates and simulations of physician-patient encounters in evaluating medical students' progress. In addition, several professional schools have moved to the competence model as the basis for curriculum revision and renewal.

These are portents and trends, not measures of a consensus that has already developed.

Bringing the Consensus to Life

BUILDING COALITIONS

The nature of the performance model strongly suggests that new coalitions will emerge. The field is not in touch with itself at present (see Chapter One). Continuing educators serving engineers, hospital administrators, lawyers, physicians, social workers, business people, nurses, accountants, corrections personnel, architects, librarians, teachers, and the allied health professions have concentrated their efforts on the specialized knowledge that distinguishes them from one another rather than on performance issues they commonly confront. There is even less contact among those who serve professionals and executives in different provider groups (higher education, professional associations, employing organizations and the for-profit sector). Not many NUCEA and ASTD members attend one another's meetings and it is not likely that any organization historically associated with the self-interests of a single provider group can convene and sustain a network of the field's principal stakeholders.

The stakeholders in the field include: individual professionals and executives; leaders of business, industry, and other organizations that employ executives and professionals; persons representing the public trust in matters of professional standards and safety; professional association leaders concerned with accountability and continuing education; members of the helping professions whose clients are executives and professionals; training and development representatives of major corporations; and the higher education community, including not only continuing education and professional-school leaders but those, as well, who represent the research base for understanding performance. These stakeholders are well represented on the local, state, and national levels and many of them have interacted in collaborative, though episodic, efforts such as the projects at the University of Chicago and Pennsylvania State University. The stakeholders are also to be found in personal networks but these are highly idiosyncratic.

The performance model touches the self-interests and concerns of all the stakeholders. It frees and empowers consumers to make more discriminating choices among continuing education opportunities. It provides organization leaders with insights into the relationship between individual and group performance and it demonstrates the benefit of employers articulating a strategy within which they will support individual continuing education choices. It disabuses policy makers of the myth that society is assured of professional competence by mandating updates in knowledge and skill. It opens a dialogue with the helping professions that deal daily with a spectrum of performance-related issues. It urges earlier involvement of training and development professionals in the organizational decision-making process and points to the need to make the educational assumptions of noneducators explicit.

The performance model changes providers' roles from *instructing* executives and professionals through isolated educational experiences that are thought to be in and of themselves complete, to *assisting* organizations and individuals to be more sophisticated in directing their own learning. The performance model leads providers away from a production mentality and toward complex *teaching-learning conversations* that connect educational designs smoothly with organizational and individual agendas. The performance model connects whole new categories of educational program possibilities to professional and executive performance, thus giving providers an unusual opportunity for growth and diversification. It offers providers relatively more financial stability during pauses in growth and mild recessions. It identifies a new, lively, and unforced role for liberal arts colleges and may lead other agencies, such as group practices in clinical psychology, to conclude that they have a role as continuing education providers. The threat of changed circumstances and the neutrality of a new perspective offer an opportunity for former competitors to become collaborators.

The performance model links research in the social sciences with organization and individual performance and, in so doing, opens new career paths for social science PhDs in service of organizations and professions. It demonstrates that business and the professions are appropriate constituencies for more than just professional schools.

The performance model is neither prescriptive nor reductionist. As a descriptive model, it must include all demonstrably significant performance-related variables. It is therefore a model open to shaping by all the stakeholders and, thereby, to broad ownership.

The major interests in the field have much at stake in moving beyond the update and competence models. *The national and regional discussions of the nature of performance and the educational model that serves its elements have already occasioned sentiment favoring the creation of a permanent organization open to all those who serve the interest of performance among executives, professionals, and their organizations.* The existence of an organization open to providers, organizational and individual consumers, interested members of the helping professions, researchers, and the like would usefully broaden the discussion of performance, bring many into contact with the considerable research base already available, and accelerate the adaptation of innovation. The American Association for Adult and Continuing Education's new commission on continuing education for the professions might become such an organization.

FOSTERING ACTION RESEARCH

Conduct of descriptive research related to the competence model, and the survey instruments and interviews related to identifying what executives and professionals really do for a living, educate those who are surveyed. Prescriptive and often romantic myths about professional life are harder to sustain after persons have inventoried the situation-to-situation tasks that are the content of a week or month at the office, hospital, school, or engineering firm. Guided self-analyses of critical incidents in performance are revelatory moments when, for the first time, professionals and executives note the frequency with which cultures and human-development issues are as deeply influential as knowledge and skill mastery.

While such insights continue to occur here and there as professional associations, universities, or employers experiment with competence-based continuing education or conduct research on the elements of performance, *the founding of action-research centers for the study of performance in business and the professions* (see Chapter Four) *can accelerate the formation of a new consumer consensus as well as provide superior settings for the development of continuing educators.* Such centers can bring together the literature and practices of the field appropriate to the performance model and even offer technical assistance in return for cooperative research opportunities.

EMPOWERING CONSUMERS

Providers interested in forming wiser and more demanding consumers have a number of opportunities to do so. Continuing educators, together with resource persons drawn from human development, can *offer instruction in self-directed learning to students in professional schools, as well as practicing professionals.* Students' study skills may experience some immediate benefit, but the longer-range benefit is the creation of a generation of professionals who are sophisticated in the ways of reflective practice. In addition to enhancing professional-school students in self-directed learning, continuing educators can organize opportunities for them to reflect with seasoned veterans on the nature of performance over the career span, the interaction between individual performance and the cultures and contexts that enhance or depress it, the sustaining of performance through anticipable life crises, the need for periodic reinterpretation of professional commitment, and the like. At first, such opportunities may have to be provided as a cost to the continuing education unit. To the extent that students and practitioners begin to value their effect, more equitable ways of financing these experiences surely can be found.

Providers can offer enriched versions of practice audits (see the Pennsylvania State project in Chapter Two) *and guided self-assessment centers.* For professionals and executives who never seem to have quite enough time, the opportunity at various career points to take stock, to sort things out, to build a learning agenda for the next few years is more critical to performance than an equivalent commitment of time to some specialized educational program. While much of the reflection may be spent in assessing the relative importance of new professional knowledge, skill and technology, a successful self-assessment or practice audit occasions broader reflection on the interplay of culture, contexts, and human development with performance. For a professional at a particular career juncture, for example, the decision to seek a fresh challenge may be more productive than a decision to master new state-of-the-art technology while remaining trapped in a practice setting that no longer holds much personal meaning. Such broader practice audits and self-assessment centers require additional resources (organization behaviorists and industrial psychologists, for example), but experiments such as De Paul University's self-discovery workshops not only pay their own way but attract clients who might not otherwise have been drawn to a particular provider.

In more popular form, many of the useful perspectives of the performance model can be described, over time, in communications such as newsletters through which many providers already communicate with their professional and executive registrants.

HELPING THIRD-PARTY PAYERS

Continuing educators can offer employers approaches to increasing the cost-benefit ratio of their continuing education, training, and development dollars. Given the approximately $60 billion that organizations spend on educational opportunities, corporations, private nonprofit organizations, public agencies, and institutions are extremely interested in ways to find performance-related value in educational opportunities. The approaches can address the design of organization-wide continuing education strategies, the contribution of recent research on individual and ensemble performance, the contributions of the helping professions and the like.

EXPLICATING THE MODEL'S PROCESSES

With the restructuring of American corporate life, the increase of mergers among professional firms and the dramatic shift in the culture of major institutions such as hospitals, the issue of executive and professional "portability" has arisen. Why is it that some executives and professionals appear to flourish in highly varied organizational cultures and settings of practice while others are completely undone by such transitions? What are the skills of mind, the patterns of human development, the conceptual frames of reference, the interpersonal skills critical to executive or professional success *across* cultures? The process employed by educational research and design in responding to this new issue is of interest to employers, human-resource/personnel professionals, other continuing educators, and even to consumers. *Explaining the genesis of such a program to the field* is yet another way in which to bring a consensus about the performance model to life.

USING THE PERFORMANCE MODEL AS A CRITICAL THEORY

Each step of program design and evaluation, particularly those steps in which consumers participate, can be examined from the perspective of the performance model. During needs analysis conversations with organization leaders or individual executives and professionals, this approach emphasizes specification of the impact learning is expected to make and the collaborative responsibility of the organization to reinforce learning by preparing other forces in the environment (policies, practices, personal styles, etc.) in support of its intended impact. Evaluation instruments, even those that seek opinions about the value of an update or competence-oriented program, can survey learners in ways that also teach them. At the conclusion of a program a registrant can be asked, "Was registration in this program a reflection of your organization's needs and objectives? Do you have a plan for integrating this experience with the daily operations of your firm? Is your boss committed to this course of action?" Six months later a registrant can be asked, "What difference did this program make to your firm's performance? Was your registration in this program part of a larger personal learning strategy? What difference did it make to your own performance? If the program failed to have the impact you had imagined, what were the key contributing factors? Did personal factors outside your occupational setting enhance or diminish the impact of the program?"

Timing, timing, and timing are the three most important elements in guiding change. The many signs that consumers are smarter, dissatisfied, self-directed learners in pursuit of a unifying conception of the role of education in performance give those in the field a unique opportunity to help shape a new consensus around the critical determinants of performance. In so doing, the performance model is played out for the field of continuing education itself. The culture in which continuing education professionals and their organizations are embedded will have been orchestrated to demand and support a new and different level of performance by continuing education providers. Continuing educators and their organizations, therefore, will set a new performance-oriented learning agenda for themselves. Continuing education consumers will evaluate its effectiveness.

References

BLOCKSTEIN, WILLIAM L. "Interdisciplinary Continuing Education," *Mobius* 3 (3), 1983.

BROOKFIELD, STEPHEN D. *Adult Learners, Adult Education and the Community*. New York: Teachers College Press, 1984.

———. "Self-Directed Learning: A Critical Review of Research." In *Self-Directed Learning: From Theory to Practice,* edited by Stephen D. Brookfield. New Directions for Continuing Education, no. 25. San Francisco: Jossey-Bass, 1985.

———. *Understanding and Facilitating Adult Learning*. San Francisco: Jossey-Bass, 1986.

FREIDSON, ELIOT. *Professional Powers: A Study of the Institutionalization of Formal Knowledge*. Chicago: University of Chicago, 1986.

HOULE, CYRIL O. *Continuing Learning in the Professions*. San Francisco: Jossey-Bass, 1980.

LYNTON, ERNEST A. "Reexamining the Role of the University," *Change* 15 (7), 1983.

MCNEILL, WILLIAM H. "The Care and Repair of Public Myth," *Mythistory and Other Essays*. Chicago: The University of Chicago Press, 1986.

REINGOLD, NATHAN. "Definitions and Speculations: The Professionalization of Science in America in the Nineteenth Century." In *The Pursuit of*

Knowledge in the Early American Republic, edited by Alexandra Oleson and Sanborn C. Brown. Baltimore: The Johns Hopkins University Press, 1976.

RUDOLPH, FREDERICK. "The Power of Professors: The Impact of Specialization and Professionalization on the Curriculum," *Change* 18 (3) 1984.

SCHON, DONALD A. *The Reflective Practitioner.* New York: Basic Books, 1983.

TOUGH, ALLEN M. "Major Learning Efforts: Recent Research and Future Directions," *Adult Education* 29 (4) 1978.

———. *The Adult's Learning Projects: A Fresh Approach to Theory and Practice in Adult Learning.* Toronto: Ontario Institute for Studies in Education, 1979.

WYMAN, THOMAS H. "Business Again Looks to Liberal Arts Majors," *New York Times,* July 12, 1986.

NINE
Some Modest Next Steps

Providers Working within the Update Model

THERE IS OPPORTUNITY IN THE PERFORMANCE model, not reproach or threat, for those who provide professional and business persons with learning updates. No providers who are currently enjoying success in refreshing professionals' or executives' baseline knowledge and skills or in bringing new knowledge, skills, and technology to their attention need fear a steep decline in demand. Nothing can substitute for proficiency in essential knowledge and skills. With an appropriately evaluative eye on issues such as retention and impact, providers need not integrate their educational planning with analyses of actual job functions in the competence frameworks being developed for many professional and business roles. Nor must the providers of updates be concerned with other major influences upon personal performance, such as individuals' learning and coping skills, their developmental balance and the influence of environments and cultures of practice. It is not necessary for update providers to be concerned with performance as a group or organizational phenomenon in order to provide individuals with worthwhile learning experiences.

What has been described as the update model can and does stand by itself. However, updates favor those executives and professionals who select wisely. For when the update stands alone, consumers have the responsibility of relating it to the competence required by real-world job functions. When it stands alone, business and professional people and their organizational leaders have the responsibility for judging the likelihood that an update will sustain or enhance actual performance. When providers in their curiosity and self-interest inquire into the reasons thoughtful persons have in selecting specific refreshers or updates, they tune in on the meanings that the programs have within the competence and performance frameworks of those individuals and their organizations. Whether these meanings are based on actual experiences of utility or not, when they are brought to providers' attention they influence the ways providers subsequently remarket the programs or modify their content. Thus, the successful update is indirectly enhanced by the competence and performance perspectives implicit in the market research findings of providers. Perceptions and experiences of utility will, by word of mouth, also influence who will be in the classroom for subsequent presentations of the program. The larger patterns of life with which a successful program is integrated seldom fail to influence it.

Providers can ask program registrants whether assessment centers, practice audits, self-inventory instruments, professional competence or proficiency frameworks, counselors, or organizational learning agendas influenced their selection. Following up where indicated, providers can study processes, instruments, and schemas that are well established in some professions and businesses. When selection criteria appear to be idiosyncratic, providers can look for patterns by forming relationships with professional and organizational leaders. The knowledge providers gain in this fashion will facilitate identification and design of updates, which from their beginning can have intentional links with competence or performance. As a result, successful updates can be enhanced by clearer statements about their applicability, improved program coherence, and easier assessment of impact.

The competence and performance models also offer providers working within the update model the opportunity to extend and diversify their present programs. Generic updates can be tailored to competence needs specific to several professions and contexts while they continue to be offered in their more general mode. An update offered to the general public, "Inflation Accounting under the New Tax Code," for example, could also be tailored in separate offerings for investors, stockbrokers, real estate brokers and appraisers, bankers, accountants, CPAs, certified financial planners, tax attorneys, senior executives, administrators of for-profit hospitals, farmers, and small business owners. The special information pertinent to each field of application or professional specialty can be added to an instructional core, which remains the same in each case.

By tapping into competence or performance frameworks under development or already in use by professions and organizations, update providers will be better positioned to judge the relative demand for new program ideas. In some cases the program idea and the market will present themselves simultaneously, greatly reducing marketing costs and risks. Pharmacists have identified the interaction between the patient and the pharmacist as critical to the profession's mission and the individual pharmacy's financial success. Communications skills, particularly those of listening and of persuasion, are key elements for the pharmacist in that interaction. Knowing this may lead a provider not only to develop communications skill-building programs for pharmacists but also to identify similar needs among divorce lawyers, physicians, dieticians, physical therapists, bank loan officers and the like.

As update providers become familiar with competence and performance frameworks, new streams of programs may result. For example, some knowledge and skill updates for individuals may have organizational implications. "New Principles of Microbial Control of the Hospital Environment" represents a package of knowledge, skills, and technological information that is intended for implementation in organizations with complex structures, employee populations, patterns of accountability, and patient/treatment environments. With impact or performance in mind, a program such as "Managing Innovation and Change in Hospital Support Services" becomes a natural companion piece. Many popular informational programs could have companion programs on implementation.

Some providers will discover that their cumulative improvements in analyzing demand and designing programs have, over time, brought them to operate within the more inclusive models of competence or performance. Others will move to the competence or performance model deliberately, through periods of inquiry, planning, and implementation marked by collaboration with organizations and professional groups. Within several years, many providers will have performance-model relationships with some individuals and organizations and specialized competence-model relationships with other constituencies while continuing to refresh and update persons' knowledge and skills.

Providers Working within the Competence Model

The analysis of job functions is firmly linked with competence assessment as a productive way to shape learning agendas that include refreshers and updates as well as preparation for new mid-career roles. These learning agendas often address professionals and executives as problem solvers. Take N's case: "I'm responsible for directing the work of other professionals for the first time. If I were as proficient in motivational skills as I should be, the professionals I supervise would do what is required without such a struggle. I need to improve my supervisory skills."

Other learning agendas address business and professional people as problem framers who frequently need to view phenomena through many frames of reference, both wide-angle and close-up, in order to reach a wise and prudent definition of the problem to be addressed. Take C's case: "I'm responsible for supervising the work of 35 other professionals. They are resisting my leadership. I'm not sure whether it's their problem, my problem or something quite different that's at play. If it's my problem, do I lack supervision skills or the capacity to think about the leadership challenge imaginatively enough? There are probably ten different ways to think this through and I just know one or two."

The ways of teaching and learning analytical strategies appropriate to N's situation are complex but well known. The chances are that C will define the problem she faces in ways that contain the elements of a lasting solution: organization culture and structure, individual competence and behavior. The prognosis is hopeful because of the analytical facility C displays in forming provisional frames of her situation. This facility makes C potentially a very versatile executive and professional.

Compare the frame of reference implicit in N's problem solving with the several ways in which C approached her situation. In the case cited, N's analysis may be correct, but it relies upon a single lens for seeing the heart of the matter. Providers can respond to N's expressed need without necessarily accepting his analysis. Providers can design programs on motivational or supervisory topics in ways calculated to begin to build in N the higher order reasoning skills demonstrated by C. Building on seminal efforts, such as those at Alverno College (Chapter Two), one next step for many competence-related providers is redesign of programs that will continue to address expressed needs while leading learners toward greater cognitive versatility.

Proficiency in interpersonal relations is an important dimension of executive and professional competence. It may be of relatively greater or lesser significance, given differing functions and contexts, but even lab-based scientists, veterinarians, and coroners must function well in some highly interactive settings. Approaches to enhancing interpersonal skills through formal classroom exercises and one-on-one learning relationships are well known and widely used. Role playing and the use of videotaped simulations have been effective innovations. Learning gains are often lost, however, for lack of reinforcing arrangements. New behaviors need to be practiced. Improvements in formal approaches could include weekly or even monthly follow-ups for students to return for practice and the motivation that results from confirmations of progress. Providers working within the competence model and their client organizations could mutually agree on reinforcing strategies including supervisor cooperation in creating a reassuring atmosphere in which learners practiced new skills or a system of temporary assignments that called for the exercise of the new skills.

There are research steps already being taken by some that others working within the competence model might consider. Among persons with the same professional specialty, what are the differences in competence demanded by differing contexts of practice or of corporate culture? Are differences in competence required in differing career plateaus? The practice audit, assessment centers, and the behavioral event and critical incident interview protocols are promising vehicles for these lines of inquiry.

Executives and professionals who select a program developed on the basis of the competence model may not be operating out of the same framework, nor is it necessary that they do so. Some will benefit even though it was the appeal of a topic or a celebrated speaker that drew them. Others will benefit although they understand that competence is only one of the variables critical to the quality of their performance. The analysis of job functions, the specification of competence required by the functions, and the assessment of individuals' competence are useful processes whether or not they are included in the larger framework of the performance model. Nevertheless, organizations experienced in competence approaches and naturally curious about why apparently equally competent individuals and groups do not perform at the same level of effectiveness will begin taking steps to understand the influence of environments and cultures of practice upon the actuation of competence. The tools of the competence model are well suited to identify the life skills that see some professionals and executives safely through developmental crises without greatly diminished performance.

While some who are working within the competence model will want to continue to specialize in developing competence frameworks and related educational experiences, they can take some modest steps to enjoy the benefits of working relationships with counseling firms, mid-career assessment centers, universities, and professional associations, which collectively address both the social and the personal strands of performance's double helix.

Providers Planning to Design a Performance Model

Developing the capacity to offer individuals guided self-assessment opportunities is the center of the continuing education performance model. Organizations that can do so will have put the most important piece of the performance model in place. The performance triage is a reasonable next step for universities, associations, and employers that already take a developmental approach and provide or make reference to fundamental counseling, placement, and assessment services. It is also the approach likely to generate the richest assortment of needs and responses.

Some providers may wish to establish a reputation by working primarily on performance as a group or organizational phenomenon. In such cases, the group or organization engages in the triage with a view toward developing a common learning and development agenda. A modest step in this case is to draw together organizational leaders with general operational responsibilities and those with human development or personnel portfolios for conversations about the relationships among organizational cultures, policies, structures, and resources with respect to performance. What are reliable baselines or proxies of performance? What are the crucial variables in both high performance and low effectiveness? How good are the organization's skills of learning and reflection, of problem framing and problem solving? What is the quality of the organization as a teaching/mentoring system? How well does the organization weather its developmental storms? Representatives of appropriate research bases and practical experience such as consulting firms, counseling practices, professional associations, and higher education are likely candidates to join in the conversation.

UNIVERSITIES

In both the wide-angle and the close-up focus of the performance model, needs analysis and program development are more surely accomplished within a long-range teaching–learning relationship including but not limited to the employing organization, professional groups, and universities. A university, particularly a state institution in collaboration with a governor's office, state agencies responsible for occupational and professional relicensure, or regional economic development bodies can convene the major professional and business stakeholders with a view toward identifying the strengths each brings to developing triage opportunities, setting learning agendas, and providing educational opportunities.

University-based continuing educators can benefit from membership in the American Society for Training and Development, where conversations about competence and performance have had a long history.

Universities might focus the lenses of the social sciences on a single major employing organization or professional service. Anthropology, education, history, human development, political science, public policy, and sociology might provide new insight into performance as a social phenomenon.

Universities might incrementally build their continuing education advising and career counseling services toward the comprehensive assessment services of the performance triage.

PROFESSIONAL ASSOCIATIONS

The process of developing an associational position paper on the influences at work in professional performance might trigger discussion and debate that would acknowledge factors of significance lying beyond the traditional realm of professional competence. Official acknowledgment that fully competent people do not always perform very well would go far toward enlarging the window through which performance issues are viewed by professionals themselves.

A professional association might design and offer continuing education programs that would draw attention to the relationship between the ways professionals organize themselves for service and the quality of services rendered. Another association might develop an inventory of community resources for dealing with common impairments and the stress of life transitions and personal tragedies, suggesting by so doing that personal difficulties can have a devastating effect on professional performance. Yet another association might alert its members to local educational opportunities dealing with successive plateaus of human development so that the members might have a framework for anticipating rough spots in professional as well as private life.

ACCREDITATION BODIES AND RELICENSURE AGENCIES

These groups and agencies could recognize the legitimacy of any learning or developmental activities carried out in service of performance agendas worked out under responsible guidance. If a learning experience has a demonstrable relationship to the quality of personal performance, the burden of proof is with those who would not permit it to be counted toward mandatory continuing education requirements or relicensure standards. Hours spent in liberal learning, in investigating alternative ways of structuring professional services, or in strengthening personal coping skills can be demonstrated to have a more direct relationship with actual performance than an equal number of hours in learning experiences with no objective beyond that of keeping up. A number of accrediting bodies honor learning that falls outside the profession's traditional base of knowledge and skills. On the other hand, an accrediting body could decide to continue recognizing only those providers or programs that fall entirely within a profession's traditional knowledge and skills because the accrediting body perceives itself to have no competence in judging other sorts of learning. Such an accrediting body might at the same time acknowledge that other agendas may serve professional performance equally well.

In looking at the crazy-quilt pattern of mandated continuing education, those in accreditation or relicensure could take a modest step by exercising restraint with regard to additional burdens. More is not always better.

Accrediting bodies might create categories of special note for programs with demonstrable relationships to the knowledge, skills, traits, and behavior proven to distinguish superior performance. Providers could be given a reasonable amount of time in which to prepare selected programs for review in the new performance category. Those providers whose programs found their way into categories of special note would enjoy a beneficial position within the constituencies they serve.

EXECUTIVES AND PROFESSIONALS

Grocery shoppers avoid falling prey to at least some of the compelling temptations of store layout and product displays by carrying a shopping list. Executives and professionals can reduce the power of clever direct-mail announcements of faddish seminars scheduled in inviting locations by making out a list of continuing education priorities. So much the better if the list reflects experience of their own performance and its context more than it embodies the imperatives of new information and technology or the myths of the profession or of the business culture.

Continuing education consumers could serve themselves and the field better if they demanded enough information about a continuing education program to warrant a reasonable judgment about its relatedness to their performance. More sophisticated individual and organizational consumers are ultimately the field's best quality control system.

Linking continuing education with performance requires no special magic, just the dedicated focus of major stakeholders taking one modest step at a time.

Appendix

The Role of Colleges and Universities in Continuing Professional Education

A Position Paper of the National University Continuing Education Association

"The Role of Colleges and Universities in Continuing Professional Education" is one of several position papers commissioned by the NUCEA Board of Directors for the purpose of identifying the best ways for NUCEA and its member institutions to exercise leadership in the 1980s. This paper presents some general principles and issues significant to continuing professional education. It recommends some positions to be adopted, and some opportunities for leadership for NUCEA.

General Principles

1. The primary responsibility for learning rests with the individual professional.

The single most important variable in the mix of continuing professional education is the individual professional: his or her motivation, prior experience, sense of what is required by changing circumstances or conditions of employment, and quality of judgment in choosing appropriate educational experiences. Continuing professional education should be a tool for the development of individual professionalism and competence, not a substitute for it. Self-directed continuing professional education also should be viewed as a preferable alternative to disciplinary action by the professions or legal action by the public. (However, care must be taken to ensure that continuing professional education is not seen as a substitute for

NOTE: Drafted by Philip M. Nowlen, the University of Chicago, and Donna S. Queeney, Pennsylvania State University. Adopted by the NUCEA Board of Directors on January 18, 1984.

professional regulation; participation in continuing professional education cannot be used as evidence of practitioner competence.)

2. The role of continuing professional education is to provide those opportunities for learning and reinforcement that professionals require to improve or acquire skills or knowledge, or to broaden the scope of their education. The following characteristics of the profession and the professional should be addressed in providing these educational opportunities.
   a. The profession's central mission
   b. Practitioners' performance-related knowledge
   c. Practitioners' needs for broad self-enhancement and enrichment
   d. Special benchmarks such as recredentialing and relicensure
   e. Special attributes of the profession
   f. The profession's standards of ethical practice, and ethical questions raised by new knowledge and skills

The agendas of both learners and providers generally are more limited than the characteristics above suggest. Most continuing education programs address a narrow band of specialized knowledge and skills, usually focusing on what is perceived to be a lack of critical technical knowledge. On the other hand, breakdowns in professional performance again and again are attributed to failure in qualities of leadership, team building, management, problem-solving skills, etc.

3. Continuing professional educators must have a comprehensive understanding of professionals' career pathways through the life cycle on a profession-by-profession basis to provide productive educational experiences that are cost effective for the practitioner.

The educational demands of the professional who is a seasoned veteran differ markedly from the mid-career professional's needs. These in turn are sharply different from the requirements of professionals holding their first jobs. Similarly, the mix of new information, experiential knowledge, and wisdom will be quite different at each of these career stages.

4. In addition to traditional classroom instruction, learning based on inquiry, practice, and reinforcement should be employed in providing continuing professional education. Knowledge of different adult learning styles should be an integral part of program design. Attention should be given to matching teaching techniques to learning objectives.

Varied instructional approaches can stand alone or can be used as reinforcing experiences for traditional instruction. In selecting instructional approaches, continuing professional educators should be aware that some professions have developed their own distinctive ways of learning, and that certain techniques are particularly suited to specific learning objectives.

It also should be noted that professional performance is not mechanistic. Professionals learn techniques and adapt them to their practice style. Because of this, one cannot expect perfect congruence between what is taught and what is practiced; the changes that occur in practice may be modifications of what is taught.

5. Professions and institutions of higher education should collaborate on the design, provision, and reinforcement of performance-oriented continuing professional education as appropriate.

The actual impact of continuing professional education on performance cannot be confidently asserted by any of the many providers currently competing with one another. The development of programs with clearer and greater impact on performance will require the sensitive collaboration of many groups including professional associations, employers, universities, government agencies, and foundations. Existing constraints to such collaboration within certain professions must be identified and dealt with.

Further, an important facet of individuals' continuing professional education comes from reinforcement of that education. Continuing professional education might be seen as a combination of instruction and reinforcement, collaboratively provided.

It must be recognized that optimum continuing professional education cannot be provided by universities alone. Because universities do not return to the work setting with the professional, they cannot provide reinforcement as can the professional association or the employer. Neither can it be assumed that universities are better providers of continuing professional education than are other entities; all have their strengths and weaknesses. Identifying appropriate opportunities for collaboration and the optimum roles of the various potential providers is critical.

6. The establishment of cooperative self-directed continued learning, involving both faculty members and professionals, should begin in the professional schools during preprofessional education.

The importance of continuing professional education should be stressed during initial professional preparation with emphasis on the need for ongoing learning throughout one's professional life.

Issues for Discussion

PROVIDER AND PRACTITIONER SELECTION OF CONTINUING PROFESSIONAL EDUCATION PROGRAMS

The field is a confused and disorderly marketplace. There is competition among providers, programs, and professional groups, and career competition motivates many practitioners who enroll in programs. Even the issues compete for attention and energy. While such competition is healthy, the need to define quality in continuing professional education frequently is lost in the midst of it. Questions of concern include:

a. How can continuing professional education have the greatest impact on professional practice?

b. What are effective procedures for self-directed learners and continuing professional education providers to use in selecting and defining the service and performance goals to be pursued through continuing professional education? What is the role of needs assessment in this process, and how can it best be incorporated?

c. What steps should be taken to ensure that continuing professional education is of high quality? One option, but surely not the only one, is the licensure or regulation of continuing professional education providers. Also to be considered is whether or not continuing professional education can best do its job by remaining divorced from credentialing and licensing matters.

d. What is a reasonable division of responsibilities between continuing education units, professional schools, and professional associations in provision of continuing professional education? What are the most appropriate roles of each? How can functional collaborative relationships between these groups be achieved?

The issues surrounding selection of programs takes continuing professional education beyond a simple extension of professional school curricula and links its future to inquiry and methodologies drawn from the social sciences.

MANDATORY CONTINUING EDUCATION FOR RECERTIFICATION AND RELICENSURE

The role of continuing professional education in credentialing for continued practice merits close examination. While continuing education providers' enrollments increase as a result of mandated continuing education, it is at the cost of accepting some degree of responsibility for maintaining professional performance standards and, consequently, some degree of blame if the public fails to perceive that it is better served by the profession. This caution is particularly critical when one recognizes that performance is affected by a number of factors beyond knowledge and skills. Since few providers can demonstrate that specific educational programs affect practitioner performance or enhance competency, care must be taken that continuing professional educators do not purport to accomplish something they cannot deliver.

THE ROLE OF THE ACADEMIC FACULTY IN CONTINUING PROFESSIONAL EDUCATION

Obtaining full-time faculty-member participation in the provision of continuing professional education often is difficult. It is common to find institutional policies that restrict faculty member participation in university-based continuing education, either in regard to a ceiling on earnings or a limit on contact hours. Because restrictions on teaching or consulting outside of the faculty member's institution are less common, continuing educators find access to faculty members at other institutions easier than access to the faculty at their own institutions.

Faculty members' obligations for community service, or continuing education, as part of their full-time responsibility to their university are not clear. It commonly is acknowledged that effective teaching in professional schools requires faculty involvement in corresponding professional fields. Yet the view that faculty member's responsibility to the professions ends with the last day of class in professional school continues to persist. Definition of what constitutes satisfactory discharge of obligations in the area of continuing professional education is needed, as is adoption and implementation of policies to provide appropriate recognition and reward for such activities. Involved in this aspect of the issue are credit toward promotion and tenure as well as adequate financial compensation.

A further dimension of the economic issue is that competition for faculty members among providers of continuing professional education has had an inflationary impact on the range of fees faculty members have come to expect. Sometimes this has the effect of raising faculty compensation demands to an excessive level and hence raising the price of the continuing-education program to the professional. The constituency able to be served under these conditions may be at variance with the constituency envisioned by the institution's mission.

NUCEA Positions

On the basis of the principles presented in the first portion of this paper, and with regard to the issues outlined above, NUCEA takes the following positions:

1. The relationship between mandatory continuing education and professional practice is not fully understood. Therefore, emphasis should be placed on individual professionals' responsibility for maintaining their ability to work competently throughout their career rather than on mandated continuing professional education.

2. Continuing education professionals, appropriate professional schools, and local and national professional associations should collaborate to set an agenda of crucial issues and to elaborate relevant continuing professional education needs. Such collaboration would more ade-

quately serve the professions. This should be done with a view toward improving the cost/benefit ratio for providers and professionals alike.

3. Institutions of higher education should do everything possible to reduce the barriers of political, financial, and organizational concerns as related to full-time faculty members' participation in the provision of continuing professional education. Institutional compensatory policies should be modified where necessary to provide incentives for faculty members who wish to participate in continuing professional education programs. Continuing education professionals should record and file evaluations of faculty teaching, research, and service with the same degree of rigor that is applied to the evaluation of faculty members fulfilling more traditional assignments.

Opportunities for NUCEA Leadership

The role of the Division of Continuing Education for the Professions should be expanded to collaborate with and form a network of professional association-based continuing education. Membership of other nonprofit and profit-oriented continuing professional education professionals and their associations should be solicited. As part of NUCEA annual national and regional conferences, the division should encourage meetings planned jointly by higher education and association-based, continuing education professionals to focus on topics that can be explored collaboratively and activities that foster professional association–higher education networks. In this manner NUCEA and its member institutions can serve as "engineers of collaboration" among the professions. Continuing education has the capacity to provide outstanding programs for a variety of professions working together, serving a number of professions in a combined effort.

Believing that NUCEA should recognize outstanding continuing professional education leaders and programs with a prestigious national award, the Division of Continuing Education for the Professions initiated an awards program in 1985. Annual awards are given for exemplary programs, program developers, and continuing professional education instructors. Programs having demonstrated effects on professional performance, and service and evaluations of programs that lead to significant improvements in program design also should receive attention, as should associations and universities engaged in collaborative efforts that provide models to others in the field. Unusually effective leaders should be recognized for careers that have made a difference.

NUCEA should bring to the attention of its member institutions the opportunities for research projects relevant to continuing professional education, and for integration of research findings into ongoing activities of the continuing professional education field. For example, the field is in need of baselines to define various performance levels (for example, excellence, marginality, inadequacy); far more should be known about actual practice of the professions and their subspecialties. Disciplines from the social sciences such as organization behavior, sociology, and social psychology could be productively involved.

NUCEA should encourage the development and testing of new models of contextual needs analysis. Models should be developed and tested to assist professionals who share a work setting such as a health clinic, family-services agency, or even continuing education office, to analyze the collective performance points at which they require change facilitated by continuing education. Information should be disseminated through continuing education programs for professionals in various practice situations.

NUCEA should promote the development of techniques in providing and coordinating mentoring in professional settings. Professionals often find themselves providing or receiving mentoring, often occurring randomly and mixed in outcome. NUCEA member institutions should develop and test more deliberate and guided mentoring models that marry the individual professional's career path with the present needs and likely future scenario of the discipline to which the professional belongs.

The relationship between the humanities and professional performance bears closer scrutiny. Some NUCEA member institutions, together with selected professions, should take the lead in pursuing the nature of this relationship. Higher-order reasoning and the critical skills of mind essential to professional performance are structured largely before admission to professional schools by prior pursuit of the liberal arts. Consideration should be given to encouragement of restructuring or sharpening these skills by renewed study at various points in professionals' careers.

NUCEA member institutions should offer information to employers of professionals to enable them to apply objective criteria to educational opportunities for their employees. The opportunity exists to educate a large segment of the continuing professional education consuming public. Frequently, employers of professionals are the "third-party purchasers" of continuing professional education.

Through the Division of Continuing Education for the Professions, NUCEA should assume a leadership role in the establishment of voluntary standards for advertising and promoting continuing professional education programs.

Summary

NUCEA recognizes the field of continuing professional education as an area of increasing importance to all of higher education. The association believes that, in striving to meet the educational needs of professional practitioners, educational institutions must address the principles and issues discussed in this paper. These include:

The primary responsibility for learning rests with the individual professional.

Continuing education professionals should provide profession-specific continuing professional education designed to have an impact on practice.

Continuing professional education should utilize modes of instruction appropriate to the specific professional group being addressed.

Collaboration between continuing education departments, professional schools, and professional associations in the design and provision of continuing professional education is highly desirable.

The role of the academic faculty in the provision of continuing professional education requires university recognition, definition, and clarification.

NUCEA's role in addressing these issues is primarily that of a catalyst, encouraging the bringing together of persons and institutions concerned with continuing professional education. NUCEA stresses the importance of research in the field, and of recognition of successful and innovative efforts, institutions, and individuals.

Index

The abbreviations *"t"* and *"f"* following page numbers indicate that the indexed material is contained in a table or figure, respectively.